W9-CML-001

A TEACHER'S GUIDE TO

PERFORMANCE-BASED LEARNING AND ASSESSMENT

Educators in Connecticut's Pomperaug
Regional School District 15, serving the
towns of Southbury and Middlebury

K. Michael Hibbard
Linda Van Wagenen
Samuel Lewbel
Stacey Waterbury-Wyatt
Susan Shaw
Kelly Pelletier
Beth Larkins
Judith O'Donnell Dooling

Elizabeth Elia
Susan Palma
Judith Maier
Don Johnson
Maureen Honan
Deborah McKeon Nelson
Jo Anne Wislocki

Association for Supervision and Curriculum Development
Alexandria, Virginia

The Authors: Educators in Connecticut's Pomperaug Regional School District 15: K. Michael Hibbard, Linda Van Wagenen, Samuel Lewbel, Stacey Waterbury-Wyatt, Susan Shaw, Kelly Pelletier, Beth Larkins, Judith O'Donnell Dooling, Elizabeth Elia, Susan Palma, Judith Maier, Don Johnson, Maureen Honan, Deborah McKeon Nelson, and Jo Anne Wislocki. Address correspondence to K. Michael Hibbard, Assistant Superintendent, Region 15 Schools, 286 Whittemore Road, P.O. Box 395, Middlebury, CT 06762. Telephone: (203) 758-8250; fax: (203) 598-3559; e-mail: mhibb@aol.com.

Association for Supervision
and Curriculum Development
1250 N. Pitt Street • Alexandria, VA 22314
Telephone: (703) 549-9110 • Fax: (703) 299-8631

Gene R. Carter, *Executive Director*

Michelle Terry, *Assistant Executive Director, Program Development*

Ronald S. Brandt, Assistant *Executive Director*

Nancy Modrak, *Managing Editor, ASCD Books*

Carolyn R. Pool, *Associate Editor*

John Somers, *Project Assistant*

Gary Bloom, *Manager, Design and Production Services*

Karen Monaco, *Senior Designer*

Tracey A. Smith, *Print Production Coordinator*

Cynthia Stock, *Desktop Publisher*

Printed in the United States of America.

ASCD Stock No. 196021

4/96
$24.95

Library of Congress Cataloging-in-Publication Data

A teacher's guide to performance-based learning and assessment / authors, educators in Connecticut's Pomperaug Regional School District 15, Southbury and Middlebury ; K. Michael Hibbard...[et al.].
  p. cm.
  Includes bibliographical references and index.
  ISBN 0-87120-261-1 (pbk.)
  1. Competency based education—United States. 2. Competency based educational tests—United States. I. Hibbard, K. Michael. II. Pomperaug Regional School District 15 (Middlebury and Southbury, Conn.) III. Association for Supervision and Curriculum Development.
LC1032.T43 1996
371.2'7—dc20   96-9979
                                            CIP

00 99 98 97 96   5 4 3 2 1

A Teacher's Guide to Performance-Based Learning and Assessment

ACKNOWLEDGMENTS

This book is dedicated to the educators, students, and parents of Connecticut's Pomperaug Regional School District 15 who have worked together to improve teaching and learning through performance-based learning and assessment. Louis Esparo, Region 15 Superintendent of Schools, and the Board of Education have provided leadership, encouragement, and the support necessary to sustain the long-term change that has resulted in improved student performance.

We acknowledge the support of colleagues in many organizations: the Connecticut State Department of Education; Education Connection, the Connecticut Middle Grades Project; the New Haven, Connecticut Public Schools' Program for Minority Student Achievement; the Newtown, Connecticut Public Schools; Quinnipiac College; the Minneapolis, Minnesota, Public Schools/Minnesota State Department of Children, Families, and Learning; the Association for Supervision and Curriculum Development's Consortium for Expanding Student Assessment; the Maryland Assessment Consortium; the National Staff Development Council; the New England League of Middle Schools; and the Council of Chief State School Officers. These colleagues have been our "critical friends" who have provided essential feedback to Region 15 over the years as our teachers and administrators learned how to make, use, and teach others about performance-based learning and assessment.

THE AUTHORS ARE REGION 15 EDUCATORS

K. Michael Hibbard, Assistant Superintendent

Linda Van Wagenen, Teacher, Memorial Middle School

Samuel Lewbel, Teacher, Rochambeau Middle School

Stacey Waterbury-Wyatt, Teacher, Middlebury Elementary School

Susan Shaw, Teacher, Middlebury Elementary School

Kelly Pelletier, Teacher, Gainfield Elementary School

Beth Larkins, Teacher, Rochambeau Middle School

Elizabeth Elia, Teacher, Gainfield Elementary School

Judith O'Donnell Dooling, Principal, Memorial Middle School

Susan Palma, Teacher, Pomperaug Elementary School

Judith Maier, Teacher, Pomperaug Elementary School

Don Johnson, Department Chair of English, Pomperaug High School

Maureen Honan, Special Education Teacher, Pomperaug High School

Deborah McKeon Nelson, Teacher, Rochambeau Middle School

Jo Anne Wislocki, Teacher, Pomperaug High School

REGION 15 ADMINISTRATIVE TEAM

Louis J. Esparo, Superintendent of Schools

K. Michael Hibbard, Assistant Superintendent

Joan Quilter, Director, Student Services

Donna Popowski, Assistant Director, Student Services

Edward Arum, Business Director

John Voss, Principal, Pomperaug High School

Judith O'Donnell Dooling, Principal, Memorial Middle School

Aldro Jenks, Principal, Rochambeau Middle School

John Mudry, Principal, Gainfield Elementary School

Richard Gusenburg, Middlebury Elementary School

Linda Tourtellotte, Principal, Pomperaug Elementary School

Jim Agostine, Assistant Principal, Pomperaug High School

Michael Audette, Assistant Principal, Memorial Middle School

Lauren Robinson, Assistant Principal, Rochambeau Middle School

Yolande Bosman, Region 15 Director of Foreign Language

Nancy Carney, High School Chairperson, Social Studies

Dale Drzwecki, Region 15 Director of Art, Technology Education, Home Economics, and Business Education

Don Johnson, High School Chairperson of English

Ernest Mazaika, High School Chairperson of Math and Science

Annette Rhoads, Region 15 Director of Music

Beth Robinson, Region 15 Director of Guidance

Joseph Velardi, Region 15 Director of Physical Education, Health, and Athletics

CYCLE OF LEARNING AND THE CYCLE OF LEARNING WITH GEARS IN THE FRAME

K. Michael Hibbard, Region 15 Public Schools, Middlebury, Connecticut

and

Martha Waibel, Minneapolis Public Schools/ Minnesota State Department of Children, Families, and Learning,

GRAPHICS

Marilyn Kaminski, Region 15 Public Schools, Middlebury, Connecticut

Gretchen Usawicz, Region 15 Public Schools, Middlebury, Connecticut

Xuan Vu, Minneapolis Public Schools, Minnesota

INTRODUCTION

MONDAY MORNING IN A PERFORMANCE-BASED CLASSROOM

The quiet of the weekend is shattered as a wave of students pours eagerly into the classroom. "Good morning," "Hi," "What are we doing today?" The questions begin even before the students are seated at the desks that fill the room in groups of four. It's Monday morning, and the class is about to embark on a new performance-based learning task. Eyes focus on the teacher now standing by the easel, on which he has neatly written a list of criteria with a bold blue marker.

"You will recall that on Friday we brainstormed some possible topics and products for our next unit. Your task," announces the teacher from beside the easel, "is to . . ."

After several minutes and a number of questions for the teacher, each group sends up a representative to get copies of the *Performance Assessment Task*. Each group's "organizer" immediately begins a discussion of how the group members might approach the task, what they might create, and how they might assess their work. "How about we . . ." "What if we . . ." "No, that's not it, let's . . ." The teacher walks around listening as each group's recorder begins to list ideas.

"Before we go any further, let's use your lists to develop a *Performance Task Assessment List* for how we will evaluate our products. Can we do that now?" asks the teacher.

From a closet in the rear of the room, the teacher removes some *Models of Excellence* or "benchmarks," which in this case are products from a similar task completed earlier in the year by another class. Students examine the products and ask questions about the samples, which, though similar in design to what is required for this task, demonstrate a wide range of options and possibilities.

Returning to the easel, the teacher points to a set of criteria for a unit similar to this one. The criteria include standards to demonstrate skills and concepts appropriate for the age and grade level of the students. The list was developed from the school district's curriculum goals for the subject and grade level. A paper copy of the criteria sits in a folder on the bookshelf, but the teacher chooses instead to use a computer disk to bring up a *generic assessment list* for the type of project being planned. Taking specific content from the planned unit and incorporating students' suggestions, the teacher will *tailor* the generic list to meet the needs of the unit and the class. He will distribute the resulting assessment list to students tomorrow. The list will clearly spell out what is expected for a top performance so that the teacher, students, and parents will all know exactly what the task will entail, what students will be responsible for, and when and how it will be completed.

[handwritten margin note: students can know the curriculum & why they're learning what they're learning]

PERFORMANCE LEARNING AND THE WRITING OF THIS BOOK

Regional School District 15 covers the towns of Middlebury and Southbury, Connecticut. Over

the past seven years, our teachers and administrators have worked to develop performance learning in our classrooms.

We don't claim to have all the challenges of other school districts, nor do we claim to have all the answers or to have solved all the problems of education. *Performance-based learning and assessment is not a panacea—but we have found this strategy to be successful, valuable, and beneficial for our students.* We wrote this book as a collaborative effort between classroom teachers and administrators for the purpose of sharing what we have learned. In the following chapters, we describe what performance-based learning is and how to use tools such as performance tasks, task assessment lists, rubrics, and portfolios.

Just as we do with our students, we began by defining our task, in this case the completion of this book. Next, we developed an assessment instrument that keyed into the specific content and skill objectives for our book (see the task and list that follow). After you have read the book, we ask that you return to our list and help us assess whether we met our objectives.

PERFORMANCE LEARNING TASK FOR THE STAFF OF REGION 15

BACKGROUND

As teachers and administrators of Region 15, we have worked together for about seven years to create an approach to teaching and learning that balances basic instruction with performance-based learning and assessment. Both literal understanding and application are important in the model. We have found strategies to construct engaging performance tasks that are well connected to the content, process skills, and work habits of the curriculum. We have embedded these tasks in our instruction to serve as excellent learning activities and opportunities to assess student performance. We found strategies to use list-driven analytical assessment tools to foster professional dialogue among educators, to improve communication to students, to coach effective student self-assessment, and to help parents support learning. The bottom line is that student performance has improved, as measured by the Connecticut State tests in grades 4, 6, 8, and 10; by the Scholastic Achievement Test (SAT); and by a variety of Region 15 measures including the regionwide student portfolio.

TASK AND PURPOSE

Our task is to write a book to be published by the Association for Supervision and Curriculum Development (ASCD) on the topic of how performance-based learning and assessment can be used within and among the disciplines throughout the grade levels. This book is not about constructing curriculum. The book we write is intended to help other educators embed performance-based learning and assessment within their curriculums.

AUDIENCE

The audience for our book will be classroom teachers across the spectrum of grade levels and disciplines who want to learn strategies for creating and using performance-based learning and assessment. The audience will also include educators responsible for leading and managing long-term change to improve student performance.

PROCEDURE

1. A team of volunteers from each of the six schools in Region 15 will compose the committee that will write this book.

2. The team will define its task and create an assessment list to be used both to structure the writing and assess the final product.

3. The team will employ strategies of cooperative learning to balance groupwork and individual writing.

4. The team will develop a "time and task management plan" for writing the book. Our work must be in the hands of ASCD by September 1, 1995.

Performance Task Assessment List for the Book for ASCD on Performance-Based Learning and Assessment

S = Extremely Well Done   T = Excellent   O = Good   W = Needs Work

Element	*Rating*
For each chapter, the following assessment is made:	
1. The text and examples answer the question posed in the title of the chapter.	_____
2. Explanations are clear.	_____
3. Vocabulary is appropriate to the reader.	_____
4. Sufficient examples and models are provided.	_____
5. The material in the chapter provides information that can be the basis of good discussions among teachers and administrators.	_____
6. The reader is provided with enough guidance to "get started."	_____
The following assessment is for the "overall" book.	
7. The sequence of chapters is logical.	_____
8. The sequence is complete; important parts do not seem to be missing.	_____
9. Overall, the book has helped me feel capable of getting started.	_____
10. This approach to performance-based learning and assessment will help me improve both student and teacher performance.	_____

TO OUR AUDIENCE:

Please send us your ratings of the elements of this book. Comments will also be appreciated. Feedback helps us learn.

Thank you.

SEND TO:

K. Michael Hibbard

Assistant Superintendent

Region 15 Schools

286 Whittemore Rd.

P.O. Box 395

Middlebury, CT 06762

Phone: (203) 758-8250; fax: (203) 598-3559

E-mail: mhibb@aol.com

Note: Assessment lists developed for grades 1–12, to be used with discipline-based and interdisciplinary performance tasks, are available from Region 15 Schools at the above address. Performance tasks in many disciplines for grades 1–12 are also available.

WHAT IS PERFORMANCE-BASED LEARNING AND ASSESSMENT, AND WHY IS IT IMPORTANT?

In the act of learning, people obtain content knowledge, acquire skills, and develop work habits—and practice the application of all three to "real world" situations. Performance-based learning and assessment represent a set of strategies for the acquisition and application of knowledge, skills, and work habits through the performance of tasks that are meaningful and engaging to students.

BALANCE IN LITERACY

Performance-based learning and assessment achieve a balanced approach by extending traditional fact-and-skill instruction (Figure 1). Performance-based learning and assessment are not a curriculum design. Whereas you decide what to teach, performance-based learning and

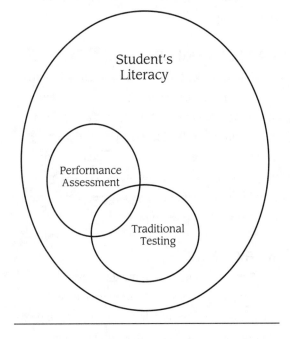

FIGURE 1. Student's Literacy

Student's Literacy

Performance Assessment

Traditional Testing

assessment constitute a better way to deliver your curriculum. Teachers do not have to "give up" units of study or favorite activities in a performance-based classroom. Because authentic tasks are rooted in curriculum, teachers can develop tasks based on what already works for them. Through this process, assignments become more authentic and more meaningful to students.

Traditional testing helps answer the question, "Do you know it?" and performance assessment helps answer the question, "How well can you use what you know?" These two ways of looking at literacy do not compete; the challenge is to find the right balance between them (Figure 2).

CONTENT KNOWLEDGE

The subject area content can come from already defined curriculums or can be enhanced by the adoption of a set of themes or topics by the department, grade-level team, school, or school system.

PROCESS SKILLS

Higher-order thinking or process skills can come from the various disciplines, such as writing or proofreading from language arts or math computation and problem-solving skills. Other process skills cut across subject area lines or may be identified as areas of need based on standardized testing (e.g., analogies, categorizing information, drawing inferences, etc.).

WORK HABITS

Time management, individual responsibility, honesty, persistence, and intrapersonal skills, such as appreciation of diversity and working cooperatively with others, are examples of work

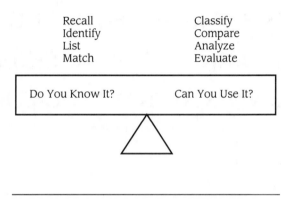

FIGURE 2. What Is the BALANCE?

Recall	Classify
Identify	Compare
List	Analyze
Match	Evaluate

Do You Know It?   Can You Use It?

habits necessary for an individual to be successful in life.

PERFORMANCE TASKS

Performance tasks build on earlier content knowledge, process skills, and work habits and are strategically placed in the lesson or unit to enhance learning as the student "pulls it all together." Such performance tasks are not "add-ons" at the end of instruction. They are both an *integral part of the learning* and an *opportunity to assess the quality of student performance*. When the goal of teaching and learning is knowing and using, the performance-based classroom emerges.

Performance tasks range from short activities taking only a few minutes to projects culminating in polished products for audiences in and outside of the classroom. In the beginning, most performance tasks should fall on the short end of the continuum. Teachers find that many activities they are already doing can be shaped into performance-learning tasks.

Two initial concerns of teachers moving toward performance-based classrooms include the amount of time needed for performance tasks and the subjectivity traditionally associated with teacher assessment and assigning "grades."

TIME

The initial move to any new method involves an investment in time. The development of performance-assessment tasks is no exception. With a little practice, however, teachers find that they can easily and quickly develop performance tasks and assessment lists. This process is further simplified as teachers and schools begin to collect and maintain lists of generic tasks and assessments that teachers can adapt for individual lessons. Teachers find assessment lists a more efficient way of providing feedback to students than traditional methods, thus saving time in the long run. Finally, as students work with performance assessment, the quality of their work improves, reducing the time teachers must spend assessing and grading student work.

EXAMPLES OF PERFORMANCE TASKS

Performance tasks should be interesting to the student and well connected to the important content, process skills, and work habits of the curriculum. Sometimes students can help in constructing these tasks and assessment lists. The following are three performance tasks that call for graphs:

(Upper Level) Middle or High School (Provide the students with a copy of a speeding ticket that shows how the fine is determined.) Say to students: "How is the fine for speeding in our state determined? Make a graph that shows teenagers in our town how much it will cost them if they are caught speeding. Excellent graphs will be displayed in the Driver's Education classroom."

Elementary School (At several specified times during the school day, students observe and count, for a set length of time, the number of cars and other vehicles going through an intersection near the school.) Say to students: "The police department is considering a traffic light or a crossing guard at the intersection near your school. Your help is needed to make graphs that show how many vehicles go through that intersection at certain times of the day. Excellent graphs will be sent to the Chief of Police."

Primary School (In view of the class, place 10 caterpillars in a box. Place a flashlight at one end, while darkening the other by folding over the box top.) Say to students: "Do caterpillars move more to the light or more to the dark? Make a graph that shows how many caterpillars move to the light and how many move to the dark part of the box. Your graphs will be displayed at Open House."

PERFORMANCE TASK ASSESSMENT LISTS

Performance task assessment lists are assessment tools that provide the structure students need to work more independently and to encourage them to pay attention to the quality of their work. Assessment lists also enable the teacher to efficiently provide students with information on the strengths and weaknesses of their work. In creating performance task assessment lists, teachers focus on what students need to know and be able to do. One result is that teachers can more consistently and fairly evaluate and grade student work. Information from performance task assessment lists also helps students set learning goals and thus helps teachers focus subsequent instruction. Parents can also use assessment lists to monitor their student's work in school and to help their children check their own work at home.

Handwritten margin note: Who Benefits: Teachers: consistency, fairness, focus. Students: set goals, know objectives. Parents: know objectives, can be more involved

EXAMPLES OF PERFORMANCE TASK ASSESSMENT LISTS

This chapter includes several examples of assessment lists; the first three are lists for assessing student-made graphs. (These lists and other illustrative materials are shown as "Exhibits" at the end of the chapters and are numbered consecutively.)

The upper-level format (Exhibit 1) is used in middle and high school. It lists the important elements and provides three columns of lines. On the first column of lines, the teacher indicates the points each element is worth. Some elements receive more points in order to focus students' attention on skills in need of improvement. These point values are based on the objectives of the task or lesson. Some elements receive more points because they are more important. These point values are determined by the teacher or could be decided by the class and the teacher together.

Students get this assessment list, with the points possible for each part of the task listed "up-front," as they begin a performance task—which in this case calls for a graph. At this point, students are also shown several examples of "excellent graphs," either done by previous students or from professional sources such as magazines or texts. These models serve as "benchmarks" (see next section), which the teacher can use to illustrate sections of the assessment list. This "no guess no excuse" approach allows students to see the importance of each element and use the list and benchmarks to guide their own work. The list also aids students in time management because they can see what the most important elements are in constructing graphs.

Before they submit their work, students do a final inspection of their own graphs and complete the self-assessment column. During this self-assessment step, students often find ways to improve their work. Peer assessment can also take place at this time. The assessment list can be customized to add an extra column for this purpose. Experiences with peer assessment often improve students' self-assessing skills.

The final step is for the teacher to assess the work and, at the same time, evaluate the student's self-assessment. When discrepancies are found between the student's self-assessment and the teacher's assessment of the student's work, the teacher may decide to hold conferences with the students who need work on improving the accuracy of their self-assessment.

The teacher can also assign a grade, using the teacher's column on the assessment list. For example, earning 90 percent of the points possible might be an *A*, 80 percent a *B*, and so on. The assessment provides detailed information about the quality of each component of the work, while the grade identifies "overall" quality. The teacher determines the relative importance of each activity in determining an overall grade point average, just as teachers do with traditional assessments.

The elementary format (Exhibit 2) is used for children in the upper elementary grades (3rd-5th). It lists several important elements of the graph and describes three levels of quality for each: *terrific, OK,* and *needs work.* Just as with the upper-level format, students are provided with the assessment list "up-front" and shown models of excellent graphs appropriate for this age level. This format also asks the students to assess their graphs "over-all" and justify that opinion based on the details discovered through element-by-element self-assessment.

The third format is for children in the primary grades (Exhibit 3). Student self-assessment and teacher assessment are a part of the format of the elementary and primary assessment lists as well. These children color the face and draw hair or a hat on the face that represents the quality of their work—*terrific, OK,* or *needs work.* The teacher indicates agreement or disagreement and talks with the child about his work and self-assessment.

COMMON FRAMEWORK OF ASSESSMENT LISTS

When teachers at a grade level, school, or school district use and adapt similar assessment lists for student work such as graphs, students encounter a common framework for learning

from subject to subject, from grade to grade, and from school to school. Overall, student performance is improved by this common focus and consistency. The details that performance tasks provide and the interaction between the student's self-assessment and the teacher's assessment focus the student's attention on the elements of quality for the various skills and content that they encounter throughout their education.

MODELS OF EXCELLENT WORK: BENCHMARKS

Students need to see examples of excellent work, or "benchmarks" of quality, for their grade and ability level. Besides using an assessment list to learn about the specific elements that will be used to assess the quality of their work, students must see what quality looks (sounds, feels, smells, or tastes) like. Over time, teachers collect sets of excellent work such as graphs, nonfiction writing, solutions to open-ended math problems, and designs for science experiments from students. Flawed or not-so-excellent work may also be used in the process of teaching students how to use the assessment lists and benchmarks.

Let's look at three benchmark graphs for the three performance tasks described earlier: Exhibit 4 shows a graph about caterpillars in the dark versus light (graph made by a primary student); Exhibit 5 shows a traffic count in front of school (made by an elementary student in the 3rd-5th grade); and Exhibit 6 shows traffic fines for speeding (made by a middle or high school student).

CYCLE OF LEARNING

How would you feel about learning all the rules and skills of a sport, spending months sweating yourself into good physical condition, but never actually playing the game? How much is traditional schooling like this? Schooling frequently centers on individual concepts, facts, discrete skills, and work habits. But how often does a student encounter opportunities to "put it all together," the way work is done in the "real world"? How often does a student actually get to step on the field and play "for real"?

To play basketball, you need to practice dribbling the ball, passing, and shooting; but to really learn the game, you need to actually "play ball!"

Similarly, it is important to learn how to ask questions, to organize data, to compute, and to write; but to make these skills meaningful, students need opportunities to use such skills in meaningful ways.

COORDINATION OF TASKS AND ASSESSMENTS

The Cycle of Learning is a model for "playing the whole game." Consider the high school-level performance task, "Freedom and Responsibility" (Exhibit 7). Students are provided with data on the number of eligible voters and the number that actually voted in local, state, and federal elections over the past 10 years. The task is to "write a persuasive letter to the editor of your local newspaper, supported by a graph, that describes your opinion. . . . Your purpose is to persuade your audience, not to antagonize." The assessment list the students use (Exhibit 8) al-

lows the students to check their organization, clarity of writing, use of supporting data, and other elements of effective persuasive writing. The assignment is a real task—the letter will go to a real editor; and the assessment is part of the learning process, or cycle (see Exhibit 9, "The Cycle of Learning").

The Cycle of Learning shows the steps through which the learner will go to complete the "Freedom and Responsibility" task in Exhibit 7. Steps 1–4 of the cycle are structured through performance task assessment lists. For this task, students will use the assessment lists for persuasive writing and for creating a graph.

Both *during* and *at the end* of these four steps, the student uses performance task assessment lists provided by the teacher or made by the student, such as that in Exhibit 8. The student is also asked to evaluate her work—to make a judgment about the degree to which the writing and graph represent her best effort to meet the requirements of the assignment. The student's answer leads the student toward setting goals for further improvement of writing and graphing.

Many performance learning tasks will be only parts of the Cycle of Learning, while others will take the student through the entire cycle. As the student completes projects that engage the entire cycle, the student's work improves and she feels more and more capable of being successful with this kind of work. As the valid self-perception of capability grows, the student is more willing to expend the energy to begin and complete a quality product. The Cycle of Learning thus becomes a cycle of improving student performance.

MESHING WITH THREE TYPES OF COMPETENCIES

Any learner successfully completing the Cycle of Learning has used a combination of competencies:

- Competencies from the "disciplines" include knowledge from such areas as the arts, humanities, language arts, physical health/health, science, math, and technology.
- Interpersonal competencies include communication skills, cooperative learning, and courtesy.
- Intrapersonal competencies include work habits such as organization, time management, and persistence.

All three types of competencies are the "gears" that mesh with the "Cycle of Learning Gear" (Exhibit 10). When all competencies are working together, the Cycle of Learning turns. When one or more competencies do not work, the Cycle of Learning does not turn well. Schooling includes improving student discipline-based competencies, interpersonal competencies, and intrapersonal competencies.

THE ENVIRONMENT FOR THE CYCLE OF LEARNING

The Cycle of Learning engages the student of any age in a process that is strongly influenced by the learning environment of the classroom, school, school district, state/region, and nation. Administrators, teachers, and other adults can provide support and encouragement in the form of time, resources, encouragement, and support of creativity and risk-taking. When the adults in the students' environment are themselves enthusiastic, reflective learners who constructively resolve the inevitable conflicts that occur during the change process, the students are more likely to employ these strategies as they learn how to be capable, self-motivated, independent, lifelong learners. Thus, the policies and practices of all the stakeholders in the performance of our youth create the "frame," which can either support the long-term changes necessary to improve performance or incapacitate these efforts.

Exhibit 1. Performance Task Assessment List for a Graph

| | | ASSESSMENT POINTS | | |
| | Points | Earned Assessment: | | |
Element	Possible	Self	Peer(?)	Teacher
1. An appropriate type of graph (line or bar) is used.	_____	_____		_____
2. Appropriate starting points and intervals are used for each axis.	_____	_____		_____
3. There is a main title for the graph which clearly states the relationship between the axes.	_____	_____		_____
4. An appropriate scale is used on each axis depending on the range of data for that axis.	_____	_____		_____
5. Axes are clearly labeled.	_____	_____		_____
6. The independent variable is put on the (X) axis, and the dependent variable is put on the (Y) axis.	_____	_____		_____
7. The data are plotted accurately.	_____	_____		_____
8. The graph should reflect uncertainty of measurement.	_____	_____		_____
9. Trends or lack of trends are depicted on the graph.	_____	_____		_____
10. An appropriate key or legend is part of the graph.	_____	_____		_____
11. The lines or bars use the space of the graph well.	_____	_____		_____
12. Appropriate techniques such as color, texture, or clarifying labels are used to make the graph easier to understand.	_____	_____		_____
13. The whole graph uses the space given it on the paper well.	_____	_____		_____
14. The graph is neat and presentable.	_____	_____		_____
15. The graph is easy to interpret.	_____	_____		_____
Total:	_____	_____		_____

Exhibit 2. Performance Task Assessment List for a Graph
Elementary School

1. **Heading**
   T: I included my name and the date.
   O: I included my name and the date but they are in the wrong place.
   W: I did not include my name or the date.

2. **Title**
   T: The title tells exactly what the graph is about. The title includes a short statement of what I changed and what I measured.
   O: The title tells what the graph is about.
   W: The title is missing or it tells little.

3. **Labeling the Data**
   T: Each axis has a name that explains what that axis is and the data has units.
   O: The axes need names that are more clear and/or the data needs units.
   W: The names for the axes and/or the units for the data are missing.

4. **Selecting a Scale for Each Axis**
   T: Each axis has a scale that fits the data in the data table.
   The scales help use the whole graph well.
   O: The scales for one or both axes need to be improved.
   W: The scales are missing or they are incorrect.

5. **Drawing Lines or Bars on the Graph**
   T: The lines or bars are drawn accurately and very neatly.
   O: There are some mistakes or the work is a little messy.
   W: There are many mistakes and/or the work is very messy.

6. **Use of Space and Color**
   T: The whole graph uses the space well. Color or some other technique is used so the graph is easy to read.
   O: The space is not used too well and color or some other technique could be used better so that the graph is easier to read.
   W: The graph needs a lot of work on the use of space and color.

7. **Key or Legend**
   T: The key or legend is very clear.
   O: The key or legend is OK.
   W: The key or legend needs a lot of work.

Did I do my best work?

Terrific   OK   Needs Work

Exhibit 3. Performance Task Assessment List for a Graph
Primary Grades

1. Did I draw the things in columns?

Terrific   OK   Needs Work

2. Did I make a separate column for each different kind of thing?

Terrific   OK   Needs Work

3. Did I print words to tell what each column is?

Terrific   OK   Needs Work

4. Did I use color?

Terrific   OK   Needs Work

5. Is my graph drawn neatly?

Terrific   OK   Needs Work

Exhibit 4. Do Caterpillars Like the Light or the Dark?

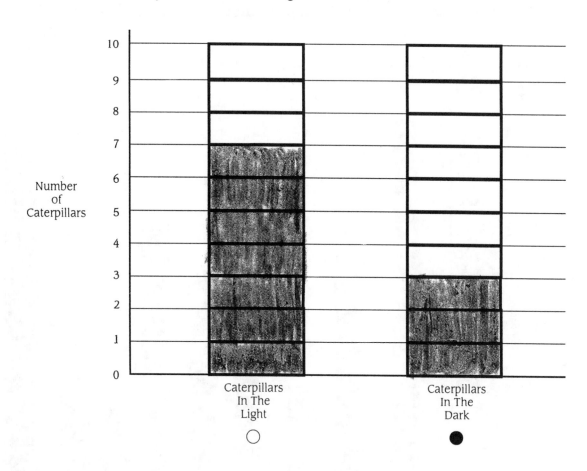

Exhibit 5. The Number of Vehicles Going Through the Intersection of Oak and Philmont Near Washington Middlebrook Elementary School

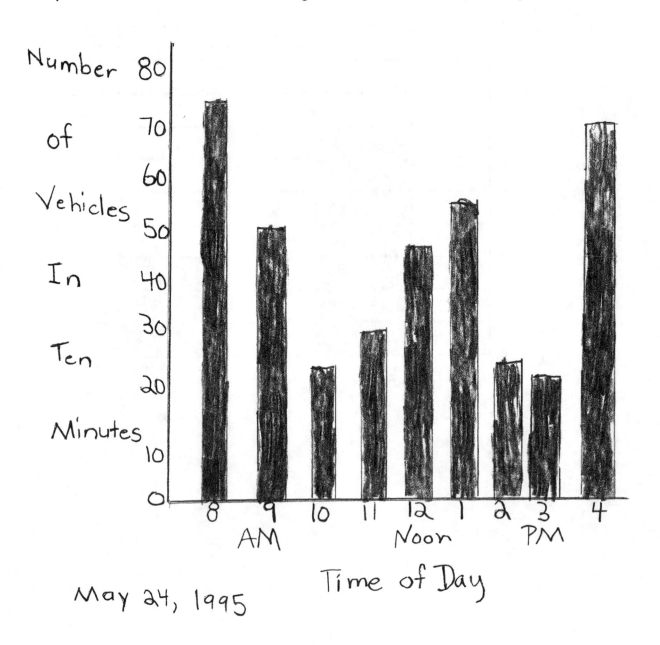

Exhibit 6. Your Fine in Connecticut and Vermont When Speeding

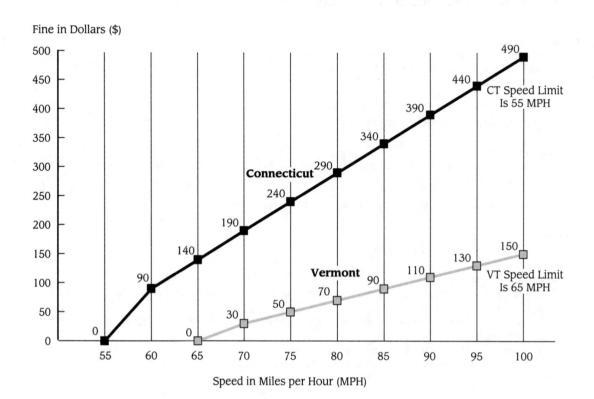

Fine in Dollars ($)

Speed in Miles per Hour (MPH)

– No maximum fine in CT
– Maximum fine is $350 in VT

Exhibit 7. Performance Task
Freedom and Responsibility in America

Background

"Be more responsible!" is a phrase often directed to teenagers by adults. But how well do adults "walk their talk?" We live in America, the most free and democratic country in history. Almost every citizen has the freedom to vote.

– Is it also the responsibility of eligible American citizens to vote?
– To what degree do the adults in your community carry out their freedom and responsibility through voting?

Task and Purpose

Write a persuasive letter to the editor of your local newspaper, supported by a graph, that describes your opinion on these questions.

Your purpose is to persuade your audience, not to antagonize them.

Audience

Your audience is adults who read the local newspaper.

Procedure

1. Organize and analyze the data you were given and brainstorm possible persuasive arguments for your letter.
2. Decide on the most appropriate type of graph to display this information in a way which supports your arguments.
3. Write a first draft of the letter and graph.
4. Complete the necessary steps of the editing process to produce a finished letter and mail it to the editor.

Exhibit 8. Performance Task Assessment List
Persuasive Writing—Freedom and Responsibility in America
Grade 9

		ASSESSMENT POINTS	
	Points	Earned Assessment:	
Element	Possible	Self	Teacher
1. The writer introduces and clearly states a position.	_____	_____	_____
2. The position is supported by at least four main points.	_____	_____	_____
3. Each main point is supported by at least three relevant, accurate, and specific pieces of information.	_____	_____	_____
4. It is clear that most of the main points and supporting details came from the reference materials.	_____	_____	_____
5. Information from personal experience or data from sources other than the reading materials is provided as additional support to the argument.	_____	_____	_____
6. The main point(s) of the opposing arguments is/are listed and refuted.	_____	_____	_____
7. The argument is made to a specific audience. The writing is crafted to appeal to that audience.	_____	_____	_____
8. The argument is organized and has a flow from beginning to end.	_____	_____	_____
9. There is a powerful concluding statement of the writer's position.	_____	_____	_____
10. Mechanics of English are correct and the writing is neat and presentable.	_____	_____	_____
Total	_____	_____	_____

Exhibit 9. The Cycle of Learning—To Improve Performance

Exhibit 10. Improving Performance of All Stakeholders

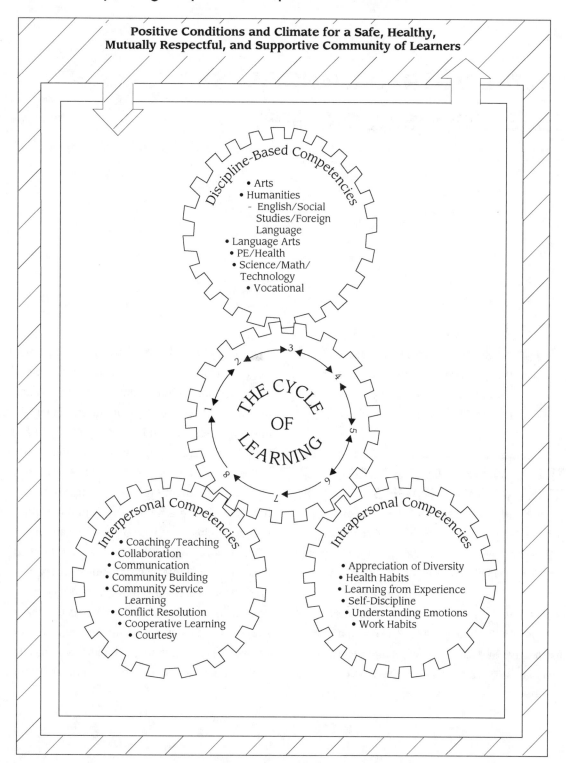

WHAT DO PERFORMANCE-BASED CLASSROOMS LOOK LIKE?

This chapter presents three case studies that portray what performance-based classrooms look like at the elementary, middle, and high school levels.

3RD GRADE CASE STUDY: "FAST PLANT GRAPHS"

It is early spring, and 24 heterogeneously grouped botanists, including several scientists with "special needs," are engaged in the study of the life cycle of plants. Plants and performance-based learning and assessment are all components of this 3rd grade curriculum. The class is 21 days into the study of "FAST Plants," a multi-disciplinary unit, using fast-growing *Brassica rapa* plants. This unit, involving hands-on

science, math, and writing, was adapted from the University of Wisconsin FAST Plants Program.

The students have planted seeds, pollinated plants, taken preliminary plant measurements, and processed data and are now preparing to take their final measurements to plot the growth of their plants on line graphs (see the performance task in Exhibit 11, "The Tall and Short of It"). The students have their "quads" (four-section miniplanters with one FAST Plant in each section) on their desks, which are grouped to serve as lab tables. Six "scientists" are gathered around each table; they are wearing lab coats fashioned out of adults' discarded white shirts. They immediately compare plants to see whose is the biggest and, of course, who has the runt. The teacher is moving from group to group

science : process skills
math : graphing
writing : summarizing, reporting

troubleshooting. She pauses to help pick up and replant a spilled quad. Since several students have limited fine motor skills, the special education teacher steps in to assist one group, who are using a flexible metric ruler to make their final measurements. Once they have completed their measurements, students will begin working on the next step of the assessment task, creation of a graph.

Earlier, during their planning time, the classroom teacher and the special education teacher had reviewed the performance task, looking for any modifications that might be necessary to meet the needs of all students. They brainstormed potential problem areas. The ability to make accurate measurements, the creation of graphs, the understanding of the terminology, and the ability to write an accurate summary were all identified as possible problem areas for special education students in the integrated class.

While explaining the task to the students, the teacher displays and discusses models of good line graphs previously done by other students. Students have already completed a quiz in which they demonstrated understanding of vocabulary terms. The students have also done many graphs as part of performance learning activities in their math classes. For the students with fine motor difficulties, one modification to the graphing activity was the use of a computer to make accurate graphs. Use of the computer ensured that all students could produce equally professional-looking graphs. Several other modifications were made where appropriate; but in the end, no modifications were made to the criteria specific to content, only to the methods used to obtain or display that information.

The classroom teacher gathers everyone together in the meeting area to explain and model the task and its assessment list step by step (see the assessment list for a "Graph of FAST Plants' Growth" in Exhibit 12). The teacher shows the students examples of the similar graphing they had done in math class. The students discuss the qualities that are necessary for a "terrific" graph.

A large group of the student scientists, armed with their lab books, make straight for the computer area to begin their graphs. The remaining scientists review the task, step by step, with the special education teacher. As the computer-generated graphs are completed, the students enter them into their lab books and write a summary about their graphs.

Although the students refer to their assessment list as a guide throughout the process, when they finish their graphs and summaries they reflect, make adjustments, and fill out their final assessment list.

The teachers were pleased that this had been a successful task. They had observed active discussion and interchange among all students about the analysis of the data and the comparison of results. Every student felt a part of the project, and all students had quality information to share. The teachers met with each student to evaluate his work, using the student's self-assessment as the basis of the discussion. The completed unit was also sent home so parents could see how their child completed each part of the unit and the assessment activities. An accompanying explanation page invited parent feedback. The bottom line was that the students' assessments demonstrated improved data collection, graphing, and writing skills.

Later that week at a grade-level meeting, the 3rd grade teachers brought samples of the graphs and the assessment lists with which they and their students had assessed the work. The students had done a better job of using titles and labels to describe what the graph was about, but they were still having problems using scales on the axes. Together, the teachers planned how to teach scaling for the next assignment calling for a graph. They also designed an assessment list that focused more attention on scaling.

A 6TH GRADE CASE STUDY: "IKEBANA"

It is early June, but there is no early summer let-down in the 6th grade. Seventy-five excited students pour into the all-purpose room with their teachers. Stacks of colorful khaki (dishes) made in art class, along with rulers and hasami (floral scissors), grace every table. Containers of lilies, alstromeria, iris, bear grass, and galax leaves are lined up in front of the stage, where a local florist prepares to guide these budding artists in the craft of Japanese floral design. His mission is not that difficult. The students have been learning about the geography, technology, history, culture, economy, and government of Japan. This activity is an authentic performance task based on content and skills learned during these studies of Japanese culture in social studies, math, science, library science, and art.

The three team teachers and the special education teacher meet frequently to plan lessons and units. They know that in the Cycle of Learning (see Exhibit 9 in Chapter 1), collaboration is an important component of learning; and

although this particular task stems from a social studies unit, other tasks will come from the science, math, or language arts curriculums. (Exhibit 13 shows the "Ikebana Arrangement" Performance Task.)

To prepare, the students have studied the culture of Japan, including customs and traditions, arts, philosophies, language, education, and religions. They have charted the paths of Buddhist monks and traders as they traveled from India, to China, and finally to Japan. Through earlier tasks and a quiz, students have demonstrated their knowledge of Shintoism, the major religion of Japan before the visiting monks and traders introduced their Buddhist customs and religion. Ikebana, an artistic and religiously symbolic arrangement of flowers, was one of the customs these newcomers brought to Japan. It was readily adopted by the people of this country because a major component of the Shinto religion was the belief in the beauty and spirituality of nature.

Once the students had demonstrated a basic understanding of some ideas from the philosophies of Shintoism and Buddhism—and familiarity with the vocabulary of Ikebana—on a quiz, the science teacher had contacted a local florist who was willing to provide materials and facilitate the Ikebana workshop. The team had applied for and received a grant from the Parent Teacher Organization to pay for materials.

In preparation, the media specialist had located books with Ikebana arrangements that would serve as "excellent models" (or benchmarks) for students to use. In subsequent years, photographs illustrating student-created arrangements could also serve as models. Working with

Enlist the help of parents & community planning task

the art and math teachers, the social studies teacher had developed an assessment list including the mathematical and artistic skills students would need to demonstrate in their floral arrangements.

As the big day approached, the 6th graders were busy using protractors and rulers to prepare for this creative but highly structured task in their math classes. Each main branch of the Ikebana arrangement has a specific location and each is mathematically proportional to the others. Students practiced geometry, ratios, measurement, addition, and division as they followed the task, using practice sheets provided by the math teacher. They sketched out a mathematical model in this class and then brought their drawings to the art teacher, who demonstrated how to add color, harmony, space, and form.

Students also wrote invitations to parents, asking them to attend and participate in this activity, explaining what Ikebana is and including relevant facts about Japanese culture. Some parents created their own arrangements, while others assisted the children or helped with management and organization. Some just came to observe.

As the 6th graders carefully carried their colorful products back to their classrooms, there were smiles of pleasure and squeals of delight as they completed their self-assessments. (Exhibit 14 shows the assessment list for "Creating a Japanese Floral Arrangement.") The teachers agreed that the students had mastered a number of mathematical and art skills.

After the interdisciplinary unit on Japan was over, parents were asked to provide feedback about the whole process, including how the as-

sessment lists helped the parents understand what the project was about and how to support the homework components. From the parent feedback, the teachers decided that they would make a year-long calendar of major performance tasks to be assigned.

At a faculty meeting, the 6th grade team shared their experiences with the interdisciplinary unit on Japan and highlighted how student self-assessment was improving the quality of the student projects and helping them to be more independent learners. The teachers outlined their plans to increase the involvement of students in creating assessment lists.

HIGH SCHOOL CASE STUDY: "EIGHT MILE BROOK"— HONORS BIOLOGY TASK

The gray skies and light drizzle do not dampen the enthusiasm of 18 motivated, academically successful sophomore honors biology students as they review the criteria for the stream management plan they are preparing to write. They engage in good-natured bantering as they follow a narrow path behind the high school to Eight Mile Brook, which borders the school property. Today is the day to gather water samples and record visual sightings that will provide data to be included in a report for the U.S. Environmental Protection Agency (EPA). They exhibit a playfulness and curiosity, in contrast to the more serious, sometimes passive demeanor they display in the classroom and laboratory. The students are cooperative and energetic as they carefully and skillfully collect their samplings and comment on their observations. Their playfulness masks a serious dedication to their task, which for the students, is a chance to really use the knowledge and skills they have been learning.

When the students return to the classroom, *they review lists of criteria they made for their own data charts and graphs* as they organize and analyze the data in preparation for a stream management plan each will write for the EPA (see Exhibit 15 for the "Eight Mile Brook" performance task). The procedures of the task emphasize independent thought, decision making, and problem-solving skills. Not only do the students write a plan, but they identify what types of data they will need, identify the sources of data, and write their own assessment lists for the charts and graphs they use in the plan. On completion of their work, the students received feedback on their assessment lists from their peers, the teachers, and members of the new school building committee (see Exhibit 16 for the "Eight Mile Brook" assessment list).

Later that year, several of these students met with the high school's Performance Assessment Committee to discuss plans for implementing a senior exit project. The Eight Mile Brook project was discussed as a model, and the committee was particularly interested to hear the students talk about how performance tasks and assessments lists used for the past several years of their schooling had prepared them for this "real work."

A FOCUS ON STUDENT WORK DEFINES THE PERFORMANCE-BASED CLASSROOM

Performance tasks give students opportunities to have fun and to use what they have been learning. Assessment lists provide a common framework through which students, teachers, and parents study student work and plan together to improve performance.

Exhibit 11. Elementary School
Performance-Based Learning and Assessment Task:
The Tall and Short of It

Background

The Wisconsin FAST Plant professors are doing research on the size of FAST Plants as they grow. They are interested in collecting data on the heights of growing FAST Plants and getting students to write about why they think some plants grow taller than others.

Task

You have been hired by the University of Wisconsin for your expert knowledge in the area of growing FAST Plants. ← *Lead-In*
Your job is to observe and measure the growth of two plants in your quad—the tallest and the shortest ones. You must record these measurements on a growth chart and then make a line graph from the chart. A summary of this graph will then be used to report your findings, which will be sent back to the Wisconsin FAST Plants professors. This summary will inform the professors of any information or conclusions you came up with about why the two plants were the shortest or the tallest. ← *Expanding perception of authorship*

Your Audience

The brilliant professors at the University of Wisconsin are your audience. (Remember—your job is at stake!!!)

The Purpose of Your Investigation

The purpose of your work is to collect and record measurement data (height of FAST Plants) and write a paragraph report on why you think the plants grew as they did.

Materials Needed

One quad of FAST Plants (the tallest and shortest plants), a centimeter ruler, a growth chart, graph paper, lined paper, pencil, crayons, and, of course—your checklists for a line graph and a summary about the graph to help guide you toward the best job you can do.

Procedure

1. Select the tallest and shortest plants in your quad and measure their heights.
2. Use the data from your Growth Chart to make a line graph. Use the *Classroom Assessment List for a Graph of FAST Plants' Growth* to help you.
3. Write a one-paragraph summary of your graph. Tell what information can be learned from your graph. For example, did one plant have a bigger growth spurt between certain days? What are the ranges of measurements? Are there any patterns in how the two plants grew? What are some similarities or differences between how the two plants grew? Can you make any inferences about why one plant grew taller than the other?

Use of Classroom Assessment List: Written Summary of FAST Plants Line Graph to Help You.

Have fun! And remember—the Wisconsin FAST Plant professors expect quality work from all employees!

Exhibit 12. Performance Task Assessment List for a Graph of FAST Plants' Growth

1. **Heading**
    - T: I included my name and the date.
    - O: I included my name and the date but they are in the wrong place.
    - W: I did not include my name or the date.

2. **Title**
    - T: The title stated exactly what the graph is about. The title includes a short statement of what I changed and what I measured.
    - O: The title tells some of what the graph is about.
    - W: The title is missing.

3. **Labeling the Data**
    - T: The bottom axis has the correct dates written in for each time I measured the plants. The side axis is labeled by every 5 cm.
    - O: The axes need dates and numbers that are more clear.
    - W: The dates and numbers for the axes are missing.

4. **Drawing Lines on the Graph**
    - T: The colored dots are drawn accurately for each height and are very neatly connected using a ruler.
    - O: There are some mistakes or the work is a little messy.
    - W: There are many mistakes and/or the work is very messy.

5. **Key or Legend**
    - T: The key or legend is very clear.
    - O: The key or legend is OK.
    - W: The key or legend needs a lot of work.

Did I do my best work?

Terrific

OK

Needs Work

Exhibit 13. Middle School
Performance-Based Learning and Assessment Task
An Ikebana Arrangement

Background

Ikebana is the term used to describe Japanese floral arrangements. The arrangements have symbolic connections to the Buddhist and Shinto religions and are constructed using materials which have specific mathematical proportions and dimensions. Special attention is paid to color, harmony, space, and design, which are also very important when creating an Ikebana arrangement.

Task

You are a well-known florist who is knowledgeable about Ikebana arrangements. You have been asked to create an Ikebana arrangement for a reception to be held for Japanese business people who are in your town to negotiate a trade deal with a major U.S. company.

Audience

Your audience is the Japanese business people and members of the U.S. company.

Purpose

The purpose of this task is for you to experience an art form from another culture as part of the study of Japan and for you to practice and apply basic math skills such as measurement, addition, division, estimation, and geometry to a real-life situation.

Procedure

1. Use the performance list for creating an Ikebana arrangement.
2. Study the vocabulary and philosophy of Ikebana in social studies classes.
3. Research Ikebana in reference books and look at models.
4. Practice using a protractor in math class.
5. Complete the "Ikebana Practice Sheet" in pairs and check results with another pair in math class.
6. Complete the Ikebana Assessment List in preparation for making the arrangement in math class.
7. Take the model you designed in math to your art class to learn about color, harmony, space, and design. Add these elements to your model.
8. Write an invitation to your parents to attend the workshop in language arts class.
9. Use your plans and knowledge to create an Ikebana arrangement on the workshop day.
10. In class, use the assessment list to evaluate your creation.

Exhibit 14. Performance Task Assessment List
Creating a Japanese Ikebana Floral Arrangement

	ASSESSMENT POINTS		
	Points	Earned Assessment:	
Element	Possible	Self	Teacher

The Drawing

1. The diagram of the plan for your arrangement shows the three distinct main lines made up of flowers or branches. | _____ | _____ | _____ |

2. The Shin, Soe, and Hikae are in correct geometrically relationship to one another and to the center line in the kaki. | _____ | _____ | _____ |

The Arrangement

3. The Shin (heaven) is correctly placed in the kaki (dish). | _____ | _____ | _____ |

4. The Soe (man) is correctly placed. | _____ | _____ | _____ |

5. The Hikae (earth) its correctly placed. | _____ | _____ | _____ |

6. Additional flowers or foliage (assistants) are placed around the Shin, Soe, and Hikae. All assistants are of a proper length. | _____ | _____ | _____ |

7. The arrangement shows artistic elements of color, harmony, space, and form. | _____ | _____ | _____ |

Total | _____ | _____ | _____ |

Exhibit 15. High School
Performance-Based Learning and Assessment Task
Environmental Impact of Building a New School on Eight Mile Brook

Background

Recently, Region 15 approved the construction of a new elementary school on a parcel of land adjacent to Eight Mile Brook in Southbury, CT. The area slated for development, unfortunately, is partially composed of wetland habitat. Over the past several weeks, debate has been increasing over the fact that the wetland area is scheduled to be replaced by athletic fields for the new school. Eight Mile Brook runs along the edge of the proposed site of the new fields. One side cites the school's and community's need for more athletic fields, while the other side questions the need for such facilities, as well as the impact of such development on the biodiversity of the local area.

Task

Your task is to collect data about the conditions of Eight Mile Brook and make a proposal for a management plan which will safeguard it when the new school is being built.

Audience

The audience for your report is the U.S. Environmental Protection Agency (EPA) and the building committee for the new school.

Purpose

The purpose of your study is to convince EPA officials and the community volunteers on the new school building committee to implement your plan to protect Eight Mile Brook.

Procedure

1. Review the assessment list for the management plan you will write.
2. Write a time and task completion plan for your project so that you will be able to get work done and the report written on time.
3. Identify the types of information and data you will need.
4. Identify the sources of this information and data.
5. Practice the analytic techniques you have been learning to study water quality.
6. Write your own assessment list for such products as graphs, data charts, and maps which will be part of your final report.
7. You will be working as part of a team to collect the type of data assigned to you. All data will be shared with all team members. Each person will write a management plan for the protection of Eight Mile Brook in building the new school.

Exhibit 16. Performance Task Assessment List Position Paper for the Management Plan to Protect Eight Mile Brook in Southbury

Element	Points Possible	Earned Assessment: Self	Earned Assessment: Teacher
1. The problem is identified.	5	_____	_____
2. The methodology of the study is summarized.	15	_____	_____
3. Diagrams, maps, graphs, and charts are effectively used to present data.	15	_____	_____
4. Relevant scientific concepts are used accurately.	20	_____	_____
5. Scientific vocabulary is explained.	10	_____	_____
6. Information from personal experience is used to augment information from resource materials.	5	_____	_____
7. The conditions of Eight Mile Brook are summarized concisely.	10	_____	_____
8. Recommendations for protecting Eight Mile Brook are made.	20	_____	_____
9. Diagrams and drawings support the descriptions of recommendations.	15	_____	_____
10. All recommendations are justified.	20	_____	_____
11. There is a powerful concluding statement of the writer's position.	5	_____	_____
12. The mechanics of English are correct and the writing is neat and presentable.	10	_____	_____
Total	150	_____	_____

HOW ARE PERFORMANCE-BASED LEARNING AND ASSESSMENT TASKS CREATED?

3

Define task in relation to standard(s)
• what should students know & be able to do •

may need to redefine standard

may need to modify task

~ FEEDBACK ~

Create Performance Task: Make Assessment List: Provide benchmarks •

Evaluate student work
Plan future work

may need to modify areas

Flowcharts can be helpful in creating and following many complex processes. The flowchart for developing performance-based learning and assessment tasks and assessment lists provides a framework within which teachers and administrators can organize their work (see Exhibit 17 at the end of this chapter). The process starts with defining what students should know and be able to do; continues with creating performance tasks, making assessment lists, providing models or benchmarks, and embedding the tasks in instruction; and ends with evaluating student work and planning future work. Although the process is presented in a linear format, it is actually nonlinear. Each component in the flowchart interacts with every other element, creating many feedback loops.

WHERE DO THE IDEAS COME FROM?

Performance-based tasks are perfect for capturing attention and motivating children of any age. Students need real-life tasks and connections to personal experiences, as well as choices that show mastery and competence, to motivate them to learn. Although writing and test taking are important skills, other modes of expression and assessment, such as role playing, simulations, debates and oral/visual presentations, are also important if students are to be truly prepared for the real-world experiences they will face after graduation. But where do teachers get their ideas for creating these tasks? Where do the content and skills around which assessment tasks are built come from?

USING THE TEXT

One of the first questions teachers ask is, "How do I cover work in the text and do performance tasks as well?" Clearly, the answer is to choose a section of the text and design a task that covers the same material. For example, according to the curriculum, students in a social studies class are required to learn about the resources of Canada from material that is located in a chapter of their textbook. The chapter includes information on the country's multitude of agricultural and mineral products, how agriculture and industry affect the economy, and how a nation's surplus leads to trade. The teacher might set up a task based on The World Trade Agreement and ask students to promote Canada's products and technology to leaders of one of the developing countries that joined this new trade group. Students might choose the country, using almanacs to see what products it needs. The task might include writing persuasive letters, including charts, graphs, and maps, to leaders of these developing nations and designing a presentation to promote Canada's products and encourage trade. The presentation is done in front of class members. This idea can be a refreshing change from "Read the text and answer questions."

Another way to use the text is to set up a task where students rewrite and illustrate sections of their textbooks either to teach younger children or to make them more appealing to their own age group.

CURRICULUM IDEAS

Another question a teacher might ask is, "How do I connect these tasks to the curriculum?" The answer is to use skills already required by the curriculum. For example, if the curriculum requires all students to be able to write a persuasive essay by 8th grade, a teacher could find samples of authentic articles that show two points of view on a particular issue that would be of interest to students, perhaps on a controversy in their town or a question on student rights or education. Students choose sides, find details and facts to support their positions, and debate the issue with peers. Reversing perspectives helps all students understand both sides of the issue. They can then respond by writing editorials addressing the public, the school board, or government officials and mailing them. The important point is that students have used the performance task to demonstrate a real skill or concept from the curriculum.

Many teachers use themes to organize their curriculum. Performance tasks are embedded in the unit to allow students opportunities to use the content, process skills, and work habits relevant to the thematic unit.

Following is an example of a sequence of curriculum organized around conceptual themes, questions, and performance tasks:

Two Conceptual Themes

I. The environment affects people, and people affect the environment.

II. Patterns can be found in changes of matter and energy.

An Essential Question Derived from Each Theme

I. How do people adjust their lives because of the factors in their environment?

II. How can changes be better understood through using graphics to show their patterns?

Sample Units of Instruction

A. **Weather**

Focus questions connecting the unit topic to the essential questions:

I.   How do people protect themselves against the weather?

II.   How does water move through the environment?

Performance tasks:

I.   Select one type of dangerous weather. Write a safety pamphlet or produce a video for the people in your community explaining how that weather is dangerous and how to protect yourself from it.

II.   Write and illustrate a story or create an interactive computer experience for children about the trip of a water molecule through the environment.

B. **Insects**

Focus questions connecting the unit topic to the essential questions:

I.   How do insects help and harm people?

Performance task:

I. & II. Make a display or a multimedia presentation, accompanied by a research report, that shows the life-cycle of an insect that is important to humans. Match the stages of the life-cycle to the ways that particular insect helps or harms humans. Explain how humans can protect themselves from these insects. The posters or other displays will be exhibited in the public library.

The two themes work to organize learning within or among disciplines and may stay the same for several grade levels or even for the entire continuum of grades, K–12. Themes are in-tended to become "lenses" through which the student will study the world. Essential questions are more specific and are written at the developmental level of the learner and connect the theme to the units of study for the year. Units of study are planned that are engaging to students and well-connected to the essential questions for that year. Focus questions are very specific versions of the essential questions, and they direct the learners' attention to the details of information to come.

Performance tasks engage the students in interesting projects to use content knowledge, process skills, and work habits to "answer" the focus questions of that unit. There is a clear connection between the content of performance tasks, focus questions, essential questions, and broad themes. Students are shown all of these elements so that they will begin to build a "cognitive" framework within which they can continue to learn.

CURRENT EVENTS

Some of the best authentic tasks stem from current events. By keeping an eye on the news, teachers can help students see the relevance of what they are learning to the real world. By reading with an eye toward adapting current events to the classroom, teachers quickly begin to identify articles that might provide the background information to share with students and options for a task. Frequently the article itself will provide ideas for a task students can perform, as well as a purpose for that task. For example, during the Canada unit mentioned earlier, the idea for a task might come from a magazine article that compared the impact of world trade on the local economy in your state with that of a province in Canada, rather than the textbook. Information in the article about different trade or business organizations might provide ideas for the task, a product, and an audience for that product.

By providing an audience, a realistic format, or intended product for the task, we can make sure that abstract issues and concepts become grounded in real, concrete tasks that are connected to real and relevant issues. Elections provide a particular wealth of information for creating tasks from current events. Students can write and perform radio spots, debate as they role-play candidates, and design campaign materials. Newspapers often provide the platforms of each candidate, which students can use for research.

LITERATURE

Responding to literature through literal understanding, conducting analysis, making connections, and evaluating the quality of the literature are central processes in performance-based learning tasks related to literature. For example, Exhibits 18–21 show performance tasks and assessment lists that guide student thinking in the explication of a poem and in poetry reading (these can be used in middle or high school).

Performance tasks embedded in the curriculum can use literature as a context to explore themes from social studies and geography. For example, middle school students reading *The Big Wave* by Pearl Buck learn about and discuss the devastating effects a tidal wave has on a Japanese village community. Students can find articles about other natural disasters, such as floods, fires, and hurricanes, and discuss the im-

pact on the affected communities. Related tasks might focus on either written newspaper articles or "on the scene" televised reports. Inventions or new technology to eliminate or counteract the affects of a disaster, or a simulated speech given by a leader whose country has been affected, are other possibilities. A journal of a "victim," with facts, pictures, and feelings, could be generated as an authentic performance task as well. (Exhibits 22 and 23 show a performance task and assessment list for "When Disaster Strikes.")

At the high school level, similar formats could be used with books from different time periods. Tasks related to a reading of *A Tale of Two Cities* or *Hiroshima* could include debates and eye-witness accounts to demonstrate an understanding of the issues and themes presented. Novels such as the *Andromeda Strain, A Brave New World*, or *Animal Farm* could be related to contemporary events in a similar fashion.

Other interdisciplinary performance tasks provide opportunities to connect literature with science or math. The performance task, to create a life-line map of a fictitious character or a past or present leader, integrates graphing with the analysis of literature. The performance task that analyzes Jack London's story, *To Build a Fire,* in the context of the physiology of hypothermia, connects science and the analysis of character development. (Exhibits 24 and 25 show performance tasks and assessment lists for a "Life-Line Map" using important people, past or present, or fictitious characters; Exhibits 26 and 27 show tasks and lists for "To Build a Fire" and "Hypothermia.")

Other ways to connect literature with other disciplines include the use of children's books—

with middle and high school students. An effective performance task puts the learner into the role of a member of a book selection committee for a local elementary school charged with evaluating a book such as Eric Carle's *The Very Hungry Caterpillar* (see Exhibits 28 and 29 for the task and assessment list for "Reviewing Children's Books for the Library"). This task requires the student to use knowledge of insect structure and function and life cycles. A follow-up performance task is to write a children's book that is both entertaining and scientifically correct (see Exhibits 30 and 31, "Writing a Science Book for Children").

Finally, the genre of writing fiction provides a wealth of opportunities for developing engaging performance tasks. For example, one task that many students find appealing is to write a sequel to a novel they have read—taking their cue from *Star Trek* and *Star Wars* movie sequels. (See Exhibits 32 and 33 for the task and assessment list for "Writing a Sequel.")

FINE, PERFORMING, AND TECHNICAL ARTS

Art, music, and other fine and performing arts are models of performance-based learning and assessment. For example, a performance task called "So You Want to Be a Song Writer" and an assessment list for writing a song can engage students in an application of what they have been learning about music (see Exhibits 34 and 35). The task and assessment list give students a structure through which to create and discuss their work. The performance task, "Original 12 Bar Blues," is another example of shaping activities in music into more engaging and better

connected performance-based learning and assessment tasks (see Exhibits 36 and 37 for the task and assessment list). The assessment list for "Original 12 Bar Blues," like many middle or high school-level lists, has categories and subdivisions to enable students to handle complicated performance tasks.

Other projects in the fine and technical arts can be enhanced by creating authentic audiences for student work and by creating assessment lists. For example, in the performance task "Nonobjective Painted Design," students are told: "You have been asked to submit some of your work to a graphic design company interested in hiring part-time student artists." (See Exhibits 38 and 39 for the "Painted Design" task and assessment list.) Another project involves designing a science center for an elementary school. (See Exhibits 40 and 41 for the task and list for "Orthographic [Multiview] Pictorial.")

LARGER WORLD MATERIALS

Teachers have found many ways to use real-world materials like advertising circulars, travel brochures, phone books, and recipe books to create performance tasks. A multiple-page grocery circular can generate many math tasks. Upper-elementary grade students can be given a budget and asked to feed a family of four for a week. Gathering and applying coupons can add interest to the task as the students total up their savings. Comparison shopping using two circulars enhances both math and reading skills. Restaurant menus offer similar opportunities. The performance task, "Consumer Decision Making: Restaurants and Senior Citizens," engages students in mathematical analysis and writing. The task asks students to find out if the senior citizen menu "is really a good deal"—and to make this determination to help an elderly relative. (For this task and its assessment list, see Exhibits 42 and 43.)

Other real-world sources of information abound. Travel brochures can be used as both models and information sources for students who are studying countries. They are especially helpful for students who have trouble showing what they know through more traditional formats like reports and tests. Phone books provide a wealth of information in many subject areas; and they include maps, government listings, time zones, and a wealth of vocabulary. Recipe books are excellent for generating math tasks using fractions and measurement. The task, "Cookbook Algebra," asks the student to use algebra to analyze how long it takes to cook varying amounts of food in the oven or microwave. (See Exhibits 44 and 45 for the "Cookbook Algebra" task and assessment list.)

Advertisements in print and on television are an endless source of opportunities for students to use math problem-solving skills. A claim for how many Americans eat each day in a nationally known hamburger chain was the source for the performance task called "Fast Food Math." (See Exhibits 46 and 47 for the "Fast Food Math" task and assessment list.)

MATH TASKS FROM MENUS

Menus are treasure troves of performance tasks in math. The following series of performance tasks are based on a regular menu and the senior citizens' menu from a local restaurant. The first task is a simple, constructed-response task; and the final example is a fully authentic performance task requiring math and communi-

cation skills. Senior citizens are the real audience because student work evaluated to be "excellent" is actually given to the senior citizens in the community.

Math Tasks

1. What is the sum of the following amounts of money?

$4.95

$2.15

$1.55

2. You have five dollars. Can you buy the following food items with the money you have? (Use the menu given to you.) If you will have any money left after you buy this food, exactly how much money will you have left? If you need to borrow, exactly how much money will you need to borrow? (Assume that there is no food tax and that you do not leave a tip.)

Bacon Cheeseburger Supermelt

Chocolate Fribble

Happy Ending Butterscotch Sundae

3. What is the most popular lunch that your friends would buy from this menu? How much would the most popular lunch cost?

4. This restaurant has a regular menu and a special menu for senior citizens. Do the senior citizens save money by using the senior's menu?

5. This restaurant has a regular menu and a special menu for senior citizens. Is this a "good deal" for senior citizens? Do an analysis of the "deal" for senior citizens and write a newspaper article about what you find. This newspaper article could be published in the weekly newspaper distributed to homes of senior citizens living in your town.

SHAPE YOUR BEST ACTIVITIES INTO PERFORMANCE TASKS

For teachers who are new to performance tasks, probably the easiest place to start is with projects and activities you already use. These can frequently be redesigned as performance tasks. A 1st grade class normally looks at photographs and videos of chicks developing inside their eggs. Instead of just making a poster or drawing pictures, the students could create a display for a children's museum, make a picture book for preschoolers, or design a poster for a nature center. High school physics and music students could create a video or live performance for younger students demonstrating how and why various instruments produce their sound.

Creating authentic tasks for students helps them connect the content, skills, and work habits they learn in the classroom to the larger world. As a result, teachers can use an unlimited number of real-world sources in developing tasks. All it takes is a little imagination and creativity, traits we all should foster and model for our students.

FOUR APPROACHES TO CREATING ENGAGING AND WELL-CONNECTED PERFORMANCE TASKS

Performance tasks must be well connected to the curriculum so that the time spent on these tasks is directed at accomplishing your goals for student performance and meeting the needs of your curriculum, whatever they happen to be. But tasks also must be engaging to students so that they will enter the task with the interest and enthusiasm necessary to sustain their efforts. In short, tasks must be engaging or "nifty" (see Figure 3). Four approaches for creating nifty, well-connected tasks are called "The Inside-Out Strategy" (Figure 4), "The Outside-In Strategy"

(Figure 5), "Planning Backwards," and "The Cycle of Learning" (see Exhibit 9).

INSIDE-OUT STRATEGY

1. Start with an engaging activity, perhaps one you already do with students. For example, students enjoy speculating about the natural environment of a "creature" that was part of the 1993–94 Statewide Connecticut Academic Performance Test (CAPT) for 10th grade. Using an "inside-out" strategy (see Figure 4), you will start with the activity and look for places to connect it

---

FIGURE 3. Performance Task

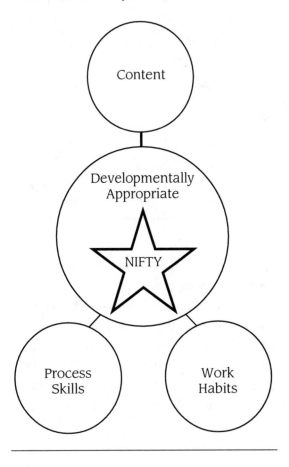

FIGURE 4. Inside-Out Strategy

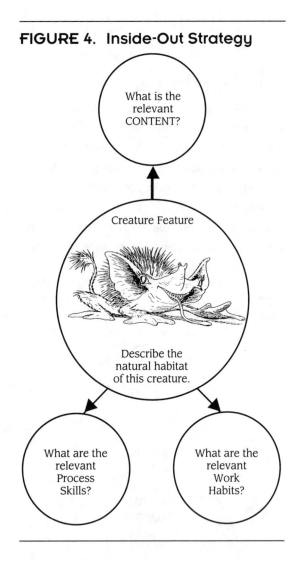

the Advancement of Science [AAAS] *Bench-marks of Science Literacy*; see References.) These connections included two in which students are required to demonstrate understanding of the following concepts:

- Living organisms have needs that are met through specific structures in specific environments.

- Animals and plants have a great variety of body plans and internal structures that contribute to their being able to make or find food and reproduce.

Our curriculums also include science and communication process skills and work habits. These include:

- Technical drawing and writing
- Organization
- Attention to detail

3. Select an audience, such as younger students or readers of *National Geographic*, for the students' work and write the task as shown in the "Creature Feature" performance task (see Exhibit 48). Specifying the audience focuses the task. Students are more likely to write a scientific description of the environment if they are *writing to a real audience to explain science concepts,* thus further enhancing the quality of the work.

4. The last step is to write an assessment list that makes the curriculum connections to the important elements of content, process skills and work habits that you identified. (See Exhibit 49 for the assessment list for "Writing in Science.")

"out" to the content, process skills, and work habits of your curriculum.

2. Survey your curriculums to identify specific objectives from the disciplines most connected to this task. For the "creature" task, we found several connections to our curriculums in Connecticut's Region 15. (Our science themes are derived from the American Association for

OUTSIDE-IN STRATEGY

You already have identified the connections to the curriculums and are searching for an engaging performance task. In other words, you are starting with the curriculum and moving into a task. To illustrate, we will start with the same curricular connections we just explored in the "Creature Feature" and will look to develop a new "nifty" task for our students (Figure 5).

1. Brainstorm some examples of real or imaginary organisms, machines, or other inventions that carry out specific functions within specific environments. Some examples are:

- Organisms: Alligator snapping turtle, flea (magnified 100 times), mole rat, giant sloth, horn bill, tapeworm (magnified 10 times), types of bats, types of ants, types of spiders
- Machines and inventions: Types of bicycles; types of baseball gloves; types of stereo speakers; types of shoes; types of hammers; types of scissors, shears, and clippers; types of strategies for security seals on food or medicine containers

2. Rewrite the "Creature Feature" task to fit the new example.

3. Choose an audience.

4. Consider letting students choose their own examples and audience. "Nifty" is in the eye of the beholder, and students are the judge of "niftyness." Involving students in helping to create performance tasks increases the chance that "niftyness" will be achieved.

5. Select or design a format for the final product, such as a written explanation supported by technical drawings, models, posters, and electronic media or oral presentations.

FIGURE 5. Outside-In Strategy

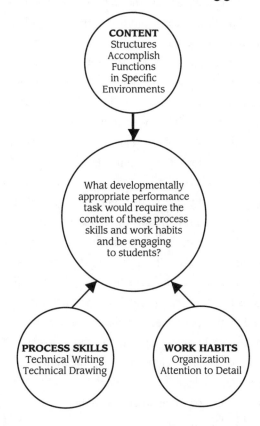

PLAN BACKWARDS

A final project or a "Senior Exhibition" is an example of an exit-level performance task that could come at the end of a course or segment of schooling. Such an "exit-level" performance task requires the most sophisticated use of the content, process skills, and work habits to be required of the student, and can be viewed as a culminating activity—as final exams or a semester "term paper" have traditionally been used.

Science teachers in a school district, for example, could plan together for the type of exit-level performances desired as "targets" for their sequences of courses. One such exit-level performance could be to ask students to explain and illustrate the concepts "Form Follows Function" and "Function Follows Form." Such a task would include the two concepts demonstrated earlier in a student's career, such as the completion of the "Creature Feature" task (see Exhibits 48 and 49). The format for an exit-level product might be left to the student and might include a museum display, an illustrated book, a video, a CD-ROM, or an oral presentation with visuals. Whatever their choice of format, students must show mastery of the science and communication skills that have been central to the curriculum and their experiences through tasks over the course of the semester or their school career. In addition to their science teacher, the audience for their final work could be a panel of students and adults, or some other real audience external to the class or school.

Once an "exit-level target" is identified, the science staff works backward to plan one-year or multiple-year sequences of performance tasks that not only involve the students in learning the content but also in learning how to communicate to various audiences through varied formats. The "Creature Feature" or other similar tasks assess the degree to which students understand and can explain how function dictates structure. Other tasks about the structure of the earth or the structure of atoms assess the degree to which students understand and can explain how structure directs function. Some tasks call for technical writing and drawing, some require

models and oral presentation, and others may ask for museum displays. Over time, students build a repertoire of communication formats, many of which mimic tasks they may be called on to perform in the adult workplace or in college.

Each "preliminary" performance task is engaging and well connected to the curriculums and systematically builds a foundation for the "exit-level" performance task that is itself also engaging and well connected to the curriculums of the school and district.

Performance task assessment lists promote a systematic development of content, process, and work habit skills. The assessment lists for the "exit-level" project should be developed by the student and approved by the teacher and mentor. In this way, the student also demonstrates that she has internalized the necessary criteria and can clearly identify "excellence."

CYCLE OF LEARNING STRATEGY

The Cycle of Learning (see Exhibit 9) defines authentic work for a learner of any age. Individual and group work are balanced. Academic content, interpersonal skills, and intrapersonal skills mesh together to produce real products for real audiences.

Initially, a math task asking students to compare the costs of food between regular and senior citizen's menus (see Exhibit 42) evolved into a more complex Cycle of Learning task, "Consumer Decision-Making Newsletter," which student teams would publish as a guide to "best buys in pizza, groceries, automobiles, stereo systems . . . and roller blades." The task requires students to make decisions about topics to be

[handwritten marginal note:] Teachers begin by choosing a large culminating activity. All prior tasks must build up to final project.

covered and the best ways to do research, present their findings, and use effective graphics or other illustrations. The task also asks students to develop both group and individual management plans, described on the "Management Plan" assessment list. (See Exhibits 50–55 for the "Consumer Decision-Making Newsletter" performance task and its associated assessment lists and management plans.)

EMBEDDING PERFORMANCE TASKS IN YOUR CURRICULUM

Creating performance tasks that are both "nifty" and well-connected to your curriculum will take some time. Collaboration among teachers within a school or school district can make the process more efficient.

EMERGING ANCHOR TASKS

At an early stage, some tasks are "nifty" but not well connected, some are well connected but do not engage students, and others are both "nifty" and well connected. As the teachers' skills in creating these performance tasks increase, more "nifty" and well-connected tasks are embedded in the curriculum just where they belong to help the students learn how to use their knowledge, skills, and work habits. After fine-tuning these performance tasks for two or three years, teachers may agree to designate the best ones as "anchor tasks" to be required by all teachers using that curriculum. The "anchor tasks" now become common experiences for students, and data from their performance can be used to study the performance of groups of students in a school or school system. Figure 6

shows emerging performance tasks turning into anchor tasks.

ANCHOR TASKS ARE THE "BEST HITS"

After using and refining performance tasks, teachers at the same grade level in the school or school district can select the tasks that are the most engaging to students and best connected to content knowledge, process skills, and work habits of the curriculum. Those performance tasks are designated as "anchor tasks" and will be done in the same way by all the teachers who use them. This "common experience" includes a specified distribution of points on a common assessment list. Student performance on anchor tasks enables educators to provide and assess a common learning and assessment experience for all students at a grade level.

WHAT ARE SOME AUDIENCES FOR STUDENT WORK?

Usually the audience for student work is the teacher or other students in the classroom; however, many other potential audiences exist. Changing the audience for student work both motivates the student and prepares the learner for doing real- world work that always has a real audience. Teachers can foster independence by allowing students to select the audience from time to time. Some potential audiences include:

- Younger students
- Students in other schools, school districts, states, or countries
- A principal, secretary, custodian, cafeteria worker, or bus driver
- Next year's teacher

FIGURE 6. Emerging and Embedded Performance Tasks

Emerging Performance Tasks

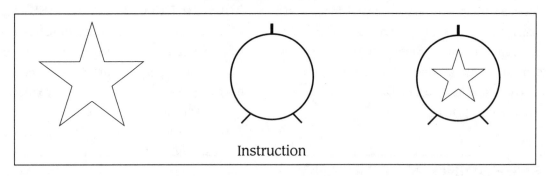

Instruction

Embedded Performance Tasks

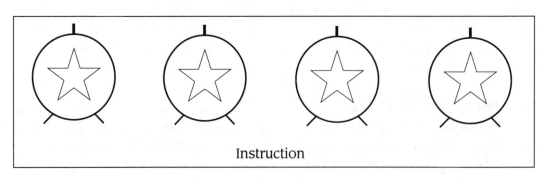

Instruction

Emerging Anchor Performance Tasks

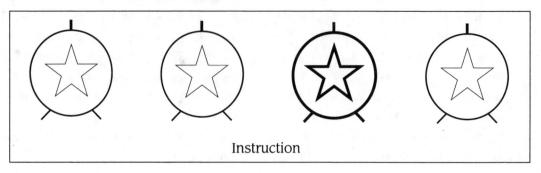

Instruction

Time in Years

- An adult in the community with an interest in the topic of the performance task
  - An adult at home
  - A professional such as a scientist or artist

WHAT ARE SOME FORMATS FOR STUDENT WORK?

Many different types of formats exist for the work students do as a part of performance tasks. The following is a list of such formats made by a districtwide team of teachers working in grades 1–12. Teachers will recognize many of them as types of projects already in place. This wide assortment of types of student work allows options for how students use their content knowledge, process skills, and work habits to show how they can use what they have learned. Other teacher teams will no doubt have other formats to add to this list.

Analysis Map of a
  Leader
Autobiography
Bulletin Board Display
Business Letter
Cartoon or Comic
Cause and Effect Essay
Children's Book
Cinquaine Poem
Collage
Composing and
  Performing a Song
Consumer Decision
  Making
Data Table or Chart
  Display
Drawing or Illustration,
  Creative

Drawing or Illustration,
  Technical
Editorial
Ethnic Food
Event Chain Graphic
  Organizer
Experiment, Designing
  and Troubleshooting
Expository Essay
Fairy Tale
Folk Tale
Friendly Letter
Geographic Game
Grant Application
  Simulation
Graph, Bar or Line
Graph, Bar Using Algebra
Graph, Pie of Circle

Graph, Picto-
Graphic Design
Group Work
History Book Chapter
Hyperlearning Stack
Idea Web Graphic
  Organizer
Information Problem
  Solving
Interview
Invention
Issue Controversy
Journal, Geographic
Lab Report
Land Use Survey
Letter Asking for
  Information
Letter to the Editor
Management Plan for a
  Group Project
Management Plan for
  an Individual Project
Map
Math Problem Solving
  with Algebra
Math Problem Solving
  with Arithmetic
Math Problem Solving
  with Geometry
Math Problem Solving
  with Statistics

Models
Newspaper Article
Observing
Oral Report with
  Visuals
Pamphlet
Peer Editing
Persuasive Writing
Geographic Portfolio
Poster
Reading Journal for a
  Novel
Research Report
Science Fair Display
Scrap Book
Skit
Slide Show or Photo
  Essay
Song with Music and
  Lyrics
Story Problem, Creating
Survey
Time Line Graphic
  Organizer
Travel Brochure
Tribute or Eulogy
Venn Diagram
Video
Weather Map
Writing Fiction
Writing Nonfiction

Teachers review the menu of student work formats in planning performance tasks. A science task might ask the student to demonstrate how the structure of a machine is related to the function of transferring energy to do some specific type of work. Options for the ways in which the students can show their knowledge include written reports, inventions, models, skits, and drawings. A social studies task developed to let students show what they have learned about the question, "What does it mean to be an American?" could allow the students to choose from product formats such as a song, a folk tale, a persuasive essay, a museum display, or a slide show to demonstrate how they can use what they know. Planning for a variety of formats and allowing students opportunities to choose whether they write a story, create a graphic organizer, perform a skit, compose a song, do a scientific experiment, collaborate with others, or work alone support the "multiple intelligences" of the students in your classroom.

Grade-level teams of teachers or districtwide curriculum committees can designate a set of formats as core so that all students have a chance to learn the particular skills involved with various types of projects. Providing real audiences for performance-based projects helps the students learn how to communicate with different audiences. Over the course of several years, students can develop a repertoire of strategies to use their content knowledge, process skills, and work habits to create products that inform, persuade, and entertain a variety of audiences.

Exhibit 17. Flow Chart for Developing Performance-Based Learning and Assessment Tasks and Assessment Lists

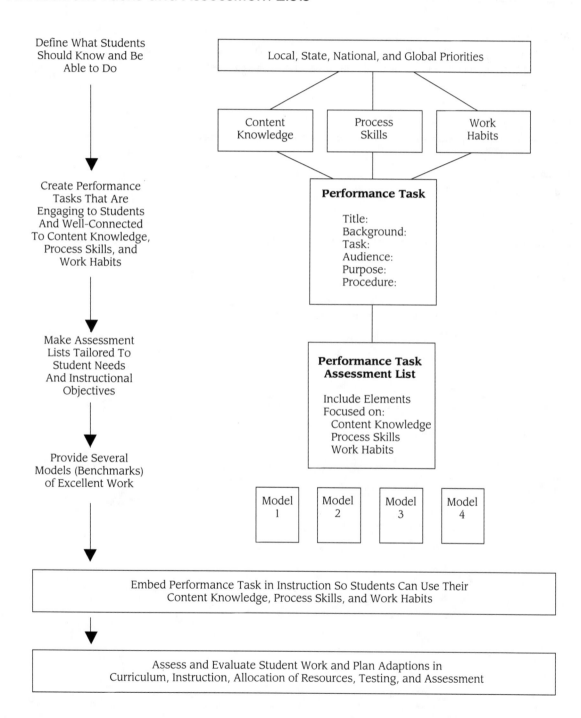

Exhibit 18. Performance Task
Explication of a Poem

Background

The literary society of the public library has invited you and your class to join them for an afternoon of discussion of poetry and refreshments. This group offers several large scholarships each year to students planning on continuing their education in the humanities.

Task

Your task is to select a poem for which you will write an analysis for the literary society.

Audience

Your audience is the members of the literary society.

Purpose

The purpose of your work is to demonstrate to the literary society how skillful you are in the explication of a poem.

Procedure

1. Use the assessment list of an explication of a poem.
2. Select a poem. Each person in the class must select a different poem.
3. Complete your analysis.

Exhibit 19. Performance Task Assessment List for an Explication of a Poem

Element	Points Possible	Earned Assessment: Self	Earned Assessment: Teacher
		ASSESSMENT POINTS	
1. Poem is typed or printed out—Double Spaced.	7	_____	_____
2. Poem has notation for a line-by-line analysis of various poetic devices (rhythm, meter, rhyme, imagery, simile, metaphor, personification, paradox, form, symbolism).	7	_____	_____
3. Poem has notation for how the most important poetic devices contribute in the poem's theme.	5	_____	_____
4. Outline/Rough Draft for the paper is complete.	5	_____	_____
5. Introduction of Essay: Clear statement of topic and thesis.	10	_____	_____
6. Body of Essay: At least 3 important poetic devices are discussed and related to the poem's theme. Each device is developed in one paragraph.	60	_____	_____
7. Conclusion: A well-developed paragraph to wrap up paper. Extremely thoughtful.	10	_____	_____
Total	100	_____	_____

Exhibit 20. Performance Task
Poetry Reading

Background

Your school has a video studio that broadcasts directly into the homes of the residents of your town. An analysis of the programming of that station has shown a lack of literary programs.

Task

Your task is to help produce an on-air poetry workshop for the members of your community. You will select and read a poem which will be videotaped for public broadcast.

Audience

The audience is the people in your community.

Purpose

The purpose of your work is to entertain the members of the community.

Procedure

1.   Use the assessment list for reading a poem.
2.   Prepare your poem.
3.   Make an appointment and videotape your reading.

Exhibit 21. Performance Task Assessment List
Poetry Reading

Element	Points Possible	Earned Assessment: Self	Earned Assessment: Teacher
Pre-performance			
1. It is evident the poem has been carefully selected.	20	_____	_____
2. It is evident the speaker thoughtfully rehearsed.	10	_____	_____
Performance			
3. Speaker introduced and concluded his or her performance, including the title of the poem, the author, a brief statement about what led to the poem's selection, vocabulary that might be helpful.	5	_____	_____
4. Speaker was not dependent upon the script.	5	_____	_____
5. Speaker enunciated clearly and fluidly.	5	_____	_____
6. Speaker used his or her voice artistically, varying pace, quality, pitch, and force to reflect a mood and help the listener grasp the meaning.	20	_____	_____
7. Speaker's volume was appropriate.	5	_____	_____
8. Speaker's performance was appropriately animated (with facial or other gestures), not lifeless, mechanical.	10	_____	_____
9. Speaker is aware of, not overwhelmed by, the musicality of the poem.	5	_____	_____
Overall Effectiveness of the Performance			
10. This was a pleasure to hear. Through voice and expression, the poem was brought to life.	15	_____	_____
Total	100	_____	_____

Exhibit 22. Performance Task
When Disaster Strikes

Background

Countries have been struck with natural disasters throughout history. Tsunamis, earthquakes, monsoons, hurricanes, major floods, tornadoes, droughts, and fires have killed millions; torn apart families; destroyed villages, towns, and cities; wreaked havoc on economies; and changed the course of history in hundreds of nations.

Task

You are a newspaper reporter in a country. You witnessed the death and destruction caused by a natural disaster and are asked by your editor to write a newspaper article describing the event and the effect it has on the people, the economy, the technology, the government, and the geography of the country you are working in.

Audience

The citizens who read the newspaper in this country and in other countries.

Purpose

To show the effect of natural disasters through a newspaper article.

Procedure

1. Use the assessment list for "A Natural Disaster: A Newspaper Article."
2. Choose a natural disaster that could occur in the country you are studying.
3. Research this type of disaster using reference books, text books, books in the library, newspaper and/or magazine articles, and videos.
4. Meet with a group of peers. Discuss how this natural disaster would affect families, the economy, technology, government, and the geography of this country.
5. You may also consult with adults.
6. Write the article. Remember to use the assessment list.
7. Revise and write the final draft.
8. Submit to the editor (teacher.)

Exhibit 23. Performance Task Assessment List
When Disaster Strikes: Newspaper Article

		ASSESSMENT POINTS		
	Points		Earned Assessment:	
Element	Possible	Peer	Self	Teacher
1. The headline catches the attention of the reader.	_____	_____	_____	_____
2. The writer's name and commercial press association appears under the headline.	_____	_____	_____	_____
3. The specific area (city, state, region) and country is noted in the date line.	_____	_____	_____	_____
4. The first sentence, or "lead" sums up the main idea of the story.	_____	_____	_____	_____
5. The first or second paragraph tells who, what, when, where, why, and how.	_____	_____	_____	_____
6. The body of the article tells how the disaster affected or will affect:	_____	_____	_____	_____
The people and their culture	_____	_____	_____	_____
The economy	_____	_____	_____	_____
The technology	_____	_____	_____	_____
The government	_____	_____	_____	_____
The geography	_____	_____	_____	_____
7. Details and elaboration (examples) are provided.	_____	_____	_____	_____
8. Quotes are used to add interest and support.	_____	_____	_____	_____
9. A picture or drawing is included.	_____	_____	_____	_____
10. There are no errors in spelling, punctuation, and grammar.	_____	_____	_____	_____
Total	_____	_____	_____	_____

Exhibit 24. Performance-Based Learning and Assessment Task Literature and Math: Life-Line Map

Background

There are defining events in each of our lives that stand out as the most important when the whole map of our life is displayed. Much can be learned about a fictional character or a past or present leader from mapping and rating these defining events in his or her life.

Task

You are a historian selecting and explaining the defining events in the life of a fictional character or a past or present leader you have chosen for this study. Your task is to construct a life-line map of events that were the most important in showing how this individual defined and acted on his or her values and beliefs. For each event you list, you will rate it on a scale of +5 to -5 according to the impact it had on the individual. You will rate each event a second time on a scale of +5 to -5 according to the impact it had on the community.

Audience

The audience for your life-line map is the members of the literary club of your local public library. Your line-line map and written explanation will be displayed in the public library.

Purpose

The purpose of your life-line map is to create a graphic display of the important events of a person's life. A graphic display is sometimes easier to understand than a long essay.

Procedure

1. Study the performance task assessment list for a life-line map.
2. Select a person such as:
     Maya Angelou from *I Know Why the Caged Bird Sings*
     Santiago from *Old Man and the Sea*
     Bigger Thomas from *Native Son*
     Willy Loman from *Death of a Salesman*
     Hester Prynne from *The Scarlet Letter*
     Others options are Malcolm X, Martin Luther King Jr., John F. Kennedy, and Eleanor Roosevelt.
     (You may suggest an alternative.)
3. Construct the life-line map with the life line on the horizontal plane and a rating scale of +5 to -5 on the vertical plane.
4. Select events from the life of the person you have chosen that show how that person defined and acted on his or her values and beliefs.
5. Rate each event according to its effect on the person. Connect these ratings with a solid line.
6. Rate each event according to its effect on the community. Connect these ratings with a broken line.
7. Write a separate paper explaining why you chose the events you chose and explain how you came to your opinion as to the effect each event had on the person and the community.

Exhibit 25. Performance Task Assessment List
Literature and Math: Life-Line Map

Element	Points Possible	Earned Assessment: Self	Earned Assessment: Teacher
		ASSESSMENT POINTS	

The Life-line Map

1. A horizontal life-line with a vertical scale of -5 to +5 is constructed to cover the life of the individual being mapped. _____ _____ _____

2. At least ____ events in the individual's life are mapped on the life-line that show how the person defined and acted on his or her values and beliefs. _____ _____ _____

3. Each event is rated on the scale of -5 to +5 according to its impact on the individual's life. A solid line connects each of these rating points in a consecutive manner. _____ _____ _____

4. Each event is rated again on the scale of -5 to +5 according to its impact on the community. A broken line connects each of these rating points in a consecutive manner. _____ _____ _____

5. Graphics are used to help describe each event. _____ _____ _____

6. A short statement explains the event and the rating it received. _____ _____ _____

7. Mechanics of English are correct and the work is neat and presentable. _____ _____ _____

**Back-up Written Explanation
(Separate from Life-Line)**

8. The impact of each event on the person's life is explained. _____ _____ _____

9. The impact of each event on the community is explained. _____ _____ _____

10. Mechanics of English are correct and the work is neat and presentable _____ _____ _____

Total _____ _____ _____

Exhibit 26. Performance-Based Learning and Assessment Task
Literature and Science
<u>To Build a Fire</u> by Jack London

Background
Jack London's story, *To Build a Fire*, is about a man struggling in the Arctic wilderness to build a fire to save his life. As the story unfolds, the man goes deeper and deeper into hypothermia.

Task
You are an expert on hypothermia and are using this story as an example of how a person behaves as hypothermia develops. Your task is to write an explanation of the physiological changes the person is undergoing that are matched to the behaviors that person is exhibiting.

Audience
The audience for your explanation of hypothermia is adults in a Red Cross First Aid course.

Purpose
Jack London's story is an interesting presentation of a person slipping deeper and deeper into hypothermia. Your explanation of hypothermia is intended to teach the students in the First Aid course how the human body changes from the beginning of hypothermia to death.

Procedure

1. Study the performance task assessment list for this task.
2. Read the story, *To Build a Fire*.
3. Devise an index system so that you can refer the reader of your explanation of hypothermia to specific passages in the story. Your explanation of what is happening to the body during hypothermia must be closely matched to the events in Jack London's story.
4. Describe the reactions of the body's cardiovascular system to the stages of hypothermia.
5. Describe the reactions of the body's neuromuscular system to the stages of hypothermia.
6. Evaluate how effective Jack London was in presenting an accurate and interesting account of how hypothermia influences behavior. Explain specific strategies Jack London used to be an effective writer.
7. Complete the self-assessment, and submit your work.

Exhibit 27. Performance Task Assessment List
Literature and Science: Hypothermia

		ASSESSMENT POINTS	
	Points	Earned Assessment:	
Element	Possible	Self	Teacher
1. The sequence of events in the story is matched to an accurate description of the sequence of events in the character's cardiovascular system.	_____	_____	_____
2. The sequence of events in the story is matched to an accurate description of the sequence of events in the character's neuromuscular system.	_____	_____	_____
3. The relationship between the structure of a body system and its function to maintain a balance to sustain life is made very clear.	_____	_____	_____
4. Technical vocabulary is used and explained.	_____	_____	_____
5. Drawings are used to add clarity to the written explanations.	_____	_____	_____
6. The information about hypothermia is indexed to the story so that the reader knows exactly how to connect the events in the story to the description of hypothermia.	_____	_____	_____
7. The evaluation of how effective the author was in describing the behavior of a person going into hypothermia is substantiated with references to specific descriptions in the text.	_____	_____	_____
8. The mechanics of English are correct.	_____	_____	_____
9. The work is neat and presentable.	_____	_____	_____
Total	_____	_____	_____

Exhibit 28. Performance Task
Reviewing Children's Books for the Library

Background
Libraries spend a lot of money each year to buy new books. The library's book review committee has asked you to serve on the library's book review committee and evaluate the quality of the science in the children's books they plan to buy.

Task
Your task is to study the book by Eric Carle called *The Very Hungry Caterpillar* and write your opinion as to whether the library should buy it.

Audience
The audience for your report is the library's book selection committee.

Purpose
The purpose of your work is to use your knowledge of science to evaluate the quality of *The Very Hungry Caterpillar*.

Procedure

1. Use the performance task assessment list for reviewing children's science books.
2. Read the book and evaluate the science in the book.
    List the science information you think is correct.
    List the science information you think is incorrect.
    List the science information you are not sure about.
3. Use the reference books to answer the questions you have about the science information in the book.
4. Write your opinion of the quality of the science in the book and make a recommendation to the library's book review committee as to whether or not they should buy *The Very Hungry Caterpillar*.

Exhibit 29. Performance Task Assessment List
Reviewing Children's Books for the Library

Element	Points Possible	Earned Assessment: Self	Earned Assessment: Teacher
1. The correct science information is listed.	_____	_____	_____
2. The incorrect science information is listed.	_____	_____	_____
3. The reasons why the science information is incorrect are explained.	_____	_____	_____
4. The decision as to the overall quality of the science in the book is clearly stated and supported.	_____	_____	_____
5. Other attributes of the book are evaluated.	_____	_____	_____
6. The decision as to the overall quality of the book is clearly stated and supported. The decision is written in the form of a recommendation to the library's book review committee.	_____	_____	_____
7. The mechanics of English are correct.	_____	_____	_____
8. The work is neat, organized, and presentable.	_____	_____	_____
Total	_____	_____	_____

Exhibit 30. Performance Task
Writing a Science Book for Children

Background
There is a good market for children's books, especially interesting science books. Schools and public libraries spend a lot of money each year adding science books to their collections.

Task
Your task is to write a book for children which is both very interesting to them and full of correct science.

Audience
The audience for your book is the children in an elementary school in your town.

Purpose
The purpose of your work is to use your knowledge of science to entertain and teach children.

Procedure

1.   Use the assessment list for writing a science book for children.
2.   Make a list of the science information you want to include in your book.
3.   Check the accuracy of your information. The science must be accurate.
4.   Plan a story line and sketch the sequence of pictures you will use.
5.   Write a first draft using the sketches.
6.   Plan the cover and give the book a title.
7.   Plan the colors you will use for your book. Your book must be very interesting for children.
8.   Read the draft of your book to a child.
9.   Make revisions and complete the final draft of the book.

Exhibit 31. Performance Task Assessment List
Writing a Science Book for Children

	ASSESSMENT POINTS		
	Points Possible	Earned Assessment:	
Element		Self	Teacher
1. The book presents the science concepts correctly.	_____	_____	_____
2. Interesting and correct details support the science concepts.	_____	_____	_____
3. Pictures and other graphics support the written statements.	_____	_____	_____
4. Science vocabulary is used and explained.	_____	_____	_____
5. The story line is organized.	_____	_____	_____
6. The cover and title catch the interest of the children.	_____	_____	_____
7. The book is creative.	_____	_____	_____
8. The mechanics of English are correct.	_____	_____	_____
9. The book is neat and presentable.	_____	_____	_____
Total	_____	_____	_____

Exhibit 32. Performance Assessment
Writing a Sequel

Background

Many movies have been so successful that one or more "sequels" are created. For example, there were at least three sequels to the movie *Rocky,* and several sequels to the film *Star Wars.* Writers of successful novels sometimes create sequels to their work as well. Mildred Taylor wrote several books as sequels to her popular novel *Roll of Thunder Hear My Cry.* Oftentimes we as readers wish that there was a sequel to a novel we have just finished reading.

Your Task

The librarian has invited you and your classmates to compile an anthology of sequels to novels that we have in the school library. She has provided several examples of sequels to help you understand the task.

Your Audience

Your peers and other students in your school form the audience for your work.

Materials

You will need pen and paper for this assignment. You may type it if you wish.

Procedure

1. Obtain a copy of the assessment list for a sequel to guide your work.
2. Read a novel that may be found in the school library. Be sure that the novel is appropriate for your reading ability. If you have doubts, ask!
3. Analyze the models that the librarian provided—using the assessment list as your guide.
4. Create a plot outline in which you brainstorm ideas for your setting, characters, exposition, rising action, climax, falling action, and resolution.
5. Write a rough draft of your sequel, making sure to include many vivid details, much description, and dialogue throughout the story.
6. Assess the story using the assessment list and make note of needed revisions.
7. Share the story with a peer for feedback and advice.
8. Revise your sequel.
9. Do a final self-assessment, make corrections, and turn it in.

Exhibit 33. Performance Task Assessment List
Sequel

| | ASSESSMENT POINTS | | |
| | Points Possible | Earned Assessment: | |
Element		Self	Teacher
1. The story is a logical continuation of the original story.	_____	_____	_____
2. The setting is vividly described.	_____	_____	_____
3. The characters are well described.	_____	_____	_____
4. The story has many details that add to the reader's ability to visualize the story.	_____	_____	_____
5. There is dialogue throughout the story.	_____	_____	_____
6. There is a logical plot with a(n):	_____	_____	_____
exposition	_____	_____	_____
rising action	_____	_____	_____
climax	_____	_____	_____
falling action	_____	_____	_____
resolution	_____	_____	_____
7. There are no unexplained "gaps" between the original and the sequel.	_____	_____	_____
8. The piece is mechanically correct.	_____	_____	_____
9. The piece is neat and presentable.	_____	_____	_____
10. The piece is especially interesting, creative, and engaging.	_____	_____	_____
Total	_____	_____	_____

Exhibit 34. Performance Task
So You Want to Be a Songwriter

Background

It's tough out there in the music world. Everyone wants to become a famous songwriter. A graduate of your school has become a successful music agent, and she will be at your school later in the year to listen to songs written by students of her alma mater.

Task

Your task is to write a song with music and lyrics.

Audience

The music agent will be your audience.

Purpose

The purpose of your work is to demonstrate your music skill and talent.

Procedure

1.   Use the assessment list for writing a song.
2.   Write the music and lyrics for your song.
3.   Practice your song and make a demo audio recording of it.
4.   Submit the sheet music and lyrics along with the demo recording.

Exhibit 35. Performance Task Assessment List for Writing a Song

	ASSESSMENT POINTS		
	Points	Earned Assessment:	
Element	Possible	Self	Teacher
1. The song is original.	_____	_____	_____
2. The pitch range is appropriate for the voice.	_____	_____	_____
3. Traditional or symbolic notation is correctly used.	_____	_____	_____
4. A rhythmic pulse can be perceived.	_____	_____	_____
5. It is written in a musical form, or in other organized structure.	_____	_____	_____
6. A variety of pitches and rhythms are used to create unity and contrast.	_____	_____	_____
7. The time signature and tempo marking are clearly indicated.	_____	_____	_____
8. The lyrics convey the intended message to the target audience.	_____	_____	_____
9. The music and lyrics work together.	_____	_____	_____
Total	_____	_____	_____

Exhibit 36. Performance Assessment Task
Original 12 Bar Blues

Background

The Blues is a type of jazz music created by African-American musicians in the United States in the early 1900s. It uses a 12 Bar form that is improvised. Common topics contained in the lyrics are love, personal misfortune, or loneliness. The musicians sing the Blues to take the blues away.

Task

You are a jazz musician in the year 1920. On Saturday night, the great Louis Armstrong is performing in local night-clubs in your hometown. He is looking for talented jazz composers that have created original Blues compositions to be featured on his first recording. This will mean instant success to the group whose entry is accepted. You decide to submit your Blues song.

Audience

Your audience is Louis Armstrong, who will select the best original Blues composition.

Purpose

The purpose of your task is to compose a 12 Bar Blues song that will highlight your knowledge of the specific style of musical composition that existed in the Jazz era.

Procedure

1. Give yourself and your partners appropriate jazz names. Also, give the group a name.
2. Use the 12 Bar Blues in the key of "A" as your form:

    A   A   A   A D D A A E D E

    Learn the A, D, and E₇ chords on the guitar. This will be your accompaniment.
3. Write the lyrics. Pick an appropriate topic that would be good for the Blues. Make sure you have 3 phrases in each verse. Remember, phrases 1 and 2 use the same lyrics, and phrase 3 is a response to the previous phrases. Try to make the end of phrase 3 rhyme with the last word in phrase 1 and 2. You must write 3 *verses.*
4. Create a melody. Since Blues is a predominately improvised form, see if you can improvise a melody for your lyrics. Try saying your words in a rhythm as you strum the guitar chords and chant them until the words and accompaniment seem to fit together. Remember, there should be some space between each phrase (like in "Joe Turner" Blues) for an improvised solo. Gradually sing the words on pitches you hear in the guitar chord. Figure out which words should be sung as "Blues" notes. Where will you use the lowered 3rd and 7th notes of the scale?
5. Arrange the performance to be creative. You could add an introduction or coda to your piece like "West End Blues." Decide which instruments you will use and play. Consider using any instruments in addition to the guitar that your classmates can play reasonably well. Determine how the lyrics should be sung (solo, duet, trio) and who will sing them.
6. Rehearse, then perform your Blues for the class.
7. Finally, assess your Blues composition and the performance.

Exhibit 37. Performance Task Assessment List
Original 12 Bar Blues

| | | ASSESSMENT POINTS | |
| | Points | Earned Assessment: | |
Element	Possible	Self	Teacher
I. Creating a 12 Bar Blues			
1. The lyrics contain appropriate themes that convey the feelings and emotions characteristic of the blues.	_____	_____	_____
2. The lyrics are in three phrases with phrase one and two being the same.	_____	_____	_____
3. A 12 bar blues form is used.	_____	_____	_____
4. Blue notes from the blues scale are used in the melody.	_____	_____	_____
5. The song is original and authentic.	_____	_____	_____
6. The pitches of the melody are correctly notated on staff paper.	_____	_____	_____
II. Performing a 12 Bar Blues			
1. Appropriate instruments were used in the performance.	_____	_____	_____
2. The ensemble stayed together.	_____	_____	_____
3. Improvisation was used between phrases.	_____	_____	_____
4. The group was prepared.	_____	_____	_____
Total	_____	_____	_____

Exhibit 38. Performance Task
Nonobjective Painted Design

Background

You have been asked to submit some of your work to a graphic design company interested in hiring part-time student artists.

Task

Your task is to create a nonobjective painted design to include in the portfolio that you will submit to the company.

Audience

The audience for your work is the creative director of the graphic design company.

Purpose

The purpose of your work is to show your skill and talent so that you will be hired for a part-time job.

Procedure

1. Use the assessment list for a nonobjective painted design.
2. Complete your plan and share it with your mentor.
3. Review your plan as needed and complete the design.

Exhibit 39. Performance Task Assessment List
Nonobjective Painted Design

| | ASSESSMENT POINTS | | |
| | Points | Earned Assessment: | |
Element	Possible	Self	Teacher
I. Planning			
1. Brainstorming has been done in order to decide on shapes, colors, etc.	_____	_____	_____
2. At least five preliminary thumbnail sketches have been completed to improve the composition.	_____	_____	_____
3. The design has balance.	_____	_____	_____
4. The design has rhythm.	_____	_____	_____
5. The design has variety.	_____	_____	_____
6. The design has emphasis.	_____	_____	_____
7. The design has unity.	_____	_____	_____
II. Execution			
1. The selected composition has been successfully transferred and enlarged to the final paper.	_____	_____	_____
2. The paint is applied using a hard-edged technique.	_____	_____	_____
3. A variety of tints and shades have been used.	_____	_____	_____
4. The chosen colors work well together.	_____	_____	_____
5. The completed design is neatly painted.	_____	_____	_____
6. I have put my best effort into this painting.	_____	_____	_____
Total	_____	_____	_____

Exhibit 40. Performance Task
Orthographic (Multiview) Pictorial

Background

The elementary school science committee needs your help in designing a science center for classrooms. The committee has a list of general specifications for the function of the science centers.

Task

Your task is to create a science center that matches the specifications and make an orthographic pictorial of it.

Audience

The audience for your work is the elementary school science committee.

Purpose

The purpose of your work is to show how you can use your skills and creativity to create a plan that will meet the needs of the elementary school science committee.

Science centers will be built based on the plans generated by you or your classmates.

Procedure

1. Use the assessment list for an orthographic pictorial.
2. Review the specifications for the science center.
3. Make a rough draft of a plan and review it with your teacher.
4. After appropriate revisions

Exhibit 41. Performance Task Assessment List
Computer-Aided Drafting
Orthographic (Multiview) Pictorial

| | ASSESSMENT POINTS | | |
| | Points | Earned Assessment: | |
Element	Possible	Self	Teacher
1. An appropriate pictorial drawing is used, and the drawing is reproduced using a CAD package.	_____	_____	_____
2. The scale is accurate.	_____	_____	_____
3. Dimensioning is complete with proper dimensioning technique.	_____	_____	_____
4. The drawing is neat and presentable.	_____	_____	_____
5. An appropriate title block is used, and it contains appropriate information.	_____	_____	_____
6. Each view lines up correctly with the others and is proportionally accurate.	_____	_____	_____
7. The correct number of views are drawn.	_____	_____	_____
8. The project meets acceptable deadlines.	_____	_____	_____
9. All views are accurately revolved into place on the drawing.	_____	_____	_____
10. All angles are correctly projected.	_____	_____	_____
11. Interior and exterior views are accurately shown.	_____	_____	_____
12. A written explanation describes how the plan meets the specifications for the project.	_____	_____	_____
Total	_____	_____	_____

Exhibit 42. Performance Task
Consumer Decision-Making: Restaurants and Senior Citizens

Background

Have you noticed that restaurants often have special prices for senior citizens? Do senior citizens really get a good deal at these restaurants?

Task

You have an elderly relative who eats at Happy's Restaurant and asked for your advice as to whether the restaurant's senior citizen menu is really a good deal. Your task is to study the regular menu and the senior citizen menu and determine the "value" of the special arrangement for senior citizens at Happy's Restaurant.

Audience

The audience for your study and written summary is your elderly relative.

Purpose

The purpose of your analysis and written summary is to show how to use logical mathematical procedures to examine the "value" of the senior citizen menu at Happy's Restaurant.

Procedure

1.   Review the assessment list for Consumer Decision-Making: Restaurants and Senior Citizens.
2.   Make a list of criteria you will use to compare the regular and senior citizen menus of Happy's Restaurant.
3.   Use the criteria to analyze each menu.
4.   Organize the data from your analysis.
5.   Display the data in a graph or graphs.
6.   Write a summary of your findings for your elderly relative. Include appropriate graphs.

Exhibit 43. Performance Task Assessment List
Consumer Decision-Making: Restaurants and Senior Citizens

	ASSESSMENT POINTS		
		Earned Assessment:	
Element	Points Possible	Self	Teacher
Consumer Research			
1. A list of criteria to be used to compare the regular and senior citizens' menus will provide the basis for a comprehensive and fair test.	_____	_____	_____
2. An objective test for each criteria is devised.	_____	_____	_____
3. Data are collected in a way to minimize error.	_____	_____	_____
4. The data are organized into a well-labeled graph.	_____	_____	_____
Consumer Report			
5. An introduction describes the reason for the study and briefly describes the procedures.	_____	_____	_____
6. A well-labeled graph displays appropriate data.	_____	_____	_____
7. A final statement summarizes the findings of the consumer research.	_____	_____	_____
8. Vocabulary and other elements of report are designed to communicate with the target audience.	_____	_____	_____
Overall			
9. Mechanics of English are correct and the work is neat and presentable.	_____	_____	_____
Total	_____	_____	_____

Exhibit 44. Performance Task
Cookbook Algebra

Background

Have you ever cooked a potato in a microwave oven and wondered how long it should cook? How about that ham or turkey for Thanksgiving? You have been hired by a cookbook publisher to create a set of graphs for a new cookbook.

Task

Your task is to review cookbooks and find recipes that describe different lengths of cooking time for different amounts of food such as cooking beef, roasts, or turkeys in the conventional oven or cooking vegetables in the microwave oven. Make a graph that shows the amount of time required to cook different amounts of food. Write an algebraic formula and a word formula for the slope of the line on each graph.

Audience

The audience for your graph is mathematicians who cook.

Purpose

The purpose of your graphs and algebraic formulas is to show mathematically how long to cook various amount of food.

Procedure

1. Review the assessment list for cookbook algebra.
2. Find six examples of food that takes different amounts of time to cook based on the amount of that food to cook.
3. Make a graph for each type of food that shows the amount of time required to cook different amounts of that food.
4. Write an algebraic formula for the slope of the line on each graph.
5. Write a word formula for each algebraic formula.
6. Study all the graphs you have made and their formulas. Describe what patterns you see in the relationship between the amount of time and the amount of food to be cooked.

Exhibit 45. Performance Task Assessment List
Cookbook Algebra

| | ASSESSMENT POINTS | | |
| | Points | Earned Assessment: | |
Element	Possible	Self	Teacher
For Each Type of Food Studied			
1. A well-labeled graph is constructed that shows the relationship between the amount of food to be cooked and the time it takes to cook it.	_____	_____	_____
2. An algebraic formula is correctly written and labeled that describes the slope of the line on the graph.	_____	_____	_____
3. A word formula is correctly written for that algebraic formula.	_____	_____	_____
Overall Conclusion			
4. The conclusion generalizes what has been learned about the amount of time it takes to cook varying amounts of food.	_____	_____	_____
5. The conclusion is supported with mathematics.	_____	_____	_____
6. Mechanics of English are correct and the work is neat and presentable.	_____	_____	_____
Total	_____	_____	_____

Exhibit 46. Performance Task
Fast Food Math

Background

A large national hamburger fast food restaurant chain printed an advertisement that read, "Seven percent of all Americans eat in our restaurants each day." This chain has 9,167 restaurants. There are approximately 250,000,000 American citizens.

Task

You are an employee of a consumer advocate group studying truth in advertising.

You have been asked to consider this advertisement. Do you think it is probably true or probably false? Your task is to use logical mathematical procedures to analyze the claim this advertisement made and write a summary of your opinion.

Audience

The audience for your study and written summary is the person in charge of the consumer advocate group.

Purpose

The purpose of your analysis and written summary is to show the use of logical mathematical procedures to examine claims made in advertising.

Procedure

1. Review the assessment list for fast food math.
2. Rewrite the task in your own words.
3. Make a list of all the information that is clearly given.
4. Make a list of what needs to be estimated, assumed, or found out.
5. Make those estimates and/or assumptions.
6. Get other information that you need.
7. Use your math skills to analyze the advertisement.
8. Write a summary of your findings for your boss at the consumer advocate group.

Exhibit 47. Performance Task Assessment List
Fast Food Math

| | | ASSESSMENT POINTS | |
| | Points | Earned Assessment: | |
Element	Possible	Self	Teacher
The Analysis			
1. The problem is rewritten in the student's own words to show that the student understands the problem.	_____	_____	_____
2. A list is made of the specific information that is actually given in the problem.	_____	_____	_____
3. A list is made of what needs to be assumed, estimated, or found out to solve the problem.	_____	_____	_____
4. The actual assumptions, estimations, and/or data collected are presented in a well-labeled, organized format.	_____	_____	_____
5. A clearly labeled, logical path is taken to solve the problem. All steps in the path are shown.	_____	_____	_____
6. Calculations are accurate. All units are accurately labeled.	_____	_____	_____
The Written Conclusion			
7. A conclusion is stated in one paragraph.	_____	_____	_____
8. Enough quantitative information is included in the conclusion to show that math was used to arrive at the answer.	_____	_____	_____
Overall			
9. Mechanics of English are correct and the work is neat and presentable.	_____	_____	_____
Total	_____	_____	_____

Exhibit 48. Performance Task
Creature Features

Background

You have been asked to help teach a unit to sixth graders about how animals are structured to satisfy their life functions in a specific environment such as a desert, a swamp, or a rain forest. The students have been studying different parts of the world in their Social Studies class and learning about the animals that live in different environments. The teacher asked you to use this picture of an imaginary animal and explain what you could learn about this animal's habitat and its niche just from seeing the structure of this imaginary animal.

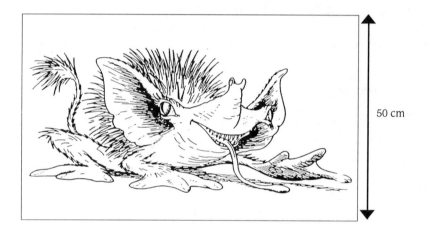

50 cm

Task

Your task is to write an explanation of the kind of environment in which this imaginary animal might live.

Audience

Write your explanation so that the sixth grader can understand you. (You may assume that the sixth grader is an excellent reader.)

Procedure

Use only the back of this paper to write your explanation. You may include drawings or diagrams to help support your written explanation. Refer to the performance task assessment list for Writing in Science.

Exhibit 49. Performance Task Assessment List
Writing in Science

		ASSESSMENT POINTS	
	Points	Earned Assessment:	
Element	Possible	Self	Teacher
1. The concept of what animals need to live is correctly explained.	_____	_____	_____
2. The concept of relating structure to function is correctly explained.	_____	_____	_____
3. Science terms are explained.	_____	_____	_____
4. At least five specific structures of the imaginary animal are used as evidence to guess about what kind of environment might be the home of this imaginary animal.	_____	_____	_____
5. You use what you know about real animals and how they are structured to function in their specific environment to support your analysis of the imaginary animal and its home environment.	_____	_____	_____
6. Diagrams are used to clarify the explanations.	_____	_____	_____
7. The writing is organized, and there are smooth transitions between ideas.	_____	_____	_____
8. The writing is neat and presentable.	_____	_____	_____
Total	_____	_____	_____

Exhibit 50. Cycle of Learning Performance Task
Consumer Decision-Making Newsletter

Background

Every day people make decisions about how to spend their money. They are concerned about getting a good deal and worry that they might not be spending their money wisely. Consumer advocates do research and provide information to consumers to help them make those decisions.

Task

You are part of a team of consumer advocates who publish a newsletter that provides information to people so that they will be wise consumers. Some examples for topics in consumer newsletters are: best buys for pizza, groceries, automobiles, stereo systems, clothing, tennis shoes, baseball gloves, bicycles, or roller blades.

Audience

You may select your own audience for your consumer newsletter. Consider writing your newsletter for people who do not speak English.

Purpose

Your job is to select a consumer product, research it, and publish your findings to help people make wise decisions.

Procedure

Group Work

1. Select an audience for your newsletter.
2. Each person in your group will research one consumer product that is important to the audience you have selected.
3. The group will put the individual research reports together into one newsletter. The newsletter will have a name and attractive graphics.
4. Complete a group work management plan and review the assessment list for the group tasks.
5. Review the assessment list for group work.

Individual Work

6. Review the assessment list for consumer decision-making.
7. Make a list of criteria you will use to evaluate your product.
8. Make a plan to make fair tests of your products.
9. Collect data and organize it.
10. Use the data to evaluate your product.
11. Write your section of the consumer newsletter. Include data, diagrams, and information that will make your findings clear to your audience.

Assessment, Grading, and Group Work

Each individual will be assessed on his or her individual section of the consumer newsletter. A grade will also be given based on the percentage of the points an individual earns on the individual performance task assessment lists. An "A" is 90–100 percent, a "B" is 80–89 percent,a "C" is 70–79 percent. Work below 70 percent is unacceptable. There are no group grades. The grade given to an individual is not influenced by the quality of the work of the other group members. There are consequences for the overall quality of the newsletter. The entire newsletter must be at the "A" level before it will be sent to its target audience.

Exhibit 51. Performance Task Assessment List for a Management Plan

| | | ASSESSMENT POINTS | |
| | Points | Earned Assessment: | |
Element	Possible	Self	Teacher
Group Planning			
1. The heading is properly completed.	_____	_____	_____
2. The list of tasks is complete.	_____	_____	_____
3. The tasks are specific.	_____	_____	_____
4. The target dates for completion of the group tasks are appropriate.	_____	_____	_____
5. A plan is made as to how the group will monitor the work of each individual.	_____	_____	_____
Total	_____	_____	_____
Individual Planning			
1. The heading is properly completed.	_____	_____	_____
2. The list of tasks is complete.	_____	_____	_____
3. The tasks are specific.	_____	_____	_____
4. The target dates for completion of each task are appropriate.	_____	_____	_____
5. Thoughtful consideration has gone into a description of the barriers to successfully completing the project	_____	_____	_____
6. Thoughtful consideration has gone into a description of strategies for overcoming those barriers.	_____	_____	_____
7. The plan is neat and presentable.	_____	_____	_____
Total	_____	_____	_____

Exhibit 52. Management Plan for Group Work

Names of Group Members: _____

_____

Date Begun: _____ Due Date: _____

Describe the group tasks to be accomplished:

Task   **Person(s) Responsible**   **Target Date**

Plan for how the group will monitor the work of each of its members:

Student Signatures: _____   _____

_____   _____

Exhibit 53. Management Plan for Individual Work

Name: _____

Task: _____

Date Begun:_____ Date Due: _____

List of Tasks to Complete   **Target Date**

Checkpoint Number 1

Checkpoint Number 2

• •

Problems Which May Cause Me Trouble   **Ideas to Overcome Those Problems**

_____   _____   _____
Student   Teacher   Parent

Exhibit 54. Performance Task Assessment List
Group Work

Element	Points Possible	Earned Assessment: Peer	Self	Teacher
		ASSESSMENT POINTS		

Name:_____

Element	Points Possible	Peer	Self	Teacher
1. The individual comes to the group prepared for the group work.	_____	_____	_____	_____
2. The individual completes all individual tasks for the group on time and with quality.	_____	_____	_____	_____
3. The individual participates in a constructive manner.	_____	_____	_____	_____
4. The individual encourages others to participate in a constructive manner.	_____	_____	_____	_____
5. The individual is a good, active listener.	_____	_____	_____	_____
6. The individual supports his or her position in a strong and thoughtful manner.	_____	_____	_____	_____
7. The individual disagrees in an agreeable manner.	_____	_____	_____	_____
8. The individual can reach compromises.	_____	_____	_____	_____
9. The individual helps the group follow directions and meet the timelines.	_____	_____	_____	_____
10. The individual promotes positive human relations in the group.	_____	_____	_____	_____
Total	_____	_____	_____	_____

Exhibit 55. Performance Task Assessment List
Consumer Decision-Making and a Consumer Newsletter

| | ASSESSMENT POINTS | | |
| | Points | Earned Assessment: | |
Element	Possible	Self	Teacher
Consumer Research			
1. A consumer product has been selected which is appropriate to the audience for the newsletter.	_____	_____	_____
2. An appropriate set of criteria has been listed by which the consumer product will be judged.	_____	_____	_____
3. A fair test of the consumer product has been designed.	_____	_____	_____
4. The procedures used for the tests are stated clearly enough for another person to replicate the tests.	_____	_____	_____
5. The data is organized according to the criteria being used to judge the consumer product.	_____	_____	_____
Subtotal	_____	_____	_____
Graphs			
6. An appropriate type of graph (line, bar, pie, or pictograph) is selected to display the data to the target audience.	_____	_____	_____
7. A title and labels are used to clearly describe what the graph is about.	_____	_____	_____
Subtotal	_____	_____	_____
The Individual Section of the Consumer Newsletter			
8. There is an interesting introduction that gets the reader's attention.	_____	_____	_____
9. The criteria for judging the consumer product are clearly stated.	_____	_____	_____
10. Procedures for conducting a fair test are briefly outlined.	_____	_____	_____
11. Results are presented in a clear, organized manner.	_____	_____	_____
12. Diagrams or other graphics help present the data.	_____	_____	_____
13. A final judgment is made about the consumer product.	_____	_____	_____
14. The mechanics of English are correct.	_____	_____	_____
15. The work is neat and presentable.	_____	_____	_____
Subtotal	_____	_____	_____
Total	_____	_____	_____

HOW DO YOU MAKE PERFORMANCE TASK ASSESSMENT LISTS?

Performance task assessment lists are created after a task has been developed. Because essential content, process skills, and work habits have been incorporated in the task during its creation, the assessment list needs to address the same content, process skills, and work habits—answering the question, "What are the elements of quality for this product?" This process allows for a clear understanding of the task and what is needed to complete it. Students, teachers, and parents all benefit from this clear communication of expectations.

GENERIC ASSESSMENT LISTS

Assessment lists can be either generic for a type of product, such as a poster, or tailored to the specific content of a particular task. A generic list reflecting the elements of quality for a poster could be used with any poster. Generic lists are not content specific. A student who wishes to develop a project using a particular format, such as a poster, might consult a generic list. A teacher creating an assessment list for a specific task can tailor the generic list, modifying it to meet the needs of the class, students, or subject area.

WHO CREATES ASSESSMENT LISTS?

Although many assessment lists are created by a teacher or a team of teachers, students can share in this process. Once students have become familiar with the process of performance assessment and assessment lists, they will begin to internalize the elements of quality for various tasks. Student creation of assessment lists for a task, individually or in a group, is a valuable learning experience for both the student and the teacher. The ultimate goal of performance-based learning is to develop self-directed, self-assessing, and self-motivated students. Whereas elementary or middle-level students may need a great deal of assistance in creating their own assessments, the process is an excellent motivational tool because it gives students a sense of control over their own learning. With practice, high school students need far less assistance.

All the required components of an assessment list should be written in language appropriate to the level of the students doing the task. Assessment lists can be modified to address the needs of individual students. Teachers can make decisions about what elements of quality to emphasize with certain students. They may also choose to alter the number of elements of quality that a modified list would contain or simplify the language in writing the list.

Most assessment lists are written in statement form. There are differences between assessment lists written for primary, elementary, middle, and high school students, based on the developmental needs of the students.

WHAT DO ASSESSMENT LISTS LOOK LIKE AT DIFFERENT LEVELS?

LISTS AT THE PRIMARY LEVEL

At the primary level, faces with big, small, or neutral smiles can be used for evaluation levels. *Note that none of these faces have frowns, but in-*

stead reflect different levels of the positive. Performance assessment lists are a positive means for reinforcing excellence at any level.

In the beginning, the assessment list might consist of two or three items such as:

- Did I draw a picture of the chickens?
- Did I draw details?

Later in the year when the teacher determines that the students are ready, the list could be expanded to include:

- Did I print a sentence about my picture?
- Did I leave spaces between my words?
- Did I read my sentence to another person?

Still later, additional items could be added as language skills improve:

- Did I use describing words?
- Did I use a capital letter to begin the sentence?
- Did I put a period at the end of the sentence?

LISTS AT THE ELEMENTARY LEVEL

At the elementary level, assessment lists are often written as a series of questions that the students ask themselves. For example, in the classroom assessment list for a poster in the primary grades, one element reads: "Does my poster tell a story?" The students would circle a *T* (Terrific), an *O* (O.K.), or a *W* (Work on It) after each question.

Using this *T-O-W* format, each component is written in three qualifying statements:

T reflects an excellent degree of performance.

O is a middle-range standard of performance,

W reflects limited performance.

The classroom assessment list for the poster at the elementary level reads:

T: Your pictures show at least 5 differences between the North and the South.

O: Your pictures show 3-4 differences between the North and the South.

W: Your pictures show less than 3 differences between the North and the South.

The degree of importance of each element on the assessment list is communicated to students during instruction and modeling of the task and the development of the assessment list. Students can also participate in this decision. The assessment list also includes a place to assess the total product, using the *T-O-W* scale.

Students in the upper elementary grades may begin working with assessment lists using points, in preparation for the middle and high school formats.

LISTS AT THE MIDDLE AND HIGH SCHOOL LEVEL

The middle and high school formats generally use a point system that denotes the relative importance of an element and is a simple means to use assessment lists in evaluation. Each component is assigned a number of points, based on instructional objectives and student needs.

When a piece of work is at the final stage, when it is to be "published" and sent to its intended audience, all elements on the assessment list are of equal importance, including spelling and mechanics.

The assessment list may also include a place for the students to assess themselves, for students to assess each other, and for the teacher to assess the students. Assessment lists and models

of excellence help students provide helpful feedback to their peers.

The writing of the assessment list is an important piece of the performance assessment process. The list is what provides the structure and organization that guides students to produce quality work. It helps students to understand their progress and to set goals. Without the assessment list, students are left to guess at what the teacher expects and how to achieve it. With the assessment list, the teacher communicates expectations to students and parents. The parent can use the assessment list to ask the elementary child working on the Civil War poster: "Show me the five differences between the North and South you have found for your poster. Is your goal to get a *T*, an *O*, or a *W*?" If the child is looking for a *T* and only has three differences, then the parent can encourage him to find two more differences between the North and South for the poster. The assessment lists help parents support the learning process.

ASSIGNING POINTS TO THE ELEMENTS ON ASSESSMENT LISTS

The assessment list format for the middle and high school has a place for possible points for each element on the list. The teacher can decide how many total points to assign the assessment list, and then how many points to assign each element in the list. (The total number of points for a list does not have to equal 100.) Elements on the list can be weighted by assigning them more or less points. Elements are weighted according to the instructional objectives of the performance task or according to the individual needs of students. The teacher also has the option of allowing the students to be involved in the process of distributing points among the elements on an assessment list.

DEVELOPING SCHOOL OR DISTRICTWIDE ASSESSMENT LISTS

Although individual teachers, departments, or teams can effectively use performance task assessments, systemic change through school or districtwide implementation will obviously bring greater benefits.

Start by selecting an important type of student work, such as nonfiction writing, graphing, writing a letter to request information, making a map, giving an oral presentation, making a poster, or writing a persuasive position statement. Inspect some samples of actual student work and similar products from the "real world" and begin to brainstorm the elements by which the work could be assessed. Consider the categories or dimensions for the elements. The dimensions describe the important categories from which more specific elements will be generated for assessment lists. Dimensions for some student work are listed in the next section.

DIMENSIONS OF SELECTED STUDENT WORK

Nonfiction Writing

1. Content (Concepts, Main Idea)
2. Focus
3. Organization
4. Support and Elaboration (Details)
5. Sense of Audience
6. Language Mechanics
7. Neatness

Writing Fiction

1. Plot
2. Setting
3. Characters
4. Dialogue
5. Descriptive Language
6. Sense of Audience
7. Organization
8. Language Mechanics and Neatness

Persuasive Writing

1. Opening Statement of Position
2. Structure of the Argument
3. Content (Concepts, Main Ideas)
4. Supporting Details
5. Closure
6. Information Sources
7. Sense of Audience
8. Language Mechanics and Presentation

Folk Tales

1. Values and beliefs of the culture.
2. Central, "bigger than life" characters
3. Culture-specific strategies of creativity and imagination
4. Culture-specific geography
5. Organization
6. Use of descriptive language
7. Drawings and other graphics
8. Mechanics of language and presentation

Responding to Literature

1. Initial (literal) understanding of the text
2. Developing an interpretation of the text
3. Making connections (between the literature and the reader)
4. Critical stance: evaluating the quality of the literature

Graphs

1. Selection of the type of graph according to the data, purpose of the graph, and the audience for the graph
2. Labels and titles
3. Scales and units of measurements
4. Use of color, texture, and other graphic devices
5. Key
6. Mechanics of English
7. Neatness and presentability

Geographic Map

1. Selects the format for the map appropriate to the purpose of the map and the audience for the map
2. Draws land forms and water forms in the correct shape and relative position
3. Draws land forms and water forms to proportion
4. Represents human activities
5. Represents natural vegetation
6. Uses colors, textures, and other graphic devices.
7. Includes quantitative data and information such as elevation and longitude and latitude with appropriate labeling
8. Titles and labels
9. Key
10. Mechanics of English
11. Neatness and presentability

Information Problem Solving

1. Asks a question to direct new learning
2. The "What do I already know about this question?" is surveyed
3. The "What do I want to know about this question?" is surveyed
4. The sources of relevant information are identified
5. Information is obtained from a variety of sources
6. The quality of the information is evaluated

7. Information is analyzed
8. Information is organized to be used

Making Observations

1. Uses all the senses safely
2. Is precise and detailed
3. Makes quantitative observations using the appropriate measurement system
4. Uses tools of measurement accurately
5. Makes qualitative observations
6. Organizes observations
7. Uses titles, labels, and keys
8. Shows units of measurement
9. Uses diagrams and scientific drawings
10. Avoids making inferences while making observations

Science Experiments

1. Observing and finding a question to investigate
2. Selecting a problem/stating a hypothesis
3. Designing an experiment to test the hypothesis
4. Analyzing data to evaluate the hypothesis
5. Communicating the outcome to a specific audience
6. Troubleshooting

Math Problem Solving

1. Formulate problems from situations and given data
2. Develop and apply a variety of strategies to solve problems—particularly multistep and nonroutine problems
3. Make and evaluate conjectures and arguments
4. Verify, validate, and interpret results and claims and generalize solutions
5. Model situations using written, concrete, pictorial, graphic, and algebraic representations
6. Express mathematical ideas and arguments with clarity and coherence

7. Use mathematical language and notation to represent ideas, describe relationships, and model situations

8. Compute accurately and make estimates with whole numbers, fractions, decimals, percents, integers, and rational numbers

9. Select and use an appropriate method for computing from among mental arithmetic paper-and-pencil or calculator

10. Use estimation to assess the reasonableness of results

Posters to Educate

1. Graphics present content accurately

2. Titles, labels, statements present content accurately

3. Impact on intended audience

4. Creativity

5. Neatness and presentability

Group Work

1. Helps the group get the task done well and on time

2. Helps the group work harmoniously

3. Supports the group through individual responsibility

Time and Task Management

1. Organizes tasks into steps

2. Makes and uses a time table for work

3. Sets priorities

4. Plans and uses strategies to overcome problems in getting the task done

CREATE ASSESSMENT LISTS FROM THE DIMENSIONS

Once the dimensions of student work have been identified, teachers write the elements in an assessment list to the degree of specificity appropriate for their students. When possible, begin by creating lists to be used by an entire department, school, or school district. Working with a multigrade level team or department is one strategy for developing such generic lists. This process provides the important perspective of input at each grade level.

Look first at the highest grade level represented. Once that "end-point" list has been created, work backwards to create developmentally appropriate lists for earlier grade levels. This procedure ensures a natural progression in skill levels toward an established goal. From this "highest level" form, assessment lists can be tailored for students of various grade and maturity levels. Figure 7 shows the progression of assessment list development. Try out your lists and revise them as necessary to make them more user friendly for students and teachers. As with most things, improvements will come with practice and use.

Exhibits 56 through 61 present a sequence of assessment lists for persuasive writing, grade 2 through high school, all derived from the dimensions for persuasive writing.

TAILORING THE LIST FOR SPECIFIC ASSIGNMENTS

Sometimes teachers need to modify an assessment list so that it is tied to the specific performance task. For example, the list for persuasive writing could be tailored to meet the special needs of a particular debate in art, math, science, social studies, literature, or an interdisciplinary topic (e.g., see Exhibit 60, which focuses on "Conflict Resolution and Persuasive Writing").

FIGURE 7. Dimensions of Student Work Provide the Foundation for a Spectrum of Assessment Lists

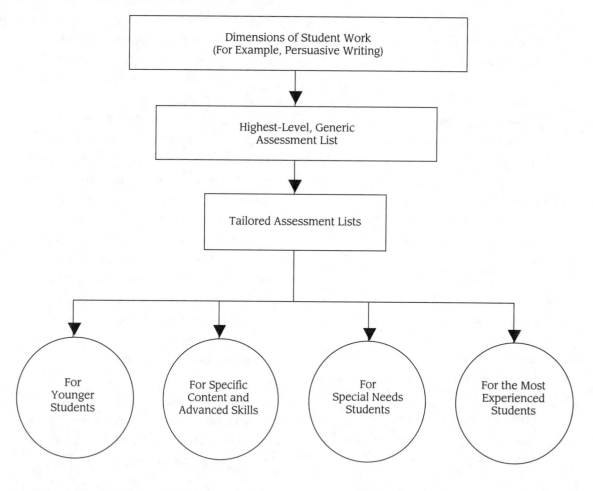

TAILORING ASSESSMENT LISTS FOR SPECIFIC CONTENT

A tailored list would include those elements of quality from the generic list and specific elements reflective of the content of the specific task. For example, a task could involve the creation of a poster that illustrates the differences between the North and the South before the Civil War. Exhibit 62 shows a generic assessment list for a poster (elementary level). A specially tailored assessment list for the pre-Civil War poster is in Exhibit 63. Whereas the generic list calls for a clear focus, appropriate curriculum content, evident purposes, and effective drawings and illustrations, the pre-Civil War poster gets much more specific.

For content, the poster might include differences in each of the following categories: economics, geography, political beliefs, education, and way of life. The illustration of accurate differences would be the major content required for the task. In the area of economics, the student could illustrate the plantation system for the South and the factory system for the North.

Categorizing the differences is a process skill involved in the task. Students would need to identify geographic information in its correct category. Clarity in presentation is an example of a necessary work habit.

Students would need to organize their poster in a clear way by determining how to delineate each category and how to situate their pictures. Each of these elements needs to be addressed on the assessment list.

Each element of the list is weighted according to its importance to the task, student needs, and instructional goals of the performance task. The element on the Civil War poster that asks for a comparison of the economic foundation of the North and South could be weighted either because it is an important concept or because the students need to work harder on the process skill of making comparisons.

In another example, the primary-level assessment list for a poster about caterpillars is derived from the generic assessment list for a primary-level poster. (See Exhibits 64 and 65 for the generic and specific assessment lists for these primary grades posters.)

Other examples are generic and tailored assessment lists for a map at the middle or high school level. (Exhibit 66 shows the generic map assessment list; Exhibit 67 shows a list for "A Physical Geography Map of Japan.")

TAILORING, WEIGHTING, AND MODIFYING ASSESSMENT LISTS

Assessment lists are not set in stone. Teachers or teams of teachers may decide to modify assessment lists for varying purposes. One way to modify a list is to weight elements in the list to focus students on specific content knowledge, process skills, or work habits.

THE DEVELOPMENT OF SKILLS OVER TIME

The assessment list in this chapter for writing a short story consists of many elements (see Exhibit 68). Elements such as characterization, plot, setting, and theme can be weighted by assigning them more points for a first draft. Shifting the weighting to elements of mood and use of language for a second draft will help shift the student's attention to those elements that should receive more attention as the short story is refined.

INDIVIDUALIZING ASSESSMENT LISTS

Teachers have the option of weighting the elements in an assessment list according to the needs of individual students. One student may need to work on clear main ideas, while another is working on supporting main ideas with details, while still another is working on style and sense of audience.

FOCUSING STUDENT ATTENTION ON CONTENT

The Creature Feature task in Chapter 3 (Exhibit 48) strongly emphasizes using the content knowledge of the life requirements of animals and how the structure of those animals is related to satisfying the life needs within specific environments. The first five elements in the assessment list (see Exhibit 49) are about the use of content and could be weighted heavily to focus the student's attention on the use of science content.

MODIFICATIONS FOR STUDENTS WITH SPECIAL NEEDS

Special education teachers can help to modify the assessment lists for use with students with special needs in general education classrooms or in a special education classroom. For example, Exhibits 69 and 70 show the unmodified and modified assessment lists for a "Geographical Picture Dictionary." Modifications have been made in the wording and in the expectations of the elements of those assessment lists.

MODIFYING THE LIST FOR INCREASINGLY INDEPENDENT AND MATURE LEARNERS

A basic objective of education is to nurture independent learning. Therefore, teachers must "wean" students away from assessment lists. A less mature learner will need the support of a more explicit and complete assessment list. As the learner matures, however, the list can become less detailed and become a list of the dimensions of the task, such as persuasive writing (e.g., see Exhibit 61). When the more mature learner thinks of the dimension, "Sense of Audience," that learner thinks about selection of vocabulary and how to state and refute the

opposition's main points. These more specific elements, which were on many previous assessment lists, are now internalized and empower the learner to be more independent.

USING ASSESSMENT LISTS WITH ENGLISH-AS-A-SECOND-LANGUAGE (ESL) STUDENTS

ESL teachers have found that translating the assessment list into the student's dominant language and using both that list and its English version in appropriate situations produces excellent results.

THE BOTTOM LINE: ASSESSMENT LISTS ARE THE KEY TO USER-FRIENDLY, PERFORMANCE-BASED CLASSROOMS

Creating and using assessment lists focuses the attention of the teacher on student performance. Assessment lists reveal the expectations of the teacher, which improves the communication between all parties in the education collaborative of school and home. Assessment lists lead the student to becoming an independent learner able to produce quality work and make decisions to improve. Assessment lists provide the connection between a task and the content, process skills, and work habits in the curriculums. Performance task assessment lists are the specific tools that make performance-based learning and assessment user-friendly.

Exhibit 56. Performance Task Assessment List
Persuasive Communication
Grade 2

1. I drew a picture of my favorite part of the story.

      Terrific   OK   Needs Work

2. I drew details.

      Terrific   OK   Needs Work

3. I wrote a sentence about my picture.

      Terrific   OK   Needs Work

4. I told the class why this was my favorite part of the story.

      Terrific   OK   Needs Work

Exhibit 57. Performance Task Assessment List
Persuasive Writing
Grade 3

1. **Opening Statement**
   T: I stated my opinion very clearly.
   Q: I stated my opinion.
   W: I did not state my opinion.

2. **Reasons for My Opinion**
   T: I gave at least three reasons for my opinion.
   Q: I gave two reasons for my opinion.
   W: I gave less than two reasons for my opinion.

3. **Explanation of My Reasons**
   T: I explained each of my reasons very clearly.
   Q: I gave some explanation of my reasons.
   W: I did not give explanation of my reasons.

4. **Closing Statement**
   T: I made a final statement that will convince people that my opinion is correct.
   Q: I made a final statement, but it is not too convincing.
   W: I did not make a final statement of my opinion.

5. **English**
   T: I used full sentences that start with a capital and end with a period.
   Q: Most of my writing is in full sentences.
   W: Most of my work is not in full sentences.

Did I do my best work?

Terrific   OK   Needs Work

Exhibit 58. Performance Task Assessment List
Persuasive Writing
Grade 5

	ASSESSMENT POINTS		
	---	---	---
	Points	Earned Assessment:	
Element	Possible	Self	Teacher
1. My position is stated clearly.	_____	_____	_____
2. I have at least two reasons to support my position.	_____	_____	_____
3. I explain each reason using details.	_____	_____	_____
4. I have a strong conclusion.	_____	_____	_____
5. I have chosen my words carefully so that I communicate well with my audience.	_____	_____	_____
6. My spelling is perfect.	_____	_____	_____
7. My punctuation is perfect.	_____	_____	_____
8. My writing is neat and presentable.	_____	_____	_____
Total	_____	_____	_____

Exhibit 59. Performance Task Assessment List
Persuasive Writing
Grade 9

| | | ASSESSMENT POINTS | |
| | Points Possible | Earned Assessment: | |
Element		Self	Teacher
1. The writer introduces and clearly states a position.	_____	_____	_____
2. The position is supported by at least four main points.	_____	_____	_____
3. Each main point is supported by at least three relevant, accurate, and specific pieces of information.	_____	_____	_____
4. It is clear that most of the main points and supporting details came from the reference materials.	_____	_____	_____
5. Information from personal experience or data from sources other than the reading materials is provided as additional support to the argument.	_____	_____	_____
6. The main point(s) of the opposing arguments is/are listed and refuted.	_____	_____	_____
7. The argument is made to a specific audience. The writing is crafted to appeal to that audience.	_____	_____	_____
8. The argument is organized and has a flow from beginning to end.	_____	_____	_____
9. There is a powerful concluding statement of the writer's position.	_____	_____	_____
10. Mechanics of English are correct and the writing is neat and presentable.	_____	_____	_____
Total	_____	_____	_____

Exhibit 60. Performance Task Assessment List for Conflict Resolution and Persuasive Writing

| | | ASSESSMENT POINTS | |
| | | Earned Assessment: | |
Element	Points Possible	Self	Teacher
Analysis of the Audience			
1. The audience is identified.	_____	_____	_____
2. The audience is described in detail using such characteristics as:	_____	_____	_____
Friendly vs. Hostile			
Informed vs. Uninformed			
Motivated vs. Unmotivated			
Other			
Analyzing Positions and Needs			
3. The position(s) of the audience is/are stated.	_____	_____	_____
4. The need(s) underlying the position(s)of the audience is/are stated and explained.	_____	_____	_____
5. Your position(s) is/are stated.	_____	_____	_____
6. The need(s) underlying your position(s)is/are stated add explained.	_____	_____	_____
Comparing and Contrasting Needs			
7. Common ground between your need(s) and the need(s) of the audience is described.	_____	_____	_____
8. Important differences between your need(s) and the need(s) of the audience are described.	_____	_____	_____
Identifying and Selecting Alternative Solutions			
9. Alternatives are listed that can meet your need(s) and the need(s) of your audience.	_____	_____	_____
10. An alternative is selected that will best meet your need(s) and the need(s) of your audience.	_____	_____	_____

(Exhibit continues on the following page.)

Exhibit 60 (continued)

Element	Points Possible	Earned Assessment: Self	Earned Assessment: Teacher
	ASSESSMENT POINTS		
	Points Possible	*Self*	*Teacher*

Persuasive Writing

11. The problem is defined in a balanced way.   _____   _____   _____

12. Common ground is described.   _____   _____   _____

13. Differences are described.   _____   _____   _____

14. An alternative is suggested and supported in a way that meets your needs and those of your audience.   _____   _____   _____

15. The writing is mechanically correct, neat, and presentable.   _____   _____   _____

Total   _____   _____   _____

Exhibit 61. Performance Task Assessment List
Persuasive Position Statement Writing

(For a High School Student Experienced in Using Assessment Lists with Much More Specific Detail)

			ASSESSMENT POINTS	
		Points	Earned Assessment:	
Dimension		Possible	Self	Other
1.	Opening Statement	_____	_____	_____
2.	Structure of the Argument	_____	_____	_____
3.	Supporting Details	_____	_____	_____
4.	Closure	_____	_____	_____
5.	Information Sources	_____	_____	_____
6.	Sense of Audience	_____	_____	_____
7.	Language Mechanics and Presentation	_____	_____	_____
	Total	_____	_____	_____

Exhibit 62. Classroom Assessment List
Poster: Elementary School

1. **Focus**
   T: The topic is very clear when you first look at it.
   O: The topic is somewhat clear.
   W: It is difficult to tell what the topic is.

2. **Main Ideas**
   T: The main ideas are appropriate to the topic and are presented correctly.
   O: Some of the main ideas used are appropriate or correct.
   W: Main ideas are lacking or are not correct.

3. **Supporting Details**
   T: Appropriate and accurate details support each main idea.
   O: Most of the details are accurate and appropriate.
   W: Few of the details are accurate and appropriate.

4. **Curriculum Connection**
   T: Much information from the curriculum has been used.
   O: Some information from the curriculum has been used.
   W: Little information from the curriculum has been used.

5. **Purpose**
   T: The purpose of the poster is very strongly accomplished.
   O: The purpose of the poster is accomplished.
   W: The purpose of the poster is not accomplished.

6. **Drawings and Illustrations**
   T: All illustrations, photographs, and drawings add to the purpose and interest of the poster.
   O: Most of the graphics add to the purpose and interest.
   W: The graphics add little, and they may even detract from the purpose and/or interest of the poster.

7. **Layout and Design**
   T: The overall organization, design, use of color, and use of space greatly help the poster to be interesting and to communicate its message.
   O: The overall organization, design, use of color, and use of space are good.
   W: The poster appears cluttered and confused and/or unorganized.

8. **Creativity**
   T: The poster is highly original and creative.
   O: The poster is original and somewhat creative.
   W: The poster is not original nor creative.

9. **Audience**
   T: The poster addresses the specific audience very well.
   O: The poster does a fair job of addressing the audience.
   W: The poster does a poor job of addressing the audience.

(Exhibit continues on the following page.)

Exhibit 62 (continued)

10. Neat and Presentable
T: The poster is very neat and presentable.
O: The poster is neat and presentable.
W: The poster is not neat nor presentable.

11. Mechanics and Sentence Structure
T: There are no errors.
O: There are few errors.
W: There are many errors.

Did I do my best work?

Terrific   OK   Needs Work

Exhibit 63. Tailored to the Topic of the Civil War
Performance Task Assessment List
Poster Contrasting the North and South Prior to the Civil War
Grade 4

1. **Focus**
   - T: It is clear that your poster is about the differences between the North and the South.
   - O: It is somewhat clear that your poster is about the differences between the North and the South.
   - W: It is unclear what your poster is about.

2. **Content**
   - T: Your pictures show 5 differences between the North and the South. (Economy, Geography, Way of Life, Religion, Education)
   - O: Your pictures show 3–4 differences between the North and the South.
   - W: Your pictures show less than 3 differences between the North and the South.

3. **Organization**
   - T: Your poster is clearly organized in two sections, one about the North and one about the South.
   - O: The organization of your poster in two sections is not completely clear.
   - W: Your poster is not organized into two clear sections about the North and the South.

4. **Audience**
   - T: Your poster is clearly understandable to your peers.
   - O: Your poster is mostly understandable to your peers.
   - W: Your poster is mostly unclear to your peers.

5. **Sentences**
   - T: You have included 10 correct sentences to describe all pictures.
   - O: You have included 6–9 correct sentences to describe all pictures.
   - W: You have included less than 6 correct sentences to describe the pictures.

6. **Mechanics**
   - T: You have no spelling or sentence mistakes.
   - O: You have 1–5 spelling and/or sentence mistakes.
   - W: You have more than 5 mistakes.

7. **Presentation**
   - T: Your poster is very neat and presentable.
   - O: Your poster is mostly neat and presentable.
   - W: Your poster is not neat and presentable.

Did I do my best work?

Terrific

OK

Needs Work

Exhibit 64. Classroom Assessment List for a Poster
Primary Grades

1. My idea for the poster fits the assignment.

2. My picture tells a story.

3. I printed a sentence that helps the picture tell a story.

Exhibit 65. Performance Task Assessment List
Poster About Caterpillars
Primary Grades
Tailored to a Unit on Butterflies

1. My poster shows where caterpillars live.

2. I drew details.

3. My picture tells a story.

4. I printed a sentence that helps the picture tell a story.

Exhibit 66. Generic Format Performance Task Assessment List Map

| | ASSESSMENT POINTS | | |
| | Points | Earned Assessment: | |
Element	Possible	Self	Teacher
1. Land forms and water forms are correct in shape.	_____	_____	_____
2. Land forms and water forms are correct in size proportion.	_____	_____	_____
3. Human activity is represented on the map.	_____	_____	_____
4. The map is drawn on a grid that accurately shows the longitude and latitude.	_____	_____	_____
5. Color, texture, and other graphic techniques help make the map interesting and easy to understand.	_____	_____	_____
6. The map includes a key or legend, and the symbols and/or colors correctly correspond to land and water forms and human activity on the map.	_____	_____	_____
7. Labels are descriptive and help make the map easy to understand.	_____	_____	_____
8. There is a title, date, and cartographer's name.	_____	_____	_____
9. The map is neat and presentable.	_____	_____	_____
Total	_____	_____	_____

Exhibit 67. Performance Task Assessment List
A Physical Geography Map of Japan
Tailored to a Unit on Japan

| | ASSESSMENT POINTS | | |
| | Points | Earned Assessment: | |
Element	Possible	Self	Teacher
1. The four major islands of Japan are labeled.	_____	_____	_____
2. The drawings of the four major islands are the correct shape and size.	_____	_____	_____
3. Cities, industrial areas, agriculture, and other human activities are represented on the map.	_____	_____	_____
4. The map is drawn on a grid that accurately shows the longitude and latitude of Japan.	_____	_____	_____
5. Color, texture, and other graphic techniques are used to make the map interesting and easy to understand.	_____	_____	_____
6. The map includes a key or legend and the symbols and/or colors correctly correspond to land and water forms and human activity on the map.	_____	_____	_____
7. The map includes labeled countries and bodies of water that either surround or are close to Japan.	_____	_____	_____
8. A compass rose is used to show direction.	_____	_____	_____
9. The map is in an authentic style.	_____	_____	_____
10. There is a title, date, and cartographer's name.	_____	_____	_____
11. The map of Japan is neat, easy to read, and colorful.	_____	_____	_____
Total	_____	_____	_____

Exhibit 68. Performance Task Assessment List for Writing a Short Story

	ASSESSMENT POINTS		
	Points	Earned Assessment:	
Element	Possible	Self	Teacher

Prewriting

1. Graphic organizers and outlines show work to explore, discover, collect, select, and focus ideas. _____ _____ _____

The Writing

Characterization

2. Character(s) developed through the following indirect means:

    A. The characters' actions and reactions. _____ _____ _____

    B. How others react to the character. _____ _____ _____

    C. Dialogue between and among characters. _____ _____ _____

    D. How characters react to their surroundings. _____ _____ _____

        Subtotal for Characterization _____ _____ _____

Point of View

3. The point of view is chosen and used to draw the reader into the events of the narration in the following ways:

    A. A good choice was made as to the level of "person": such as 1st person, 3rd person limited omniscient, 3rd person omniscient. _____ _____ _____

    B. The point of view is used consistently and creatively. _____ _____ _____

    C. The point of view is used appropriately to reveal or to conceal. _____ _____ _____

        Subtotal for Point of View _____ _____ _____

Plot

4. The action is important, entire, and appropriate to the task and its purpose. _____ _____ _____

5. The actions of the plot maintain the artistic unity of the narrative. _____ _____ _____

        Subtotal for Plot _____ _____ _____

(Exhibit continues on the following page.)

Exhibit 68 (continued)

Setting

6. The setting is effectively established and described. _____ _____ _____

7. The setting is essential to this narrative and contributes strongly to its overall effect. _____ _____ _____

Subtotal for Setting _____ _____ _____

Theme

8. The elements of the narration work together to achieve a single purpose. _____ _____ _____

Mood

9. The narrative accomplishes a single emotional effect. _____ _____ _____

Title

10. The title suggests the overall effect and purpose of the narrative. _____ _____ _____

Use of Language

11. Literary devices such as a flashback, foreshadowing, simile, metaphor, and imagery are used. _____ _____ _____

12. The choice of words is varied and creative. _____ _____ _____

13. Sentence length and structures are varied throughout the narrative. _____ _____ _____

14. The story gains from a second reading. _____ _____ _____

15. Language mechanics and grammar are appropriate. _____ _____ _____

16. The work is neat and presentable. _____ _____ _____

Subtotal for Language _____ _____ _____

Total _____ _____ _____

Exhibit 69. Unmodified Performance Task Assessment List Geographical Picture Dictionary

| | | ASSESSMENT POINTS | |
| | Points | Earned Assessment: | |
Element	Possible	Self	Teacher
1. There are at least 10 geographical terms that are defined and represented by pictures.	_____	_____	_____
2. The written text is accurate, and the content shows understanding of typical geographic terms.	_____	_____	_____
3. The graphics represent the written definitions.	_____	_____	_____
4. The graphics are interesting and appealing to children.	_____	_____	_____
5. The layout of the booklet is artistic, appealing, and well balanced.	_____	_____	_____
6. There is a cover page with the title, author, and a picture.	_____	_____	_____
7. There is a title page with the title, author, illustrator, publisher's name and city, and a copyright date.	_____	_____	_____
8. The booklet is neat and presentable.	_____	_____	_____
9. The booklet has few errors.	_____	_____	_____
Total	_____	_____	_____

Exhibit 70. Modified for a Special Needs Student Performance Task Assessment List Geographical Picture Dictionary

		ASSESSMENT POINTS	
	Points	Earned Assessment:	
Element	Possible	Self	Teacher
1. There are at least 5 geographical terms that are defined and represented by pictures.	_____	_____	_____
2. The definitions are correct.	_____	_____	_____
3. The pictures match the written definitions.	_____	_____	_____
4. The pictures are interesting and appealing to children.	_____	_____	_____
5. The layout of the booklet is artistic, appealing, and well balanced.	_____	_____	_____
6. There is a cover page with the title, author, and a picture.	_____	_____	_____
7. There is a title page with the title, author, illustrator, publisher's name and city, and a copyright date.	_____	_____	_____
8. The booklet is neat and presentable.	_____	_____	_____
9. The booklet has few mechanical errors.	_____	_____	_____
Total	_____	_____	_____

WHAT IS A RUBRIC, AND HOW DOES IT COMPARE IN FORM AND FUNCTION TO AN ASSESSMENT LIST?

A rubric is an evaluative tool designed to lay out a continuum of product quality from very excellent to very poor. Attached to each level of the rubric is a narrative describing what a product achieving that level might look like. The goal of the rubric designer is to create an instrument that might be used to place students' work on a continuum of quality. The rubric should also enable two or more teachers to view the performance in the same way. Teachers at different grade levels or teaching different subjects may also be able to use the same rubric, thereby providing a continuity of teaching and learning from grade to grade and from subject to subject.

A SAMPLE RUBRIC

There are as many types of rubrics as there are rubric designers. One simple and easy-to-use format is a six-point, two-decision rubric (see Exhibit 71, "Rubric for a Scientific Drawing").

Use of this type of rubric requires that the assessor make two separate decisions. In the first decision, the assessor decides whether the product is "good"—*T*—or "weak"—*W*. If the first decision is that the product is more like one that is excellent (*T*), then the second and final decision is made. Was the product one of those unusually excellent products that surpass the standards of excellence for the grade level (*S*), was it evenly excellent (*T*), or was it mostly excellent—lacking in one or two elements (*U*)? If the first decision was that the product was more like a (*W*), then the assessor must decide if it was evenly weak (*W*), mostly weak, but with some better elements (*V*), or very poorly done (*X*). Thus, with only two decisions, the product is placed on a six-point continuum of performance.

The rubric uses letters (*S, T, U, V, W, X*) instead of numbers. This is done to avoid using the numbers to somehow "average" performances. For example, if numbers are used, and if a student were to score a 5 on one product and a 3 on another, one might be tempted to report that the student earned an average of 4 on her work. But the scores of 1, 2, 3, 4, 5, 6 (*X, W, V, U, T, S*) are placed on a continuum of quality, and the "distances" between each of the six levels are not precisely known. Further, the distances between each of the six levels are likely to be uneven. Therefore, a rubric is more likely to be like continuum B than continuum A, and the values of two different products could not be added together to calculate a "mean" score.

Continuum A: EQUAL intervals between values:

Low Quality				High Quality	
X	W	V	U	T	S
1	2	3	4	5	6

Continuum B: UNEQUAL intervals between values:

Low Quality				High Quality	
X	W	V	U		T	S
1	2	3	4		5	6

If a student completes seven performance assessment tasks during the course of one quarter, she might earn the following ratings:

W   W   U   U   T   U   T   T

It would be incorrect to state that the student's average performance was a *U*. Instead, we might describe that student's long-term performance by reporting that she earned two *W*'s, three *U*'s, and three *T*'s. Another observation might be that the student began to earn *T*'s toward the end of the quarter, indicating that the student was becoming more proficient at performance assessment tasks as she gained practice and experience. Further, we might use the individual rubrics to draw conclusions about how the student is performing. To assign a numerical "grade" based on the student's performances during the quarter might be somewhat difficult since rubrics are primarily holistic in nature. However, if grades are necessary, teachers might assign grades as follows: *S* = A+, *T* = A/A-, *U* = B+/B/B-, *V* = C+/C, *W* = C-/D, and *X* = F.

HOW ARE RUBRICS USED, AND HOW ARE THEY DIFFERENT FROM ASSESSMENT LISTS?

Unlike the rubric, the assessment list is analytical in nature. The assessment list for a "Scientific Drawing" allows the teacher to evaluate the quality of each of the important components in a performance task, making the assignment of a numerical grade much simpler (see Exhibit 72).

Performance task assessment lists may be used for any performance task. A numerical grade is easily derived from the total points earned on the assessment list.

Rubrics are used much less often. Some teachers use them to generate a more holistic view of the work of the class. Each product is given a rubric score, and samples of work at each level are collected for use in conferences with parents or individual students. Other teachers use them to provide holistic feedback during the rough draft stages of work. Still others use them to provide holistic feedback that does not translate into a grade.

Perhaps the best use of the rubric is to help students periodically assess the overall quality of their work. After making a series of products such as posters, graphs, letters to the editor, models, or maps, the student is asked how he or she is doing overall on performance assessments. By looking at the standards of quality for their grade level, students can decide where on the continuum of quality their work fits. The student may be asked not only to assign a rubric score, but to explain why they selected that score. Because the student has used a performance task assessment list to examine the elements of each of the products, he or she can justify the rubric score. Before asking students to use the rubric to assess their own work, it is essential that they have had a significant amount of practice in self-assessment using performance task assessment lists.

Even if teachers do not use rubrics with students, they may find them helpful in selecting benchmarks, as described in Chapter 6.

Both rubrics and assessment lists have value in the instruction/assessment circle. Both help us to find answers to the questions "What do students know?" and "What can students do with what they know?" They can also be useful to the student in answering the question "How am I doing?" In any performance learning system, there is a place for both rubrics and assessment lists. Remember, performance-based learning and

FIGURE 8. A Continuum, Not a Competition

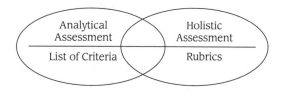

assessment are a continuum, not a competition (Figure 8).

HIGH-STAKES PERFORMANCE ASSESSMENTS USUALLY USE RUBRICS

A rubric is a tool, used in conjunction with benchmarks of student work that *show* the quality of student work described by each level of the rubric, designed to help scorers assess many pieces of student work in a highly reliable and cost-effective manner essential to high-stakes, expensive, state-level performance assessments. The rubric serves as a "shorthand" reminder to the expert scorer of the essential characteristics of each level of quality. Three such rubrics used in Connecticut to assess writing at the elementary and middle grade levels are included here. These rubrics provide general, holistic information that places the student into one of the categories of quality, but does not indicate specific areas of strength or weakness. The analytical assessment lists found in this book for nonfiction writing, fiction, and persuasive writing (see Chapter 4) are the tools invented for classroom use because they provide the details that students and teachers need to improve. (Note: The Connecticut Mastery Test (CMT) rubrics in Exhibits 73–75 are part of the "off year" tests provided to schools to support school improvement projects there. They are *identical* to the rubrics used for the statewide standardized test given in grades four, six, and eight.)

HIGH-STAKES ASSESSMENTS CAN BE PARTNERS WITH CLASSROOM PRACTICES

Most states and many school districts are using some form of high-stakes performance assessment to provide data so that the quality of student performance can be evaluated. Figure 9 shows how classroom performance-based learning and assessment and state-level high-stakes performance assessment can work together. In Figure 9, the top lever shows student performance in a "depressed" position and a high-stakes performance assessment placed to "elevate" it. Alone, the high-stakes assessment will not accomplish this goal; and educators and the public alike will be frustrated. The bottom level shows that when high-stakes performance assessment is built on a foundation of classroom performance-based learning and assessment, such as the strategies described in this book, student performance can be "elevated."

FIGURE 9. Student Learning and High-Stakes Performance Assessment

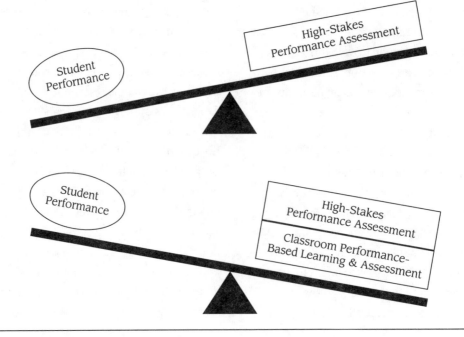

Performance tasks assessing reading comprehension will be used here as examples of how classroom and high-stakes performance assessment strategies can be partners.

RESPONDING TO LITERATURE: A HIGH-STAKES PERFORMANCE ASSESSMENT

The Connecticut Academic Performance Test (CAPT) given in April to public school 10th graders includes a measure of reading comprehension and writing called the Response to Literature. Exhibit 80 shows the "Overview" of the CAPT task presented to students; Exhibit 81 shows the "Scoring Guidelines" provided to teachers. Figure 10 shows the relationship among the four elements of reading comprehension. Initial (literal) understanding of the story is the foundation for the three remaining elements of comprehension, but it is insufficient to measure reading comprehension. The student must go *beyond literal understanding* and show skills of developing an interpretation, making connections, and taking a critical stance.

To measure student performance on this state test, a rubric is used. The rubric for Responding to Literature embodies all four aspects of reading comprehension: initial understanding, developing an interpretation, making connections, and taking a critical stance.

• A rubric score of 6 indicates that the student demonstrated excellence in all four categories of reading comprehension.

FIGURE 10. Reading Comprehension

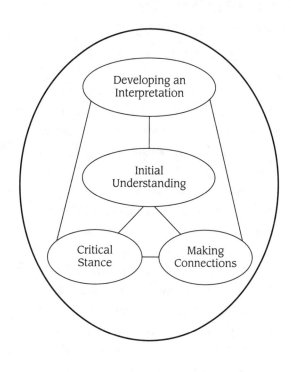

• A rubric score of 1 indicates that the student shows little or no comprehension of the material read.

• Rubric scores of 2, 3, 4, or 5 represent various levels of reading comprehension, but the specific strengths and weaknesses are not revealed by these rubric scores.

If student performance is to improve, more information is needed. This is where classroom performance-based learning and assessment, together, become a partner with the high-stakes assessment.

CLASSROOM READING COMPREHENSION ASSESSMENT TASKS AND ASSESSMENT LISTS

If reading comprehension is to be improved, it will happen because effective strategies are used day-to-day at the classroom level. The Region 15 Public School Integrated Language Arts Team (kindergarten through 12) created a set of performance tasks and assessment lists, based on the same definition of reading comprehension as that the State of Connecticut used for assessing reading comprehension on the CMT and the CAPT. Exhibits 82 through 104 show samples of those performance tasks used as learning activities associated with the literature selections that are a part of the Region 15 Language Arts, Social Studies, and Science curriculums. The assessment list for each performance task is tailored to the specific piece of literature on which the task is based, uses a developmentally appropriate format for the assessment list, and is keyed to the four elements of reading comprehension.

Exhibits 102 through 106 represent a collection of high school performance-based tasks and assessment lists in the "Responding to Literature" series. Tasks vary, from writing an essay about Maya Angelou's *I Know Why the Caged Bird Sings* to writing an "additional chapter" for Mark Twain's *The Adventures of Huckleberry Finn.*

In addition, the reading logs and the accompanying assessment list (see Exhibit 107) provide students with comprehensive self-assessment tools.

SHARPENED FOCUS, HIGHER STUDENT PERFORMANCE

Teachers in Region 15 have been approaching reading comprehension according to the elements shown in Figure 10 for many years. The Response to Literature section of the CAPT sharpened the focus of the teachers on those elements and prompted the Regionwide Integrated Language Arts Committee to produce a set of model reading comprehension performance tasks and assessment lists better connected to the elements of reading comprehension. The 10th grade state-level test was not viewed as a "high school" test, but rather a measure of how well reading comprehension was being taught and learned from kindergarten through grade 12, so all teachers have a stake in the performance of our 10th graders. The high-stakes, state-level performance task has worked as a partner with Region 15 to adapt day-to-day instruction and improve student performance. In Chapter 14, a graph of student performance on the CAPT shows that Region 15 students performed very well.

Exhibit 71. Rubric for a Scientific Drawing

S: The drawings are striking in how realistically the student has drawn the object(s.) Amazing detail is provided. A very precise scale is used consistently. The scale uses the metric system when possible. Labels are used to help convey information. The principles of artistic composition are well employed in this drawing.

T: The drawings show the details of the structure of the object(s.) The student has drawn the object(s) to a scale that is clearly marked. A metric scale is used when possible. Enough views of the object(s) are drawn to provide the viewer with a complete picture of the structures under study. Accurate details of color, pattern, and texture are shown. If appropriate, the relationship between the object(s) and its/their environment is shown. Labels are used accurately to provide needed information. An accompanying test accurately and clearly explains the science that is intended to be shown. The drawings are neat and presentable, and the space of the paper is well used.

U: The drawings are like those receiving a rating of **T**, except that there are one or two important elements that are not excellent.

V: The drawings are like those receiving a rating of **W**, except that there are one or two important elements that are well done.

W: The drawings do not show much detail of structure. The drawings are not done to a consistent scale. The scale is not metric when metric measurements could have been used. Details of color, pattern, and texture are not used well. Labels are incorrect or lacking. An accompanying text to explain the science intended to be shown is missing or inaccurate. The drawings are not neat.

X: The drawings are very poorly done.

Key: S = Surpasses the standards of excellence for the grade level; T = Evenly excellent; U = Mostly excellent, lacking in one or two elements; V = Mostly weak, but with some better elements; W = Evenly weak; X = Very poorly done.

Exhibit 72. Performance Task Assessment List
A Scientific Drawing

Element	Points Possible	Earned Assessment: Self	Teacher
		ASSESSMENT POINTS	
1. Appropriate and accurate details of structure are shown.	_____	_____	_____
2. The drawings show an appropriate number of views of the object so that all of it is represented in the drawings.	_____	_____	_____
3. All drawings use the same scale, which is clearly shown. The scale is metric.	_____	_____	_____
4. Appropriate and accurate details of color, pattern, texture, and/or other physical characteristics are shown.	_____	_____	_____
5. If appropriate, the relationship of the object of attention to its surroundings is accurately shown.	_____	_____	_____
6. If appropriate, the relationship(s) between the structure of the object of attention and its function is/are accurately shown.	_____	_____	_____
7. Labels are used accurately.	_____	_____	_____
8. An accompanying text accurately explains the science intended to be shown in the drawing.	_____	_____	_____
9. Drawings are neat and presentable.	_____	_____	_____
10. Drawings use the space of the paper well.	_____	_____	_____
Total	_____	_____	_____

Exhibit 73. Connecticut Mastery Test-Second Generation Grade 3 Scoring Manual (September 1995)

Writing Prompt: Imagine that your class went on a field trip to the zoo, and one of the animals got loose. Write a story and tell what happened next.

Rubric for Scoring Narrative Writing

NOTE: These are provided as a general guide. Do not attempt to go point-by-point when scoring papers.

Score Point: 6
Well-developed narratives; writers expand on all key events and characters
- fully elaborated with specific details
- strong organizational strategy/sequencing
- fluent

Score Point: 5
Developed narratives; writers expand on most key events and characters
- moderately well-elaborated with mostly specific details
- generally strong organizational strategy/sequencing
- moderately fluent

Score Point: 4
Somewhat developed narratives; some expansion of key events and characters
- adequately elaborated with mix of general and specific details
- satisfactory organizational strategy/sequencing
- somewhat fluent

Score Point: 3
Minimally developed narratives; little expansion of key events and characters; some details just listed
- more general than specific details
- some evidence of organization/sequencing
- some awkwardness may be present

Score Point: 2
Underdeveloped narratives; usually brief responses, details just listed
- mostly general details
- may be disorganized/weak sequencing
- may be awkward and confused

Score Point: 1
Very sparse narratives
- may have few/vague details
- too brief to indicate sequencing
- awkward and confused

Reprinted with permission from the Connecticut State Department of Education.

Exhibit 74. Connecticut Mastery Test-Second Generation Grade 5 Scoring Manual (September 1995)

Writing Prompt: Your principal has decided to start a program in which members of the community will come to your school and talk about their jobs. Write to your principal about the occupation in which you are interested and tell why you are interested in the job you picked.

Rubric For Scoring Expository Writing

NOTE: These are provided as a general guide. Do not attempt to go point-by-point when scoring papers.

Score Point: 6

Well-developed responses

- reasons fully elaborated with specific detail
- strong organizational strategy
- fluent

Score Point: 5

Developed responses

- reasons moderately well-elaborated with mostly specific details
- generally strong organizational strategy
- moderately fluent

Score Point: 4

Somewhat developed responses

- reasons adequately elaborated with a mix of general and specific detail
- satisfactory organizational strategy
- somewhat fluent

Score Point: 3

Minimally developed responses

- reasons have only a little elaboration; more general than specific details
- some evidence of organizational strategy
- some awkwardness may be present

Score Point: 2

Undeveloped responses; usually brief with details just listed

- mostly general details
- may be disorganized
- may be awkward and confused

Score Point: 1

Very sparse responses

- may have few/vague details
- too brief to indicate organization
- awkward and confused

Reprinted with permission from the Connecticut State Department of Education.

Exhibit 75. Connecticut Mastery Test-Second Generation Grade 7 Scoring Manual (September 1995)

Writing Prompt: Your principal is considering the idea that school work should be done during school hours only and that children should not be assigned homework. Write to convince your principal either for or against this idea.

Rubric for Scoring Persuasive Writing

NOTE: These are provided as a general guide. Do not attempt to go point-by-point when scoring papers.

Score Point: 6

Well-developed responses

- reasons fully elaborated with specific detail
- strong orgainizational strategy
- fluent

Score Point: 5

- Developed responses
- reasons moderately well-elaborated with mostly specific details
- generally strong organizational strategy
- moderately fluent

Score Point: 4

Somewhat developed responses

- reasons adequately elaborated with a mix of general and specific details
- satisfactory organizational strategy
- somewhat fluent

Score Point: 3

Minimally developed responses

- reasons have only a little elaboration;more general than specific details
- some evidence of organizational strategy
- some awkwardness may be present

Score Point: 2

Undeveloped responses; usually brief with details just listed

- mostly general details
- may be disorganized
- may be awkward and confused

Score Point: 1

Very sparse responses

- may have few/vague details
- too brief to indicate organization
- awkward and confused

Reprinted with permission from the Connecticut State Department of Education.

Exhibit 76. Scoring Rubric for Connecticut Academic Performance Test (CAPT) Science Open-Ended Items

Each score category contains a range of student responses that reflect the descriptions given below.

Score 3

The response is an excellent answer to the question. It is correct, complete, and appropriate and contains elaboration, extension, and/or evidence of higher-order thinking and relevant prior knowledge. There is no evidence of misconceptions. Minor errors will not necessarily lower the score.

Score 2

The response is a proficient answer to the question. It is generally correct, complete, and appropriate although minor inaccuracies may appear. There may be limited evidence of elaboration, extension, higher-order thinking, and relevant prior knowledge, or there may be significant evidence of these traits; but other flaws (e.g., inaccuracies, omissions, inappropriateness) may be more than minor.

Score 1

The response is a marginal answer to the question. While it may contain some elements of a proficient response, it is inaccurate, incomplete, and/or inappropriate. There is little if any evidence of elaboration, extension, higher-order thinking, or relevant prior knowledge. There may be evidence of significant misconceptions.

Score 0

The response, although on topic, is an unsatisfactory answer to the question. It may fail to address the question, or it may address the question is a very limited way. There may be no evidence of elaboration, extension, higher-order thinking, or relevant prior knowledge. There may be evidence of serious misconceptions.

Reprinted with permission from the Connecticut State Department of Education.

Exhibit 77. Scoring Rubric for Connecticut Academic Performance Test (CAPT) Mathematics Open-Ended Items

Each score category contains a range of student responses that reflect the descriptions given below.

Score 3

The student has demonstrated a full and complete understanding of all concepts and processes embodied in this application. The student has addressed the task in a mathematically sound manner. The response contains evidence of the student's competence in problem-solving and reasoning, computing and estimating, and communicating to the full extent that these processes apply to the specified task. The response may, however, contain minor arithmetic errors that do not detract from a demonstration of full understanding.

Score 2

The student has demonstrated a reasonable understanding of the essential mathematical concepts and processes embodied in this application. The student's response contains most of the attributes of an appropriate response including a mathematically sound approach and evidence of competence with applicable mathematical processes, but contains flaws that do not diminish countervailing evidence that the student comprehends the essential mathematical ideas addressed by this task. Such flaws include errors ascribable to faulty reading, writing, or drawing skills; errors ascribable to insufficient, nonmathematical knowledge; and errors ascribable to negligent or inattentive execution of mathematical processes or algorithms.

Score 1

The student has demonstrated a limited understanding of the concepts and process embodied in this application. The student's response contains some of the attribute of an appropriate response, but lacks convincing evidence that the student fully comprehends the essential mathematical ideas addressed by this task. Such deficits include evidence of insufficient mathematical knowledge; errors in fundamental mathematical procedures; and other omissions or anomalies that bring into question the extent of the student's ability to solve problems of this general type.

Score 0

The student has demonstrated merely an acquaintance with the topic. The student's response is associated with the task in the item, but contains few attributes of an appropriate response. There are significant omissions or anomalies that indicate a basic lack of comprehension in regard to the mathematical ideas and procedures necessary to adequately address the specified task. No evidence is present to suggest that the student has the ability to solve problems of this general type.

Reprinted with permission from the Connecticut State Department of Education.

Exhibit 78. Connecticut Academic Performance Test (CAPT) Interdisciplinary Assessment Scoring Rubric

Each score category contains a range of student responses that reflect the descriptions given below.

Score 1

Fails to take a stand that addresses the problem. The response offers no support; or emotional support only; or serious misunderstanding; or inaccurate or irrelevant support. The response lacks focus and a controlling idea; displays little or no organization; and contains frequent digressions or abrupt shifts in ideas that interfere with meaning. The response shows no awareness of audience; most ideas are difficult to follow and understand; fluency and transitions are lacking.

Score 2

Attempts a stand but fluctuates between or among positions. Only superficial support (1 or 2 ideas) is given; and ideas may be poorly developed, inaccurate, irrelevant or logically inconsistent. The response stays on topic but lacks the focus of a strong controlling idea; digressions and/or abrupt shifts interfere with meaning. The response displays little, if any, awareness of audience; many ideas are difficult to understand; fluency and transitions are lacking.

Score 3

Takes a stand but doesn't develop a clear position; the response contains limited support with only a few ideas; some information may be inaccurate or irrelevant. The controlling idea, if present, may be a simple restatement of the problem. The response shows some organization, but there may be some digressions or abrupt shifts that interfere with meaning. The response shows some awareness of audience and some transitions and fluency; however, some ideas may not be clearly expressed.

Score 4

Takes and develops a position, but the response lacks thoroughness; some information may be inaccurate or irrelevant. The response displays adequate organization with at least one controlling idea and some coherence; digressions, if present, are not disruptive. The response shows some awareness of audience; most ideas are clear and understandable; but fluency and transitions may be lacking.

Score 5

Takes a clear and thoughtful position; the position is well supported but not as completely developed as a "6" response; information is accurate and relevant. The position is well organized and contains one or more controlling ideas; but may not be as unified as a "6" response; digressions are rare. The response shows some sensitivity to audience; ideas are clearly expressed but may lack the fluency and polish of a "6" response.

Score 6

Takes a clear and persuasive position; the position is richly supported and developed with accurate and relevant information from the source materials. The position is unified and focused and contains one or more clear controlling ideas. Organization and control are sustained throughout the response. The response shows awareness of audience; ideas are clearly and effectively developed; and writing is fluent with effective transitions.

Reprinted with permission from the Connecticut State Department of Education.

Exhibit 79. Abbreviated Scoring Rubric for Connecticut Academic Performance Test (CAPT) Literature Prompts

Each score category contains a range of student responses that reflect the descriptions given below.

Score 1
- Displays very limited understanding and/or serious misunderstanding of the text.
- Displays no or very little reflective thinking about the text or his/her ability to process the text.
- Displays no awareness of or appreciation for aesthetic or literary features of the text.
- Displays no meaningful associations between the text and other texts and/or personal experience.

Score 2
- Displays a literal or superficial understanding of the text.
- Displays little, if any, reflective thinking about the text.
- Displays judgments of literary quality that are superficial, emotional, and/or personal experience.
- Displays difficulty in making association between the text and other texts and/or personal experience.

Score 3
- Displays marginally acceptable comprehension, but interpretation tends to be predictable and lacks insight.
- Displays little reflective thinking about the text.
- Displays judgments about the literary quality of the text that tend to be ritualistic and lack support.
- Displays associations between the text and other texts and/or personal experience that are superficial, lack depth of understanding, or lack support.

Score 4
- Displays a thoughtful and plausible interpretation of the text, but the interpretation lacks the insight displayed by superior and excellent readers.
- Displays some reflective thinking about the text, but no the deeper interpretations exhibited by superior and excellent readers.
- Displays judgments about the literary quality of the text, but the judgments tend to be superficial and/or not well supported.
- Displays some associations between the text and other texts and/or personal experience, but the associations tend to be routine and predictable.

Score 5
- Displays a thoughtful comprehension, but the interpretation may be less insightful than that of superior readers.
- Displays reflective thinking about the text, but may lack deeper interpretations exhibited by superior readers.
- Displays judgments about the literary quality of the text and usually supports those judgments with evidence.
- Displays associations between the text and other texts and/or personal experience, but the associations may not be as perceptive or thoughtful as those of superior readers.

Score 6
- Displays perceptive and insightful comprehension.
- Displays exceptional reflective thinking about the text.
- Displays thoughtful judgments about the literary quality of the text and supports those judgments with evidence from the text and/or personal experience.
- Displays perceptive associations between the text and/or personal experience.

Reprinted with permission from the Connecticut State Department of Education.

Exhibit 80. Connecticut Academic Performance Test (CAPT) Response to Literature Task

Overview

In this Language Arts assessment, you will read and respond to a short story. After reading this story, you will answer six open-ended questions. You will have 90 minutes to complete this test.

The purpose of the Language Arts assessment is to determine how well you can interpret a work of literature. You will be evaluated on the following:

- how well you understand the characters in the story, the problems or conflicts they experience, and why they act the way they do;
- what you think the story means—the theme the author is trying to create; and
- how well you connect the story to your experiences and to human nature in general.

Reading the Short Story (approximately 30 minutes)

Directions:

Read the story "Tears of Autumn" by Yoshiko Uchida. As you read, you may mark the selection and write notes in the margins that help you think about what you are reading. For example, you may underline, take notes, jot down questions, or draw diagrams. If you choose to take notes, you might react to the characters, note how your thoughts change, ask questions about parts that are confusing, or explain what the story means to you. Your notes will not be scored but might be helpful to you later when you answer the questions.

You may reread or refer to the story at any time during the assessment.

Note: The student is given the story "Trees of Autumn," by Yoshiko Uchida.

Reprinted with permission from the Connecticut State Department of Education.

Exhibit 81. Scoring Guidelines for Connecticut Academic Performance Test (CAPT) Response to Literature

The CAPT Response to Literature assessment is based on the belief that readers construct interpretations of a text based on elements within the text; prior knowledge and experience; and the context in which the text is read. Meaning does not reside solely within the text, but is constructed by the reader as he or she interacts with the text. This does not mean that *any* interpretation is acceptable. Rather, it opens the door to multiple interpretations, not a single "correct" interpretation, as long as those interpretations are justified. A focused-holistic scoring system will be used to evaluate a student's response to literature. The written response to all of the "items will be read in total, evaluated in terms of the enclosed rubric, and given a single overall rating. The ratings may range from a low of 1 to a high of 6.

The scoring will be "focused" in that scorers will look for evidence of four major dimensions:(1) initial understanding; (2) developing an interpretation; (3) critical stance; and (4) connection. These are described below.

The scoring will be "holistic" in that a single, overall score will be assigned to the student's entire set of responses. The following descriptions characterize each score point. However, given the weighing and balancing that are inherent in holistic scoring, a response may not contain all the characteristics of the score it receives. Scorers should not attempt to link an item with a single dimension. Although some of the items may seem to be more closely related to some dimensions than others, evidence of a dimension is more likely to cut across multiple items.

Major Dimensions to Consider When Scoring

Initial Understanding

Initial Understanding examines the student's ability to derive a general understanding of the text. Questions such as the following guide the assessment of this dimension:

- Does the student have a basic understanding of the text as a whole?
- Does the student understand important elements of the text (e.g., the main characters, actions, or events)?
- Does the student recognize inconsistencies or ambiguities in the text and attempt to deal with them?

Developing and Interpretation

Developing and Interpretation refers to a student's ability to reflect upon and interact with the text, to search for deeper interpretations of the text, and to go beyond interpreting parts of the text to search for overall meaning. The following questions guide the assessment of this dimension:

- Does the student use clues or evidence from the passage to make inferences, draw conclusions, predict events, and infer the motives of characters?
- Does the student revise, reshape, and/or deepen initial understandings?
- Does the student demonstrate emotional or intellectual engagement with the text?
- Does the student carry on an internal dialogue with the author?
- Does the student generalize beyond the text?
- Does the student engage in self-reflection?

Reprinted with permission from the Connecticut State Department of Education.

(Exhibit continues on the following page.)

Exhibit 81 (continued)

Critical Stance

Critical Stance examines the student's ability to step outside the text, to challenge the text, and/or to make judgments of quality about the parts of the text or the text as a whole. The following questions guide scorers in assessment of this dimension:

- Does the student demonstrate aesthetic appreciation of the text? sensitivity to the author's style? awareness of linguistic or literary features?
- Does the student challenge the text by disagreeing or questioning the author?
- Does the student examine the fit between the text and prior knowledge and experience, and attempt to reconcile differences when necessary?
- Does the student go beyond the text to judge its literary quality?

Connection

Connection examines the student's ability to make associations between the text and life outside of the text. Questions such as the following guide scorers in evaluating this dimension:

- Does the student make associations between the text and other texts? between the text and other works of art (e.g., movies, paintings, music, dance)? between the text and personal experiences? between the text and aspects of his/her culture?
- Does the student apply his/her understanding of people and the world to the text?
- Does the student form analogies between the world of the text and his/her personal world?
- Does the student make associations between the character's life and his/her own personal life?
- When associations are made, do they lead to autobiographical digressions or are they linked back to the text?

Reprinted with permission from the Connecticut State Department of Education.

Exhibit 82. Butterfly Life Cycle
The Very Hungry Caterpillar by Eric Carle
Grade 1

Your Task

You have read a story about the life of a caterpillar.

You have watched real caterpillars change into butterflies in science class.

Your job is to draw pictures that show the life cycle of a butterfly.

Your pictures will be put on the bulletin board for Earth Day.

Procedure

1. You have a large piece of paper divided into four parts.

2. Show the four parts of the butterfly life cycle.

3. Show details.

4. Label what you draw.

5. Write a sentence about each part of the butterfly life cycle.

Note to the Teacher:

This task involves **initial understanding** from reading the book and **connections** to the child's experiences with real caterpillars and butterflies in science class and elsewhere.

Exhibit 83. Performance Task Assessment List
Responding to Literature
The Very Hungry Caterpillar by Eric Carle
Grade 1

1. Did I draw the four parts of the butterfly life cycle?

          Terrific   OK   Needs Work

2. Did I show details?

          Terrific   OK   Needs Work

3. Did I label the parts of each picture?

          Terrific   OK   Needs Work

4. Did I write a sentence for each picture?

          Terrific   OK   Needs Work

(Exhibit continues on the following page.)

Exhibit 83 (continued)

5. Do my sentences tell what the pictures show?

Terrific   OK   Needs Work

6. Did I start each sentence with a capital letter?

Terrific   OK   Needs Work

7. Did I end each sentence with a period?

Terrific   OK   Needs Work

8. Is my work neat?

Terrific   OK   Needs Work

Exhibit 84. Responding to Literature
Memory Box
Wilfrid Gordon McDonald Partridge
Grade 2

Background

We have just finished reading *Wilfrid Gordon McDonald Partridge*, and have learned that memories can create many different feelings.

Task

Make a memory box that you might have shared with Miss Nancy.

Audience

Our 2nd grade class

Purpose

The purpose of this task is to help us to understand that things can have different meanings to different people.

Procedure

1. Find a shoebox and decorate it.
2. Choose five things to add to the box the way Wilfrid Gordon did. Be sure to use the answers he got to the question, "What's a memory?" to help you choose your objects.
3. On a note card, write the reason you chose each object (for example, I chose this object as something precious as gold because...). Use complete sentences and check punctuation.
4. Share your memory box with the class.
5. When sharing your box, be prepared to tell us if you liked Wilfrid Gordon's choices for his memory box.

When Wilfrid Gordon asked his friends at the old people's home, "What's a memory? he got many different answers.

Fill in the blanks to compare the different answers he got with the object *he* chose to go along with each one.

Question: What's a memory?

Person	Answer	Object Wilfrid Chose
Mrs. Jordon		Fresh egg
Mr. Hosking	Something from long ago	
Mr. Tippett		Medal that his grandfather had given him
Miss Mitchell	Something that makes you laugh	
Mr. Drysdale		His football

Exhibit 85. Performance Task Assessment List
Responding to Literature
<u>**Wilfrid Gordon McDonald Partridge**</u>
Memory Box, Grade 2

1. Is my memory box decorated?

2. Do I have five (5) objects in my memory box? (Connections)

3. Did I complete my guide sheet? (Initial Understanding)

4. Was each object chosen to go along with an answer to the question, "What's a memory?" from the book? (Initial Understanding)

(Exhibit continues on the following page.)

Exhibit 85 (continued)

5. Do I have a notecard for each object that explains why I chose it? (Developing an Interpretation)

6. Did I use complete sentences on the notecards?

7. Am I prepared to tell the class whether or not I liked Wilfrid Gordon's choices? (Critical Stance)

Exhibit 86. Responding to Literature
Summary Letter
<u>The Courage of Sarah Noble</u>
Grade 3

Background

You have just read *The Courage of Sarah Noble.* Sarah and her father traveled through the wilderness to build a new house for their family. In the beginning of their journey, they stopped in a settlement; and Sarah met Abigail Robinson.

Task

Write a summary letter to Abigail Robinson as if you were Sarah Noble. Tell her what happened on the rest of your trip. Include a picture of your favorite part of the journey.

Audience

Your cooperative group.

Purpose

The purpose of this task is to recall the story and write a summary letter by including the main idea and important details of each chapter.

Procedure

1. Read *The Courage of Sarah Noble.*
2. Complete the "Main Ideas and Details Organizer"
3. Writing the letter:
    _____Write a rough draft of your letter using your organizer.
    _____Include the main idea and details from each chapter when writing your letter about the journey.
    _____Be sure to explain to Abigail why your (Sarah's) cloak was so important.
    _____Edit.
    _____Make any changes needed. Be sure to use letter form.
    _____Write a final draft.
4. Include a picture of your favorite part of the journey (do not use a picture already in the book). In a sentence at the bottom of the picture tell why.
5. Be prepared to share an experience you had when you (or a friend or family member) had to keep up their courage.
6. Share your letter and experience with your cooperative group.

Exhibit 87. Performance Task Assessment List
Responding to Literature: <u>The Courage of Sarah Noble</u>
Summary Letter
Grade 3

1. The summary letter tells about the most important events. (Initial Understanding)
   T: I have included all of the important events in the story.
   O: I have included most of the important events in the story.
   W: I have included few or no important events in the story.

2. The summary letter includes details that support the main ideas. (Initial Understanding)
   T: My letter has many interesting supporting details.
   O: My letter has some interesting supporting details.
   W: My letter has few or no interesting supporting details.

3. The story events are in the correct order. (Initial Understanding)
   T: All events in my letter are in the correct order.
   O: Most of the events in my letter are in the correct order.
   W: Few or none of the events in my letter are in the correct order.

4. I explained why Sarah's cloak was important. (Developing an Interpretation)
   T: My explanation was clear, and I used an example to support it.
   O: My explanation was clear, but I didn't use an example.
   W: My explanation was unclear.

5. The letter includes the date, greeting, body, and closing.
   T: My letter includes all the important parts.
   O: My letter has 3 of the important parts.
   W: My letter has 2 or less of the important parts.

Did I do my best work?

6. Spelling
   T: I have less than 5 errors.
   O: I have between 5 and 8 errors.
   W: I have more than 8 errors.

7. Mechanics/Punctuation
   T: I have less than 5 errors.
   O: I have between 5 and 8 errors.
   W: I have more than 8 errors.

Terrific   OK   Needs Work

8. Presentation
   T: The writing is neat and presentable.
   O: The writing is somewhat neat and presentable.
   W: The writing is not neat and presentable.

9. My picture was colorful, neat, and included a complete sentence.
   T: My picture included all of the above.
   O: My picture included only two of the above.
   W: My picture included only one or none of the above.

10. I shared a personal experience of someone who keeps up the courage. (Connection)
    T: I shared an experience and provided several details.
    O: I shared an experience with few details.
    W: I didn't share an experience.

Exhibit 88. Responding to Literature
Picture Book of <u>The Lucky Stone</u>
Grade 4

Background

You have been reading the book *The Lucky Stone* and studying about slavery, in Social Studies. It is an important part of learning to be able to retell a story including all the important story elements. This is called a *summary.*

Task

Your job is to construct a picture summary that illustrates the main idea of the story and includes all story elements.

Procedure

Part 1: The Cover

Design a cover for your picture summary. It should:

_____ clearly show what the story is about

_____ have a title that states the main idea of the story

_____ be colorful and neat

Part 2: The Picture Summary

Draw a picture summary that retells each chapter of the story. Your four pictures should:

_____ show the setting of the story (where and when it takes place)

_____ include the main characters of each chapter

_____ show the main idea of each chapter

_____ include supporting details for each chapter

_____ show the correct sequence of the story (has a beginning, a middle and an end)

_____ have a title for each chapter picture that retells the main idea of that chapter

_____ have 3 or more sentences on each picture that describe them

Part 3: Beyond the Book

On the last page of the book, the author writes, "There is more to it than that, though, and someday I might tell you about that, too." Draw a picture that shows what you think happened that Tee didn't tell us. Your picture should:

_____ have a title

_____ have 3 or more sentences to describe it

Draw a picture of a story you know or an event in your life that is similar to the story in *The Lucky Stone*. Your picture should:

_____ have a title

_____ have 3 or more sentences to describe it

Exhibit 89. Performance Task Assessment List
Responding to Literature
Picture Book of The Lucky Stone
Grade 4

| | | ASSESSMENT POINTS | |
| | Points | Earned Assessment: | |
Element	Points	Self	Teacher
Initial Understanding			
Part 1: The Cover			
1. The cover clearly shows what the story is about.	_____	_____	_____
2. The cover has a title that states the main idea of the story.	_____	_____	_____
3. The cover is colorful and neat.	_____	_____	_____
Part 2: The Picture Summary			
4. My pictures show the setting of the story (where and when it takes place).	_____	_____	_____
5. My pictures include the main characters of each chapter.	_____	_____	_____
6. My pictures show the main idea of each chapter.	_____	_____	_____
7. My pictures include supporting details for each chapter.	_____	_____	_____
8. My pictures show the correct sequence of the story (beginning, middle, end).	_____	_____	_____
9. I have a title for each chapter picture that retells the main idea of that chapter.	_____	_____	_____
10. I have 3 or more sentences on my pictures that describe the pictures.	_____	_____	_____
Part 3: Beyond the Book			
Developing an Interpretation			
11. I drew a picture that shows what else might have happened.	_____	_____	_____
12. I have a title for my picture.	_____	_____	_____
13. I have 3 or more sentences on my picture that describe it.	_____	_____	_____
Connections			
14. My picture shows a story that I know or an event in my life that reminds me of the story in the book.	_____	_____	_____
15. I have a title for my picture.	_____	_____	_____
16. I have 3 or more sentences on my picture that describe it.	_____	_____	_____
Total	_____	_____	_____

Exhibit 90. <u>Owls in the Family</u>
Grade 5

After reading *Owls in the Family*, prepare the following questions for our "book chat" discussion in class. Also create a "literary postcard" for the book.

Book Chat Discussion Questions

1. What is the main problem in *Owls in the Family*?

2. Name a major event in the story. Could you have predicted that this would occur? Give examples or clues from the story.

3. If you were Billy, would you have solved the problem in the same way or would you have done it differently? Explain your ideas .

4. Read your favorite passage aloud to the group (note the page # here). Why did you choose this particular passage?

5. State your reasons (at least 3) for recommending or not recommending the book to a friend.

6. State the name of a novel in which the main problem was similar or different. Give at least two specific comparisons.

After the book chat, use the information from the above questions to write a summary of the book. Be sure to include all the information.

Literary Postcards

Create a literary postcard for *Owls in the Family* to share at the next book chat. The postcard should be completed on the large blank index card handed out in class. On the front side, draw a picture of the main setting of the book. The back should contain a note to a friend describing a situation or main character from the book. There should also be a recommendation whether to read the book or not with a reason to support your choice.

Exhibit 91. Performance Task Assessment List
Responding to Literature
<u>Owls in the Family</u>
Grade 5
Book Chat and Literary Postcard

| | ASSESSMENT POINTS | | |
| | Points | Earned Assessment: | |
Element	Possible	Self	Teacher
Initial Understanding			
1. The main problem in the novel is stated.	_____	_____	_____
2. A main character is described on the literary postcard.	_____	_____	_____
3. The setting is drawn on the literary postcard.	_____	_____	_____
Developing an Interpretation			
4. Prediction is made and supported.	_____	_____	_____
Critical Stance			
5. A passage is identified and evaluated.	_____	_____	_____
6. A judgment about the quality of the book is made and supported.	_____	_____	_____
Connections			
7. Specific connections are made between the character's actions and how the student would have reacted.	_____	_____	_____
8. Examples are used to support the connections.	_____	_____	_____
9. A comparison is made between the main problem in this novel and the problem in another novel.	_____	_____	_____
10. Specific examples are used to support the comparison.	_____	_____	_____
11. Participation in the "Book Chat" discussion was (5 fair, 10 good, 15 commendable)	_____	_____	_____
Total	_____	_____	_____

Exhibit 92. Performance Task
Responding to Literature: Journal
Sadako and the Thousand Paper Cranes
Grade 6

Every entry must include 3 words, numbered, underlined, and defined. There should be at least 5 illustrations in your journal that directly relate to the content in the chapter you choose. There must be an entry for each chapter.

Chapter 1 Entry: Prediction

Write down some good luck signs. Make a prediction about what you think might happen in the book.

Chapter 2 Entry: Setting

Tell me about the setting of the story (where and when the story takes place). Write down some examples of Japanese culture.

Chapter 3 Entry: Freewrite

Sadako had a secret. Have you ever had a secret? Write about a time when you had a secret or someone you know had a secret. What happened?

Chapter 4 Entry: Figurative Language

Write down at least 5 examples of figurative language from the story (similes, metaphors, hyperbole, etc.) and tell me what you think they mean. Did the author's use of figurative language help your understanding of the story? How?

Chapter 5 Entry: Characters

Sadako is the main character in the book. Make a character map about her.

Chapter 6 Entry: Characters

There are many other characters in the book. Choose four other characters and write a brief description of each.

Chapter 7 Entry: Research

There are many concepts and ideas discussed in this book. Choose one and research to find out more information. Some topics might be Hiroshima, World War II, radiation, atom bomb, X-rays, leukemia, etc.

Chapter 8 Entry: Comparison

Draw a Venn diagram and compare your life to Sadako's. Include elements of culture.

Chapter 9 Entry: Plot

The action in a story is called the plot. What is the problem in the book and what events lead up to the climax (the most important event).

Chapter 10 Entry: Theme

The theme is the author's statement or lesson about life. What is the theme in this book? What has the author taught you through this book?

Exhibit 93. Performance Task Assessment List
Responding to Literature: Journal
Sadako and the Thousand Paper Cranes
Grade 6

Element	Points Possible	Earned Assessment: Self	Earned Assessment: Teacher
		ASSESSMENT POINTS	
Vocabulary:			
27 words	_____	_____	_____
Chapter 1 Entry: Prediction			
Good luck signs	_____	_____	_____
Prediction	_____	_____	_____
Chapter 2 Entry: Setting			
Setting of the story (where and when the story takes place).	_____	_____	_____
Examples of Japanese culture	_____	_____	_____
Chapter 3 Entry: Freewrite			
Chapter 4 Entry: Figurative Language	_____	_____	_____
5 examples of figurative language (similes, metaphors, hyperbole, etc.) What they mean.	_____	_____	_____
Chapter 5 Entry: Characters			
Character map	_____	_____	_____
Chapter 6 Entry: Characters			
Brief description of four characters	_____	_____	_____
Chapter 7 Entry: Research			
Four facts	_____	_____	_____
Chapter 8 Entry: Comparison			
Venn diagram comparing your life to Sadako's.	_____	_____	_____
Chapter 9 Entry: Plot			
What is the problem in the book?	_____	_____	_____
What events lead up to the climax?	_____	_____	_____
Chapter 10 Entry: Theme			
What is the theme in this book?	_____	_____	_____
What has this book taught you?	_____	_____	_____
Illustrations:	_____	_____	_____
Neatness:	_____	_____	_____
Labels:	_____	_____	_____
Total	_____	_____	_____

Exhibit 94. Performance Task Assessment List
Responding to Literature: Journal Entry
<u>Sadako and the Thousand Paper Cranes</u>

		ASSESSMENT POINTS	
	Points	Earned Assessment:	
Element	Possible	Self	Teacher

Initial Understanding

1. The main characters are described (Entry #5, 6). _____ _____ _____

2. The setting is identified (#2). _____ _____ _____

3. The problem of the story is identified (#9). _____ _____ _____

4. Events leading up to the climax are identified (#9). _____ _____ _____

Developing an Interpretation

5. Prediction is made using good luck signs (#1). _____ _____ _____

6. Concepts from the book are researched to deepen initial understanding (#7). _____ _____ _____

Critical Stance

7. Figurative language is identified and interpreted (#4). _____ _____ _____

8. The theme of the book is identified (#10). _____ _____ _____

Connections

9. The theme of the book is identified and applied to their own life (#10). _____ _____ _____

10. Specific connections are made between the character's culture and the student's own life (#8). _____ _____ _____

11. Examples are used to support the connections (#8). _____ _____ _____

12. Connection is made between an event in the story and the student's personal life (#3). _____ _____ _____

Total _____ _____ _____

Exhibit 95. Responding to Literature
<u>The Big Wave</u>
Grade 6

Directions: After reading *The Big Wave*, answer the following six questions related to the novel. Read over all six questions before answering them. Answer each question as completely as possible.

1. Kino and Jiya are very close friends. Discuss three things they like to do together. Use specific examples from the book.

2. Where does this book take place? Why is this setting so important to the events that happen in this book? Use specific details from the book.

3. At the end of the book, Jiya marries Setsu and moves to the beach. Remembering his fear of the sea, why do you think he did that? Provide evidence to support your answer.

4. Did the author's use of imagery help you to understand the story? Choose a specific use of imagery in the book and explain why it was or wasn't effective.

5. Compare your culture to Kino and Jiya's. How are they different? How are they similar? Back up you answers with specific examples from the book and your life. Use a Venn diagram to plan.

6. Jiya had to face his fear of the sea and deal with loss throughout the novel. Choose a character from another book that you have read that had to deal with either fear or loss. Did they deal with it in the same way, or did they deal with it differently? Please explain using specific examples from both books.

Exhibit 96. Performance Task Assessment List
Responding to Literature
The Big Wave
Grade 6

| | ASSESSMENT POINTS | | |
| | Points | Earned Assessment: | |
Element	Possible	Self	Teacher
Initial Understanding			
1. The main characters' friendship is described.	_____	_____	_____
2. The setting is identified.	_____	_____	_____
3. Importance of setting on the main events of the story is established.	_____	_____	_____
4. Specific examples of imagery are identified.	_____	_____	_____
Developing an Interpretation			
5. Inference is made and supported about a character's actions.	_____	_____	_____
Critical Stance			
6. The identified examples of imagery are evaluated.	_____	_____	_____
Connections			
7. Specific connections are made between the character's culture and the student's own life.	_____	_____	_____
8. Examples are used to support the connections.	_____	_____	_____
9. Specific connections are made between how the character in this novel and the character in another novel deal with fear or loss.	_____	_____	_____
10. Specific examples are used to support the connection.	_____	_____	_____
Total	_____	_____	_____

Exhibit 97 Responding to Literature
Performance Assessment Task
Dialogue
The Witch of Blackbird Pond
Grade 7

Background

Dialogue is a conversation between two or more people. The words spoken by each person are set off by quotation marks. Every time the speaker changes, a new paragraph is begun.

Task

The Anderson Publishing Company has hired you to add a section to the book, *The Witch of Blackbird Pond*. Write a dialogue that might have occurred between Kit Tyler and Mr. Eleazer Kimberly when she goes to his house to plead for a second chance at the Dame School.

Audience

Your 7th grade class and The Anderson Publishing Company.

Purpose

1.   To show your understanding of the character, Kit Tyler, and how she would act in a certain situation.
2.   To correctly write convincing and interesting dialogue.

Procedure

1.   Write a one-paragraph introduction. Be sure to discuss:
     • Why this section might have been left out.
     • If you were the author, would you have left it out or included it? Support your opinion with details.
2.   Write the Dialogue:
     • Write a rough draft of your dialogue
     • Edit/revise (be sure to use correct dialogue form)
     • Write final draft
3.   Write a conclusion. Be sure to discuss:
     • How you would have handled the situation if that happened to you.

Assessment

See classroom assessment list.

Exhibit 98. Performance Task Assessment List
Responding to Literature
The Witch of Blackbird Pond
Grade 7
Writing Dialogue

Element	Points Possible	ASSESSMENT POINTS Earned Assessment: Self	Teacher
1. Quotations marks are used correctly.	_____	_____	_____
2. A new paragraph is used each time the speaker changes.	_____	_____	_____
3. Writing is grammatically correct.	_____	_____	_____
4. Dialogue is creative, thoughtful, and convincing.	_____	_____	_____
5. Dialogue is true to Kit's character (Initial Understanding)	_____	_____	_____
6. States why the section might have been left out. (Developing an interpretation)	_____	_____	_____
7. States whether you would have left it out or included it. (Developing an Interpretation)	_____	_____	_____
8. Above opinion is supported with a reason. (Developing an Interpretation)	_____	_____	_____
9. Includes a personal experience that was similar to Kit's. (Connection)	_____	_____	_____
Total	_____	_____	_____

Exhibit 99. Responding to Literature
Performance Assessment Task
Book Jacket for To Kill a Mockingbird
Grade 8

Background

When a book is published, a team of artists and writers work together to design a book "jacket." This book cover usually consists of an artist's rendering, a short summary of the plot, a brief biography of the author, and (frequently) a collection of one or two sentence comments by other authors or book reviewers.

Task

Imagine that you have been hired by a publishing company to create a book "jacket" for the book, *To Kill a Mockingbird*. The book jacket must have:

A.   A drawing on the front cover, which is *clearly* related to the book (do NOT merely *copy* the drawing on the cover). It should be your original work.

B.   A back cover that contains 4-5 "blurbs"—short (one- or two-sentence) comments about the quality of the book made by a book reviewer. For example, a blurb for *Johnny Tremain* might be "No novel more faithfully recreates Boston in the days that led up to the Revolution. The author's devoted research and style transports the reader back to the century in which the hero lived. —NY Times Book Review"
You must create these (make them up) yourself. Do NOT copy them from the back of your book.
The back cover should also contain a 3-sentence advertisement for the book's sequel (imagine that a sequel has already been written). What will it be about? How would you advertise it?

C.   A front "flyleaf" should have the summary of the book. You must write the summary yourself. PLEASE DO NOT COPY THIS FROM YOUR BOOK. You may have to continue this on the back flyleaf.

D.   A back flyleaf should contain a short paragraph comparing a main story element (characterization, setting, plot, problem, etc.) to another novel. You may also continue the book summary on the back flyleaf.

Audience

The audience for your "jacket" consists of other readers of the book.

Purpose

The purpose of your work is to attract others to read the book.

Procedure

1.   Read the book.
2.   Review the assessment list for a Book Jacket.
3.   Sketch your drawing.
4.   Draft the plot summary, comparison, reviewers blurb, and sequel ad.
5.   Check your rough drafts using the assessment list and make changes.
6.   Show your work to an impartial observer and ask for feedback.
7.   Make necessary changes.
8.   Create your final draft.
9.   Complete the self-assessment column and hand in your work.

Exhibit 100. Performance Task Assessment List
Responding to Literature
To Kill a Mockingbird
Grade 8
Book Jacket

| | | ASSESSMENT POINTS | |
| | Points | Earned Assessment: | |
Element	Possible	Self	Teacher
The Front Cover			
1. Contains a drawing which is:			
• clearly related to the book	_____	_____	_____
• original and creative	_____	_____	_____
• colorful	_____	_____	_____
2. Contains the name of the author and title	_____	_____	_____
The Back Cover			
3. Contains "blurbs" that tell what reviewers might have said about the book (created by the student)	_____	_____	_____
4. The information given in the blurbs is accurate and believable	_____	_____	_____
5. Contains an advertisement for the sequel	_____	_____	_____
The Front Flyleaf (This may be continued on the back)			
6. Contains a brief summary of the book that is:			
• clear	_____	_____	_____
• accurate and complete	_____	_____	_____
The Back Flyleaf			
7. Contains a short paragraph comparing a main story element (characterization, plot, setting, problem, etc.) to another novel. It is:			
• clear	_____	_____	_____
• complete and accurate	_____	_____	_____
• uses specific examples	_____	_____	_____

(Exhibit continues on the following page.)

Exhibit 100 (continued)

| | ASSESSMENT POINTS | | |
| | Points | Earned Assessment: | |
Element	Possible	Self	Teacher
Bonus Points			
8. The entire work is especially interesting, creative, and engaging	_____	_____	_____
The Jacket			
9. Measures 12 X 18 inches	_____	_____	_____
10. Is divided into four sections (see diagram)	_____	_____	_____
Deductions			
• spelling and grammatical errors (1 point each)			_____
• run-on sentences (1 point each)			_____
• fragments (2 points)			_____
• careless or sloppy printing/writing/drawing (up to 10 points)			_____
Total Deductions			_____
Total	_____	_____	_____

Performance Task Assessment List
Book Jacket

◀ - - 3" - - ▶	◀ - - - - - 6" - - - - - ▶	◀ - - - - - 6" - - - - - ▶	◀ - - 3" - - ▶
D	B	A	C

Exhibit 101. Performance Task Assessment List
Responding to Literature
To Kill a Mockingbird
Grade 8
Book Jacket—Advanced

	ASSESSMENT POINTS		
	Points	Earned Assessment:	
Element	Possible	Self	Teacher

Initial Understanding

The Front Cover

1. Contains a drawing that is:
   - clearly related to the book
   - original and creative
   - colorful
2. Contains the name of the author and title

The Front Flyleaf (This may be continued on the back)

3. Contains a brief summary of the book that is:
   - clear
   - accurate and complete

Developing an Interpretation

The Back Flyleaf

4. Contains an advertisement for the sequel

Critical Stance

The Back Cover

5. Contains "blurbs" that tell what reviewers might have said about the book (created by the student).
6. The information given in the blurbs is accurate and believable

Connections

The Back Flyleaf

7. Contains a short paragraph comparing a main story element (characterization, plot, setting, problem, etc.) to another novel. It is:
   - clear
   - complete and accurate
   - uses specific examples

(Exhibit continues on the following page.)

Exhibit 101 (continued)

| | ASSESSMENT POINTS | | |
| | Points Possible | Earned Assessment: | |
Element		Self	Teacher
Other			
8. The entire work is especially interesting, creative, and engaging	_____	_____	_____
The Jacket			
9. Measures 12 X 18 inches	_____	_____	_____
10. Is divided into four sections (see diagram)	_____	_____	_____
Deductions			
• spelling and grammatical errors (1 point each)			_____
• run-on sentences (1 point each)			_____
• fragments (2 points)			_____
• careless or sloppy printing/writing/drawing (up to 10 points)			_____
Total Deductions			_____
Total	_____	_____	_____

Performance Task Assessment List
Book Jacket

Exhibit 102. Responding to Literature: Poetry
Grade 9

Read the poem several times. Enjoy it. Then answer the questions below.

Nearing Again the Legendary Isle
by C. Day Lewis

Those chorus-girls are surely past their prime,
Voices grow shrill and paint is wearing thin,
Lips that sealed up the sense of gnawing time
Now beg the favor with a graveyard grin.

We have no flesh to spare and they can't bite,
Hunger and sweat have stripped us to the bone;
A skeleton crew we toil upon the tide
And mock the theme-song meant to lure us on:

No need to stop the ears, avert the eyes
From purple rhetoric of evening skies.

Questions:

1. Who is the speaker and what is the situation?

2. Identify the allusion in the poem and explain its source.

3. Compare the positive aspects of this encounter for the men and what they have gained to the negative aspects and what they have lost.

4. How effective is the author's use of irony in the last two lines of the poem? Support your opinion with reasons.

5. Explain the poet's position. Does he feel the loss is greater than the gain? Do you agree with him? Why or why not?

6. How does your knowledge of the epic enhance the meaning of this modern poem?

Exhibit 103. Performance Task Assessment List for Responding to Literature: Poetry
Grade 9

| | | ASSESSMENT POINTS | |
| | Points | Earned Assessment: | |
Element	Possible	Self	Teacher
Initial Understanding			
1. The speaker is identified.	_____	_____	_____
2. The situation is explained	_____	_____	_____
Developing and Interpretation			
3. Allusion in the poem is identified and its source is explained.	_____	_____	_____
4. Positive aspects of the encounter and what the men gained are discussed.	_____	_____	_____
5. Negative aspects of the encounter and what the men lost are discussed.	_____	_____	_____
6. Poet's position is explained.	_____	_____	_____
Critical Stance			
7. The effectiveness of irony in the poem is evaluated.	_____	_____	_____
8. Opinion about the poet's position is expressed and supported.	_____	_____	_____
Connection			
9. Specific connection is made between the student's knowledge of the 'epic' and how that enhances the meaning of this modern poem.	_____	_____	_____
Total	_____	_____	_____

Exhibit 104. Responding to Literature: <u>Fahrenheit 451</u>

Background: Students have completed a short story unit that asked them to define and apply specific literary devices including imagery. Students have read and studied *Fahrenheit 451* by Ray Bradbury.

Purpose: Requires students to analyze an author's writing style, discern his purpose and evaluate his effectiveness.

Task: Read the following passage where a character—Clarisse—experiences a reaction that shows the power of imagery.

(1) Identify the two images that become symbols in the course of the novel.
(2) Identify the one image that is more symbolic of Montag at the end of the novel.
(3) Support your opinion by identifying two ways that the image corresponds to changes you see in Montag's character in Part III of the novel.
(4) Discuss how effectively Bradbury uses imagery in this passage. Support your opinion with reasons and examples from the text.

"The girl stopped and looked as if she might pull back in surprise, but instead stood regarding Montag with eyes so dark and shining and alive that he felt he had said something quite wonderful. But he knew his mouth had only moved to say hello, and then when she seemed hypnotized by the salamander on his arm and the phoenix disc on his chest, he spoke again."

Performance Task Assessment List (for Passage Analysis)

| | | ASSESSMENT POINTS | |
| | Points | Earned Assessment | |
Element	Possible	Self	Teacher
1. Two images are listed which Bradbury later uses as symbols.	_____	_____	_____
2. One image is selected as most symbolic of Montag at the end of *Fahrenheit 451*.	_____	_____	_____
3. Defends the choice of image with 2 specific, well selected references to the changes observed in the main character at the end of the novel.	_____	_____	_____
4. Critiques Bradbury's use of imagery.	_____	_____	_____
5. Critique is supported.	_____	_____	_____
Total	_____	_____	_____

Exhibit 105a.   Performance Task/Assessment List
Responding to Literature—Expository Writing
How Do We Know Who We Are? Multicultural Identity
English IV: High School

The Task: Expository Writing

This writing assignment has two parts. Do not combine them into one essay. You may choose any two of the following. Each essay should be a minimum of 500 words. A typed copy is expected. Pre-writing—notes, graphic organizers, outline—is to be completed by _____. The first essay is due on _____. The second essay is due on _____. There will be no extensions!

Essay 1:   How do *I Know Why the Caged Bird Sings* and *Grand Canyon* show the conflict that exists between racial groups and within the African-American community because of this conflict? Focus on how identities emerge in relation to these conflicts.

Essay 2:   How do those two works demonstrate the effect of gender on identity? Show a range of relationships from both works.

Essay 3:   How do external circumstances—police helicopters and the KKK, money and the lack of it, housing, family, safety, blood on the sidewalk—affect the development of one's identity? What happens to the sense of self when life is reduced to making a left turn in Los Angeles? How do the "Grand Canyon" and "Caged Bird" function as symbols?

Performance Task Assessment List: Expository Writing for *Grand Canyon/Caged Bird* Essays: High School

| | | ASSESSMENT POINTS | |
| | Points | Earned Assessment | |
Element	Possible	Self	Teacher
1. The writing demonstrates an understanding of how identity is affected by the conflict between a minority and majority culture, gender, and/or environmental circumstances	30	_____	_____
(Initial Understanding and Connections)			
2. The thesis of the paper is appropriate and clearly stated.	10	_____	_____
3. All of the subtopics are clearly related to the thesis.	10	_____	_____
4. The subtopics are organized in a logical sequence.	5	_____	_____
5. The transitions from one subtopic to the next are smooth	5	_____	_____
6. There are enough appropriate and accurate details to support each subtopic.	20	_____	_____
(Initial Understanding and Connections)			
7. The choice of words is appropriate, varied, and "natural."	5	_____	_____
8. The mechanics and grammar are perfect.	5	_____	_____
9. There is a balance between evidence from the film and *Caged Bird.*	5	_____	_____
(Initial Understanding and Connections)			
10. The paper is typed, neat, and presentable.	5		
Total	100	_____	_____

Comments:

Exhibit 105b. Performance Task/Assessment List
Responding to Literature—Creative Writing
The Adventures of Huckleberry Finn: High School

The Task: Creative Writing

Background: You have just completed the novel *The Adventures of Huckleberry Finn*.

Task: Create an additional chapter "Huck to Finn." This chapter may be an incident that occurs between two incidents already depicted in Huck's river journey or may be one that takes place after Twain's story closes. The choice is yours. Adhere to the parameters of the following assessment list to ensure that you will do your very best writing and not make Twain spin miserably in his grave!

Performance Task Assessment List. Creative Writing: *The Adventures of Huckleberry Finn*

	ASSESSMENT POINTS		
	Points	Earned Assessment	
Element	Possible	Self	Teacher
Initial Understanding:			
1. Chapter shows accurate portrayal of character.	_____	_____	_____
Developing an Interpretation:			
2. Flows well stylistically and thematically with the existing text.	_____	_____	_____
3. Thorough and natural use of dialect and character voice.	_____	_____	_____
Critical Stance:			
4. Use of satirical elements: i.e., exaggeration, understatement, humor, caricature, irony, parody, etc.	_____	_____	_____
Connections:			
5. Chapter revolves around a key dramatic incident (humor, of course, may be used).	_____	_____	_____
6. Dramatic incident makes a statement about human nature.	_____	_____	_____
7. Proofread and polished. **MUST BE TYPED.**	_____	_____	_____
Total	_____	_____	_____

Exhibit 106. Performance Task/Assessment List
Responding to Literature—Expository Writing
Multiculturalism: English IV: High School

The Task: Expository Writing

Background: A unit on identity as reflected by the benefits and limitations of multiculturalism.

Purpose: To demonstrate an understanding of identity formation and knowledge of oneself when external conditions are restrictive and alienating.

Task: Based on your examination of three of the short stories assigned and any additional references from *inquiry* or otherwise, demonstrate your understanding of the conflicts and potential resolutions that occur when a minority culture confronts life in a dominant culture. Discuss the positive and negative consequences of assimilation for minority cultures. You might consider issues concerning language traditions and the potential tensions within the family structure of such minority groups.

Responsibilities: Two to three typewritten pages. Due date: _____. You will use an assessment list for expository writing to check your work.

Performance Task Assessment List: Expository Writing for Multicultural Paper: High School

Element	Points Possible	ASSESSMENT POINTS Earned Assessment Self	Teacher
1. The writing demonstrates an understanding of how identity is affected by the conflict between a minority and majority culture. **(Initial Understanding and Connections)**	30	_____	_____
2. The thesis of the paper is appropriate and clearly stated.	10	_____	_____
3. All of the subtopics are clearly related to the thesis.	10	_____	_____
4. The subtopics are organized in a logical sequence.	5	_____	_____
5. The transitions from one subtopic to the next are smooth.	5	_____	_____
6. There are enough appropriate and accurate details to support each subtopic. **(Initial Understanding and Connections)**	20	_____	_____
7. The choice of words is appropriate, varied, and "natural."	5	_____	_____
8. The mechanics and grammar are perfect.	5	_____	_____
9. A minimum of three stories are used.	5	_____	_____
10. The paper is typed, neat, and presentable.	5	_____	_____
Total	_____	_____	_____

Comments:

Exhibit 107. Responding to Literature Reading Log

Reading Log #1

"Myself as a reader" includes the following information:

_____ 1. List of books I have read, organized by type or author

_____ 2. List of books I keep in my personal library

_____ 3. Patterns of reading I find comfortable—minutes per day of chapters per week includes a calendar of assignments

_____ 4. How I select a particular book—cover, number of pages, illustrations, back cover, browsing in the library, bookstore, recommendation from a friend, favorite author, favorite genre

_____ 5. What I hate most about reading

_____ 6. What I hate most about reading assignments

_____ 7. My goal for 9th grade—number of books read, types of books read, challenges, pleasures, things to avoid

I deserve _____ /10 points for this entry.

Reading Log #2

Initial Understanding, chapter-by-chapter notes:

_____1. All chapters are thoroughly referenced

_____2. Most of the beginning chapters and the most important middle chapters are referenced

_____3. About 1/2 of the chapters are somewhat referenced

_____4. About 1/4 of the chapters are somewhat referenced

I deserve _____ /10 points for my chapter notes.

Reading Log #3

Graphic Organizer for the Plot

_____1. All parts of the plot are included

_____2. Most of the plot line is included

_____3. Some of the plot line is included

_____4. Little of the plot line is included

_____5. Part of the plot (or page numbers in the book) that I didn't understand are listed

_____6. The author probably chose this plot because he/she is writing about (fill in a possible statement(s) of theme)

I deserve _____ /10 points for this reading log.

Key: 10–9 = A, 8 = B, 7 = C, 6 = D, 5 or less = F.

Grade (score) is based on honest assessment of your completion of the goal, not whether you actually completed the goal. Some goals take a year to complete.

(Exhibit continues on the following page.)

Exhibit 107. Responding to Literature
Reading Log—Continued

Reading Log #4
Characterization

_____1.   The main characters are identified
_____2.   Two important examples of dialogue are included
_____3.   The major character s actions are described in the log of the plot
_____4.   The minor character s effect on the main character is described
_____5.   The change in the major character is described
_____6.   I told whether or not I found the characters believable and explained my thinking

I deserve _____ /10 points for this journal.

Reading Log #5
Page numbers that remind me of real life or another story are:

(List and briefly comment.)

I deserve _____ /10 points for this reading log.

Reading Log #6
This is the best description in the book:

(Paste or Copy Description Here)

because:

I deserve _____ /10 points for this reading log.

Key: 10–9 = A, 8 = B, 7 = C, 6 = D, 5 or less = F.
Grade (score) is based on honest assessment of your completion of the goal, not whether you actually completed the goal. Some goals take a year to complete.

(Exhibit continues on the following page.)

Exhibit 107. Responding to Literature
Reading Log—Continued

Reading Log #7

A sentence that is typical of this writer's style is on page_____.

Write the sentence here and explain why you chose it.

I deserve _____ /10 points for this reading log.

Reading Log #8

Ten interesting word choices are:

1.

2.

3.

4.

5.

6.

7.

8.

9.

10.

They create a mood of:

I deserve _____ /10 points for this reading log.

Reading Log #9

Free Choice

I deserve a grade of _____ /10 points for this reading log.

Reading Log #10

Evidence of completion of the reading goal you established in the first journal:

I deserve a score of _____ /10 points for this reading log.

Key: 10–9 = A, 8 = B, 7 = C, 6 = D, 5 or less = F.
Grade (score) is based on honest assessment of your completion of the goal, not whether you actually completed the goal. Some goals take a year to complete.

Exhibit 107. Performance Task Assessment List
Responding to Literature
Reading Log—Continued

| | ASSESSMENT POINTS | | |
Element	Points Possible	Earned Assessment: Self	Teacher
Reading Log #1	_____	_____	_____
Reading Log #2	_____	_____	_____
Reading Log #3	_____	_____	_____
Reading Log #4	_____	_____	_____
Reading Log #5	_____	_____	_____
Reading Log #6	_____	_____	_____
Reading Log #7	_____	_____	_____
Reading Log #8	_____	_____	_____
Reading Log #9	_____	_____	_____
Reading Log #10	_____	_____	_____
Total	_____	_____	_____

HOW ARE "BENCHMARKS" (MODELS OF EXCELLENCE) SELECTED?

As students complete performance tasks, teachers must look for those products that represent excellent work for the grade level. Benchmarks are products that are representative of work that most students at that grade level could strive to create; the benchmarks must be achievable by many students at that grade level. If teachers use the six-point rubric described in Chapter 5 to score these products, they should select work that was at the *T* or *evenly excellent* level, since this represents work that many students at that grade level could produce with coaching and support. Work that would be scored at the *S* level generally is so *outstanding and special* that it is beyond the scope of the average student at that grade level. (For a sample rubric, see Exhibit 71 in Chapter 5.)

Where do models come from?

- Student work
- State performance tests
- Teacher-made models
- The larger world

SELECTION BY INDIVIDUAL TEACHERS

Teachers may select benchmarks in several ways. First, individual teachers may select benchmark products for the tasks that they assign. It is a good idea to select a set of benchmarks representing a variety of levels of performance. Some teachers find that the rubric helps them to select the benchmarks, while other teachers use the more analytical assessment list. Regardless of how the benchmarks are selected, this set of products can be used to help students understand what excellent and not-so-excellent work looks like. The benchmarks may also be used to help parents understand the range of performances for the grade level, so that they may place their child's work on the continuum of quality for the grade.

SELECTION BY A GRADE-LEVEL TEAM OF TEACHERS

A second method of selecting benchmarks might involve a grade-level team. For example, in an interdisciplinary project such as the "Ikebana" task described earlier (see Exhibits 13 and 14 in Chapter 2), the entire team might select products that could be used as benchmarks for an entire grade level. A rubric is helpful again as teachers view representative samples of student work at the grade level and score them holistically before selecting the benchmark work. The professional discussion about the elements of quality helps teachers clarify their expectations for the student work. Many teachers report that the benchmarking sessions are valuable professional development opportunities that enable teachers to decide what students are capable of producing given the structures of performance-based learning. By working together to select the benchmarks of quality, many teachers find that the scoring of the products is much more reliable and valid. All teachers involved in scoring the

projects have a complete understanding of the expectations for student work.

SELECTION BY CONTENT SPECIALISTS ACROSS GRADE LEVELS

In a third method of selecting benchmarks, content specialists from several grade levels examine the students' work. Using a common rubric, these teachers may work together to select benchmark papers or products for several grades, just as teacher teams do. In this case, however, the professional discussion centers around developmental issues—how students from the several grade levels differ in the degree of sophistication or depth in their response to the task. For example, a rubric for nonfiction writing might be created for use by all middle school students. Using that rubric, language arts teachers select benchmark papers from a set of 6th, 7th, and 8th grade papers. The benchmarks for the 6th grade exemplify excellent work for that grade level. The 7th grade benchmarks will probably have similar characteristics, but will inevitably demonstrate a more sophisticated or complete response to the prompt; and the 8th grade benchmarks will also show growth in depth and quality of response over the 7th grade benchmarks. Thus, the benchmarking team will gain a more complete understanding of the progression of skills in a middle school student, and the students will have models of excellence to help them on future assignments.

USE BENCHMARKS FROM A STATE-LEVEL ASSESSMENT

The benchmarks used to score student work on state-level or other standardized performance assessments can be used at the classroom level to provide teachers and students with day-to-day models.

BENCHMARKS CAN BE FOUND IN THE LARGER WORLD

Newspaper articles, political cartoons, graphs, and consumer reports are some examples of "real" work from the larger world. Teachers can use these abundant models to identify "targets of quality" for students.

SELECT SOME BENCHMARKS OF LESS THAN EXCELLENT QUALITY

Samples of student work with "flaws" provide excellent opportunities for learning. Sometimes students can more readily understand "excellence" when they can contrast it with work of less quality. Save some of these flawed examples to use as instructional materials.

No matter how you select benchmarks, it is important that students have the opportunity to analyze models that demonstrate a variety of approaches to solving the "problem" so that students will understand the importance of divergent thinking and learning. Thus, as individual teachers, grade-level teams, or content area teams select the benchmarks, they should attempt to choose work that shows the students that there is no one perfectly correct way of approaching the task. After all, the purpose of the benchmarks is to stimulate the thinking of the students, not to prescribe the response.

HOW ARE STUDENTS TAUGHT TO USE ASSESSMENT LISTS AND BENCHMARKS?

7

Many students find that assessing their own work is not always easy. At first, they tend to either overestimate or underestimate the quality of their work. Sometimes the students have no idea what an "excellent" piece of work looks like and are confused by terms like *elaboration, detail, creativity,* and *good sentence structure.* Teachers must take time to teach students how to effectively use assessment lists and benchmarks so that they can become better *analytical self-assessors* and, as a result, to improve the *quality* of their work. As students grow in understanding of self-assessment and quality indicators, they learn to develop their own assessment lists and benchmarks, and then internalize much of the process as they are "weaned" from detailed assessment lists.

COACHING STUDENTS TO UNDERSTAND ASSESSMENT LISTS

To begin with, introduce students to assessment lists for use with products with which the students have had the most experience, such as writing, graphs, oral presentations, and posters. With younger children, the initial assessment lists should contain few items. For example, a 1st grade assessment list for drawings of caterpillars could be one item: "Did I draw details?" The list is gradually expanded as the students are ready to pay attention to more elements of their work. A 5th grader just being introduced to the use of performance assessments in a writing assignment might receive a list that contains just three items:

- Do I have a main idea?
- Do I have at least three details about the main idea?
- Did I use capitals and periods correctly?

A diverse set of examples of excellent work for that "grade level" will also accompany the use of the assessment list so that the students can "see" what the elements in the list mean. The teacher is in control of when and in which form assessment lists are used. The key is to start small and expand at a rate that is comfortable to the teacher and students.

Teachers have found several strategies helpful in introducing assessment lists to students. Successful strategies include using models, holding "show and tell" discussions, and conducting guided self-assessments.

MODELS

To create an excellent product, students need to see what excellence looks like. The assessment list and models of excellence (benchmarks) work together to define quality and help "pull" students toward the target. The models are not to be copied, nor are they the only examples of excellent work. (Students may copy or mimic models, however, as part of the learning process.) Models should help students, teachers, and parents get a better idea of what quality is. Choose either excellent models of student work models from the larger world, such as newspaper articles, posters, cartoons, experiments, and graphs.

By using overhead projections of written work and actual examples of three-dimensional products, students can identify excellent qualities. Teachers can also display models of flawed work and ask students to identify problems and offer solutions.

CLASS DISCUSSIONS—ORAL READING AND SHOW AND TELL

If the classroom climate is positive, many students will be willing to share work they've done with the class. Even some of the students whose work is not up to par may be willing to share if they will get feedback and advice to help them improve their work. For example, an assignment might be to write an introductory paragraph for a folk tale. The assessment list might detail the components for an excellent introduction. The students use the assessment list to evaluate a peer's work as that child presents it to the class. Such discussions are extremely beneficial for many students.

GUIDED SELF-ASSESSMENT

When self-assessment is done properly, students inspect their work in reference to each element on the assessment list. The students are looking for "evidence" of the degree to which they have produced quality, according to that element. Guided self-assessment helps teach students how to do this. (For example, see Exhibits 108–110, which present the performance task, assessment list, and guided self-assessment for "Writing a Nature Myth.")

TEACHING STUDENTS ABOUT WHAT POINT VALUES MEAN

Upper-level elementary, middle school, and high school assessment lists use point values (e.g., see Exhibit 109, the assessment list for a

"Nature Myth"). It is important to teach students what these point values mean. For example, if a given element is worth 15 (out of a possible 100) points, students need to understand that if they have done an average job on that element, they should give themselves only 10–11 points. A good job is worth 12–13 points; an excellent job is worth 14 points; and perfection is worth 15 points. Students can become involved in the process of deciding how many points each element in the list is worth. One of the ways for students to set and carry out their own goals for improvement is for them to weight elements in the assessment lists that are most in need of their attention. Again, the teacher is in control of when and how to involve students in distributing points on assessment lists.

PROVE YOUR POINT

When some students first encounter assessment lists, they may not make the connection between their actual work and the elements on the assessment list. These students may assess their own work without going back to their work to see if they have actually accomplished what the element on the assessment list stated. For example, they may mark the assessment list for the element of labeling the axes of the graph without actually inspecting their graph to see if they had labeled the axes. To train students to base their self-assessment on an honest analysis of their own work, require them to "prove your point" by indicating the spot on their work where they have found the "evidence" to support their self-assessment. If element 5 on the assessment list for a graph was, "The axes are clearly labeled," require that the student put the numeral 5 on his graph where he found the data to support his self-assessment. You can require as much of this "notation" as is necessary to help the students pay attention to their work as they self-assess.

PEER HELPERS

Where cooperative groups are in place, peers can be valuable assets. Peers may be asked to help their classmates succeed by comparing assessment criteria. This is a coaching opportunity to help students know what quality is. When they use assessment lists to evaluate another student's work, their purpose is to not only help their peers find areas to improve on, but to help themselves become better at assessing and understanding where a grade is coming from. When teachers view the assessment of the students, they can evaluate the progress being made by both the producer of the work and the peer assessor.

THE MATCH GAME

Although the match game can be played by younger students, it is also an excellent strategy to help other students understand how teachers assign point values to their work. The game can be played individually or in cooperative groups. The teacher chooses a model of a task a student has completed and asks permission to use the work as a model, making copies for the class. Either individually or in groups, the students assign point values to each criterion on the task assessment list as they evaluate the work. Groups win who match the point totals assigned by the teacher for each element on the assessment list. The class then discusses the teacher's explanation of the point values.

FIX THE FLAW

Give flawed work to individuals or cooperative groups. Ask them to use the assessment lists and models of excellent work to find and fix the flaws in the samples they have been given. Each individual or group can then present the flawed and the fixed work to the class.

GALLERY OF EXCELLENCE

Allow individual students to nominate work for a class "gallery of excellence." This work must be excellent according to the criteria as defined by the assessment list and the models of excellence already identified. Students must support their nominations by explaining how the work meets the criteria for excellence.

COACHING STUDENTS TO CREATE THEIR OWN ASSESSMENT LISTS

One of the best ways for students to learn about using performance task assessment lists is to guide the students through the whole process of developing an assessment list. Choose a task you would normally have the students do. An example might be writing a folk tale. (A folk tale performance task might ask students to show their understanding of how a culture's values and beliefs are represented using a folk tale format.) Give students a folk tale assessment list for their first experience with this genre. For their second or third project involving a folk tale, involve the students in creating the assessment list. In cooperative groups, brainstorm characteristics and ask students to list what they would

put into their writing of a folk tale. When each group has drafted its assessment list, allow them to view each other's lists and make improvements in their own. Groups can also revise assessment lists provided by the teacher during previous assignments. The assessment lists from all groups can be synthesized into one classroom list, or the individuals in each group can use the list created by their own group.

While the student is learning about the elements of quality for a folk tale, the first assessment list would be simple (see Exhibit 111 for an assessment list for a "Folk Tale"). Subsequent assessment lists would include more descriptive elements (see Exhibit 112, an assessment list for "A Folk Tale from Japan"). An assessment list for an experienced learner who has internalized the elements of quality would return to a more simple list of the general categories of elements or dimensions of the folk tale genre. (For an example of an assessment list for a more experienced learner—in a different literary genre—see Exhibit 61 in Chapter 4: "Persuasive Position Statement Writing.")The assessment list for an experienced learner still allows the teacher to provide feedback and a grade if necessary.

Once students have learned how to use performance assessment lists, they produce work that is far superior to that produced when they were playing the "Guess what the teacher wants" game. The work is neater, more organized, more accurate, and more nearly complete, making the job of scoring the work easier and less subjective for the teacher.

The teacher is in control of when and how to involve students in the process of creating an assessment list. The goal is to move all students closer to becoming independent learners. To reach this goal, each student must internalize the process of thinking about quality before, during, and after producing a product. Some students may be ready to make their own assessment lists before other students are. Allowing those students to move ahead and make their own lists is one way to individualize the lesson without changing the performance learning task.

MOVING STUDENTS AWAY FROM DETAILED ASSESSMENT LISTS

The final goal of performance-based assessment is to eventually move students away from assessment lists, since such tools aren't usually available in the larger world. By the time young people have completed their high school education, they should have honed their analytical skills and internalized specific criteria enough to enable them to assess their work on their own. This may not happen in your class—it usually takes years to get to this point. Use your judgment to evaluate your students' progress, and move away from detailed analytical assessment lists as soon as the students are ready.

BENCHMARKS ARE WHAT SHOW THE PROGRESSION OF QUALITY

Assessment lists and benchmarks (models of excellence) work together to define quality. Assessment lists become more detailed and cover a wider range of elements as students perform better and better. During the last several years of schooling, the lists become more simple and highlight only the dimensions or general categories of the dimensions, or elements of quality, of a specific type of work. The sequence of assessment lists for nonfiction writing from grade 1 through grade 12 shows that pattern of change (see Exhibits 113–118, assessment lists for "Nonfiction Writing"). What continues to show continuous growth are the benchmarks used to define quality. The assessment list for grade 9 nonfiction writing (see Exhibit 117) is the most detailed of all the lists. The examples of nonfiction writing that demonstrate the level of quality for each grade level and the "exit-level" performance (the benchmarks), however, continue to be of higher and higher quality.

Figure 11 shows that the assessment lists increase in specificity and comprehensiveness over the years into high school and then become less specific again as students are "weaned" away from those assessment lists. In this example, an assessment list at a set level of specificity and comprehensiveness is used for two years in grades 3 and 4, 5 and 6, and 7 and 8.

Figure 12 shows that the quality of benchmarks that define quality continues to improve each year from grade 1 through grade 12.

DECIDING AT WHAT RATE TO REVEAL THE STANDARDS OF QUALITY

The teacher is in control of when students are shown the benchmarks of student work that define the target for their work. In some cases, teachers decide to show students the target for

FIGURE 11. Assessment Lists Change in Specificity and Comprehensiveness Over Time

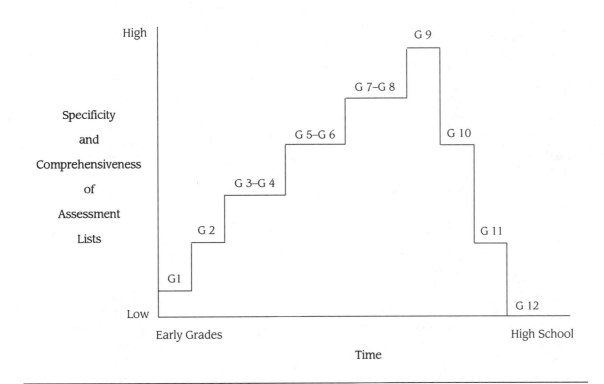

the end of that school year. In other cases, the teacher may decide to show the students benchmarks that are of an intermediate quality first and show the end-of-the-year target midway through the year. In still other cases, the teacher may decide to show students what excellence looks like for the end of a grade-level span.

SHOULD THE SAME STANDARDS OF QUALITY BE USED FOR ALL STUDENTS?

The same standards of quality should be set and fixed for all students. One measure of

growth is the student's progress towards those fixed standards. An equally valuable measure of progress is the amount of improvement that students have shown in comparison to their past work. A student beginning 6th grade performing at a 3rd grade level, as defined by the benchmarks selected by the teachers of that school, has two goals: move closer to the 6th grade level of quality and improve past performance. The teacher, while evaluating the student according to both goals, may emphasize improving past performance as a way to motivate the student. A student entering the 6th grade performing at an

FIGURE 12. The Gradual Improvement in Quality of the Benchmarks of Excellence from Grade 1 Through Grade 12

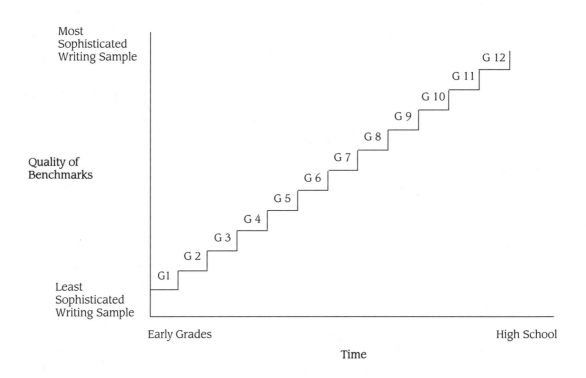

8th grade level would need the challenge of the standards for 9th grade or above. Benchmarks help the teacher set appropriate targets for individual students.

SELF-ASSESSMENT AND SELF-EVALUATION ARE THE FOUNDATION FOR SELF-REGULATION

Students learn a lot about themselves as workers through self-assessment and self-evalu-

ation; this knowledge prepares them for setting appropriately challenging learning goals for themselves. At the conclusion of performance tasks and self-assessment, teachers can engage the students in goal setting by asking them to write responses questions like these:

• On which elements of the assessment list have you improved the most? Give specific examples from your own work to back-up your opinion.

• What has helped you the most to improve? Explain.

• Which elements seem to be causing you the most difficulty?

- What can you suggest we do in class to help you continue to improve?

- List three specific ways you intend to improve this work (for the next draft or for the next time this type of work is part of an performance task.)

Another successful strategy that includes parents in the process is to ask students to write progress reports for their parents. The progress report includes a description of the work, the assessment of it, and a plan for improvement. Parents are asked to read and sign the progress report. Parents are also encouraged to write comments or a letter to their child in response to this progress report.

ASSESSMENT LISTS AND BENCHMARKS ARE TOOLS

Tools should be used for their intended purpose. Assessment lists and benchmarks link the general dimensions of a type of student work to the developmental level of the student. As the developmental level of the student changes, the assessment lists and benchmarks change accordingly. The purpose of assessment lists and benchmarks is to help the student learn to internalize the standards of quality and then use those internalized standards to produce quality work and make decisions for self-improvement. All the decisions made about how and when to use assessment lists and benchmarks should be made with this purpose in mind.

Exhibit 108. Performance Assessment Task
Writing a Nature Myth

Background

People have had a need to explain the world around them since the beginning of time. Each culture, therefore, has a body of stories—called myth—that developed to help people understand the world in which they live.

Your Task

Your class has been asked to compile an anthology of mythological works. This anthology will eventually contain stories, ballads, and essays about myth. For this task, you will be writing original myths that demonstrate your understanding of the Gods and Goddesses of Greek mythology. Use the myths in your textbook as models for your work.

Your Audience

Your peers form the audience for your work.

Materials

You will need pen and paper for this assignment. You may type it if you wish, but be sure to print out drafts and make corrections and revisions on the "hard copy" before you return to the screen. Remember: SAVE ALL DRAFTS!!

Procedure

1. Obtain a copy of the assessment list for a myth to guide your work.
2. Examine the nature myths contained in our text to help you understand what a good nature myth "looks like."
3. Brainstorm ideas for natural occurrences that might make interesting myths. Share your ideas with others before selecting the one you like best.
4. Create a plot outline in which you brainstorm ideas for your setting, characters, exposition, rising action, climax, falling action, and resolution.
5. Write a rough draft of your myth, making sure to include many vivid details, much description, and dialogue throughout the story.
6. Assess the story using the assessment list, and make note of needed revisions.
7. Share the story with a peer for feedback and advice.
8. Revise your myth.
9. Do a final self-assessment, make corrections, and turn it in.

Exhibit 109. Performance Task Assessment List For a Nature Myth

	ASSESSMENT POINTS		
	Points	*Earned Assessment*	
Element	*Possible*	*Self*	*Teacher*
1. There is a logical plot with a(n):			
• exposition	3	______	______
• rising action	3	______	______
• climax	3	______	______
• falling action	3	______	______
• resolution	3	______	______
2. The story has many details that add to the reader's ability to visualize the story.	10	______	______
3. The characters are described vividly and completely.	7	______	______
4. The setting is described vividly and completely.	7	______	______
5. There is dialogue throughout the myth and the tone is set through the use of specific and vivid words (i.e. "roared" instead of "said").	15	______	______
6. Mythological elements (gods, heroes, monsters, etc.) are used effectively throughout the myth.	15	______	______
7. The myth *shows* rather than *tells* the reader what natural occurrence is explained by the myth.	5	______	______
8. The writing is mechanically correct.	10	______	______
9. The piece is neat and presentable.	5	______	______
10. The piece is especially interesting, creative, and engaging.	10	______	______
Total	99	______	______

Exhibit 110. Guided Self-Assessment
Nature Myth

To do a "first rate" job of self-assessment, you must do more than just fill in the numbers that you *wish* that you had earned. It takes time, effort, and thought. You **cannot** do it without looking carefully at your paper.

To help you assess your paper accurately, follow the directions below carefully. Make marks right on your final draft as directed. You will notice that each item relates to the assessment list.

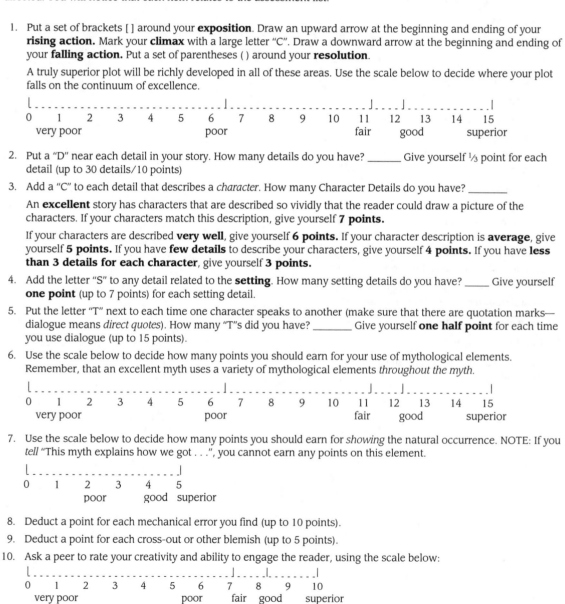

1. Put a set of brackets [ ] around your **exposition**. Draw an upward arrow at the beginning and ending of your **rising action.** Mark your **climax** with a large letter "C". Draw a downward arrow at the beginning and ending of your **falling action.** Put a set of parentheses ( ) around your **resolution**.

    A truly superior plot will be richly developed in all of these areas. Use the scale below to decide where your plot falls on the continuum of excellence.

0	1	2	3	4	5	6	7	8	9	10	11	12	13	14	15
very poor						poor						fair	good		superior

2. Put a "D" near each detail in your story. How many details do you have? _____ Give yourself ⅓ point for each detail (up to 30 details/10 points)

3. Add a "C" to each detail that describes a *character*. How many Character Details do you have? _____

    An **excellent** story has characters that are described so vividly that the reader could draw a picture of the characters. If your characters match this description, give yourself **7 points.**

    If your characters are described **very well**, give yourself **6 points.** If your character description is **average**, give yourself **5 points.** If you have **few details** to describe your characters, give yourself **4 points.** If you have **less than 3 details for each character**, give yourself **3 points.**

4. Add the letter "S" to any detail related to the **setting**. How many setting details do you have? _____ Give yourself **one point** (up to 7 points) for each setting detail.

5. Put the letter "T" next to each time one character speaks to another (make sure that there are quotation marks—dialogue means *direct quotes*). How many "T"s did you have? _____ Give yourself **one half point** for each time you use dialogue (up to 15 points).

6. Use the scale below to decide how many points you should earn for your use of mythological elements. Remember, that an excellent myth uses a variety of mythological elements *throughout the myth.*

0	1	2	3	4	5	6	7	8	9	10	11	12	13	14	15
very poor						poor						fair	good		superior

7. Use the scale below to decide how many points you should earn for *showing* the natural occurrence. NOTE: If you *tell* "This myth explains how we got . . .", you cannot earn any points on this element.

0	1	2	3	4	5
		poor		good	superior

8. Deduct a point for each mechanical error you find (up to 10 points).

9. Deduct a point for each cross-out or other blemish (up to 5 points).

10. Ask a peer to rate your creativity and ability to engage the reader, using the scale below:

0	1	2	3	4	5	6	7	8	9	10
very poor						poor		fair	good	superior

Exhibit 111. Performance Task Assessment List
Folk Tale

(An assessment list for a first experience in writing a folk tale.)

Element	ASSESSMENT POINTS		
	Points Possible	Earned Assessment:	
		Self	Teacher
1. The situation to be solved is set up in the beginning.	_____	_____	_____
2. There are two main characters. At least one is human.	_____	_____	_____
3. Each main character is developed through descriptions of at least three physical characteristics.	_____	_____	_____
4. At least five elements of the environment are woven into the story.	_____	_____	_____
5. There is an element of magic important to the development of the plot.	_____	_____	_____
6. A conclusion is reached that "teaches the lesson."	_____	_____	_____
7. Complete sentences are used.	_____	_____	_____
8. The writing is neat and presentable.	_____	_____	_____
Total	_____	_____	_____

Exhibit 112. Tailored to a Unit on Japan
Performance Task Assessment List
A Folk Tale from Japan

(An assessment list for students with experience using simpler versions.)

| | ASSESSMENT POINTS | | |
| | Points Possible | Earned Assessment: | |
Element		Self	Teacher
1. The introduction includes an authentic Japanese geographic setting and a specific period.	_____	_____	_____
2. The introduction includes at least two Japanese characters with authentic characterization and background.	_____	_____	_____
3. A problem to be solved is introduced in the first or second paragraph. The problem shows the values and beliefs of the Japanese culture.	_____	_____	_____
4. Other characteristics of the Japanese culture are evident.	_____	_____	_____

(Circle at least three that you use.)

a. CELEBRATIONS   e. LANGUAGE

b. CEREMONIES   f. FOOD

c. RELIGION   g. ARTS

d. LITERATURE   h. LEISURE ACTIVITIES

5. Other elements that affect the Japanese culture are evident.	_____	_____	_____

(Circle at least three that you use.)

a. GEOGRAPHY   d. TECHNOLOGY

b. GOVERNMENT   e. EDUCATION

c. ECONOMY   f. HISTORY

6. There are at least five characteristics of Japanese folk tales.	_____	_____	_____

(Circle at least five that you use.)

a. ORDINARY PEOPLE

b. GOOD OVERCOMES EVIL

c. MAGIC NUMBERS

d. PERSONIFICATION

e. YOUNGEST=HERO

f. EXAGGERATION

g. MAGIC TRICKERY

h. MORAL IS TAUGHT

i. PUNISHMENT OR REWARD

(Exhibit continues on the following page.)

Exhibit 112 (continued)

	ASSESSMENT POINTS		
	Points Possible	Earned Assessment:	
Element		Self	Teacher
7. The values and beliefs of the Japanese people are evident throughout the folktale. How did you do this? Give an example for each one.			
a. Proverbs:	_____	_____	_____
b. Characterization:	_____	_____	_____
c. Actions:	_____	_____	_____
8. The problems is solved. The solution seems reasonable.	_____	_____	_____
9. Drawings in the Japanese style support the story.	_____	_____	_____
10. The folktale is organized and it "flows."	_____	_____	_____
11. The mechanics of English are correct.	_____	_____	_____
12. The work is neat and presentable.	_____	_____	_____
Total	_____	_____	_____

Exhibit 113. Performance Task Assessment List
Nonfiction Writing
Grade 1

1. Did I draw a picture about the topic?

Terrific   OK   Needs Work

2. Did I write a sentence about the picture?

Terrific   OK   Needs Work

3. Does my sentence start with a capital letter?

Terrific   OK   Needs Work

4. Does my sentence end with a period?

Terrific   OK   Needs Work

Exhibit 114. Performance Task Assessment List
Writer's Guide for Nonfiction
Grade 3

1. **Focus**
   T: The author is on the topic throughout the piece.
   0.   The author is on the topic throughout most of the piece.
   W: The author is off the topic throughout most of the piece.

2. **Organization**
   T: There is an ordered sequence with a clear plan throughout the entire piece.
   0:   There is an ordered sequence with a clear plan throughout most of the piece.
   W: The piece has an unclear sequence or plan.

3. **Main Ideas**
   T: Main ideas are appropriate to the topic and are correct throughout the entire piece.
   0:   Main ideas are appropriate to the topic and are correct throughout most of the piece.
   W: Main ideas are inappropriate and/or incorrect.

4. **Details**
   T: The piece has many clear, supportive, and accurate details.
   0:   The piece has some clear, supportive, and accurate details.
   W: The piece has few or no details. The piece has inaccurate details.

5. **Visual Aids**
   T: Drawings, diagrams, or pictures are used very well to help present information throughout the entire piece.
   0:   Drawings, diagrams, or pictures are used to help present information throughout some of the piece.
   W: Drawings, diagrams, or pictures are not used; and they make the information presented unclear.

6. **The writer uses full sentences that begin with a capital and end with a period.**
   T: There are no errors.
   0:   There are some errors.
   W: There are many errors.

7. **Presentation**
   T: The writing is very neat and presentable.
   0:   The writing is somewhat neat and presentable.
   W: The writing is not neat or presentable.

Did I do my best work?

    Terrific   OK   Needs Work

Exhibit 115. Performance Task Assessment List
Writer's Guide for Nonfiction
Grade 5

Element	Points Possible	Earned Assessment: Self	Earned Assessment: Teacher
		ASSESSMENT POINTS	

The Writing

Element	Points Possible	Self	Teacher
1. Contains appropriate main ideas and facts.	_____	_____	_____
2. Maintains focus.	_____	_____	_____
3. Is well organized.	_____	_____	_____
4. Contains supporting details.	_____	_____	_____
5. Has a clearly defined purpose.	_____	_____	_____
6. Communicates well with its intended audience.	_____	_____	_____
7. Is smoothly written.	_____	_____	_____
8. Is neat and presentable.	_____	_____	_____
9. Contains correct spelling, grammar, and mechanics.	_____	_____	_____
Total	_____	_____	_____

Exhibit 116. Performance Task Assessment List for Nonfiction Writing Grade 7

	ASSESSMENT POINTS		
	Points	Earned Assessment:	
Element	Possible	Self	Teacher
1. The introduction clearly states the thesis.	_____	_____	_____
2. The introduction clearly introduces the main ideas.	_____	_____	_____
3. The concepts used are appropriate and accurate.	_____	_____	_____
4. Each paragraph has a topic sentence that is one of the main ideas.	_____	_____	_____
5. Each paragraph has appropriate and accurate supporting details.	_____	_____	_____
6. The conclusion sums up the points made in an interesting, thoughtful, and unique manner.	_____	_____	_____
7. The writer's own "voice" and style are evident throughout.	_____	_____	_____
8. The title is clear and informative.	_____	_____	_____
9. The writing is mechanically correct.	_____	_____	_____
10. The writing is neat and presentable.	_____	_____	_____
11. Visuals such as drawings, diagrams, or pictures are used in an appropriate way to add information and interest.	_____	_____	_____
Total	_____	_____	_____

Exhibit 117. Performance Task Assessment List for Nonfiction Writing Grade 9

	ASSESSMENT POINTS		
	Points Possible	Earned Assessment:	
Element		Self	Teacher
Prewriting			
1. Graphic organizer and outlines show work to explore, research, collect, select information, and focus ideas.	_____	_____	_____
The Writing			
1. The writing demonstrates an ability to interpret ideas meaningfully in context.	_____	_____	_____
2. The "big idea" of the paper is interesting and clear.	_____	_____	_____
3. All of the main ideas are clearly related to the "big idea."	_____	_____	_____
4. The main ideas are organized into a logical sequence.	_____	_____	_____
5. The transitions from one main idea to the next are smooth.	_____	_____	_____
6. There are enough appropriate and accurate details to support each main idea.	_____	_____	_____
7. The choice of words is appropriate, varied, and creates a natural voice.	_____	_____	_____
8. The mechanics and grammar are integral to the meaning and effect of the writing.	_____	_____	_____
9. Stylistic variety and choice are evident in elements of rhetoric such as diction, syntax, structure, and figurative language.	_____	_____	_____
10. The paper is neat and presentable.	_____	_____	_____
Total	_____	_____	_____

Exhibit 118. Performance Task Assessment List for Nonfiction Writing

(An assessment list for a writer very experienced in using assessment lists for nonfiction writing.)

	ASSESSMENT POINTS		
	Points	Earned Assessment:	
Element	Possible	Self	Teacher
1. Content is Accurate and Appropriate.	————	————	————
2. Organization.	————	————	————
3. Focus.	————	————	————
4. Support and Elaboration.	————	————	————
5. Sense of Audience.	————	————	————
6. Mechanics of English.	————	————	————
7. Presentation.	————	————	————
Total	————	————	————

WHAT IS A PORTFOLIO, AND HOW IS IT USED IN PERFORMANCE-BASED LEARNING?

WHAT IS A PORTFOLIO?

A portfolio is a purposeful collection of student performances that exhibits a student's effort, progress, and achievement over a period of time. It is composed of student-selected works, and it includes both a student's reflection on her performances as well as the teacher's comments about the student's reflection and work. It demonstrates what a student is able to do with knowledge and skills and how effective his work habits are. It is a way of tracking a student's progress on a variety of types of assessments throughout the year.

The following goals for a portfolio plan were developed by Connecticut's Region 15 staff as a first step in creating and implementing portfolios regionwide:

- To improve student performance
- To promote the students' skills of self-assessment and goal setting
- To present a clear portrait of the students as learners
- To provide a vehicle for communicating student progress to parents, future teachers, and community members
- To build the students' sense of responsibility for their own learning
- To build a sense of ownership and pride of accomplishment in the students
- To build the students' confidence in their abilities as learners

Other district and school-level goals for the portfolio could include the following:

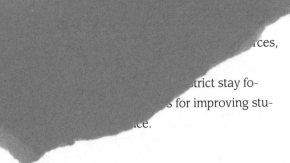

ces,

trict stay fo-
s for improving stu-
ce.

HOW IS THE PORTFOLIO INTEGRATED INTO A PERFORMANCE-BASED CLASSROOM, SCHOOL, AND SCHOOL DISTRICT?

A portfolio is a natural adjunct to a performance-based classroom because it provides a vehicle for showcasing what students have accomplished over time. The portfolio is a structure that encourages students to collect their work throughout the year, select work from this larger collection, and then reflect on what they have accomplished and what they have yet to learn. The use of assessment lists and self-assessment throughout the year provides students with much specific information about the quality of their work. This detailed knowledge empowers students to see ways in which the processes and products of their work are improving. By selecting and reflecting on their work and setting goals for future learning, students engage in the self-evaluation and self-regulation steps of the Cycle of Learning (see Exhibit 9 in Chapter 1). The triangle in Figure 13 represents the process of "analytical assessment," using an assessment list and models (benchmarks) of excellent work, used by the student and teacher for a specific piece of student work. Because the student

FIGURE 13. Analytical Assessment

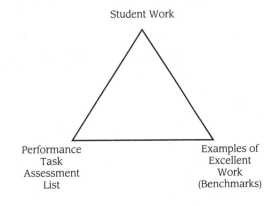

learns the details of elements of quality of each piece of work done, an "overall" assessment may begin to be done.

Samples of work over time can be collected in a working folder, and students can begin to generalize the strengths and weaknesses of their work from the patterns they see in rating elements in assessment lists task-by-task-by-task. Written reflective self-assessments help the students become explicit and specific about the patterns of change seen.

Near the end of the year, students make the final selections out of the their working folders for the portfolios and write the final reflective self-assessments. At this time, students also write learning goals for the next year. Figure 14 shows the sequence of events from the assessment of many pieces of work, to making a working folder and beginning self-reflection, to the final portfolio. The portfolio, then, encourages students to go beyond a piece-by-piece

FIGURE 14. Self-Assessment Is the Foundation for a Portfolio

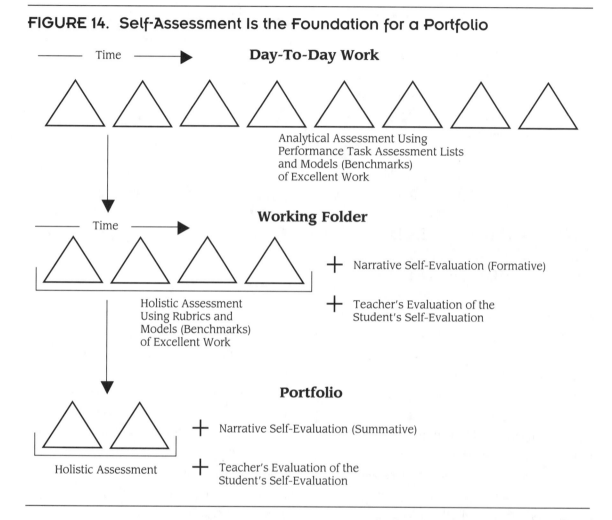

Day-To-Day Work

Time ⟶

Analytical Assessment Using
Performance Task Assessment Lists
and Models (Benchmarks)
of Excellent Work

Working Folder

Time ⟶

Holistic Assessment
Using Rubrics and
Models (Benchmarks)
of Excellent Work

+ Narrative Self-Evaluation (Formative)

+ Teacher's Evaluation of the
Student's Self-Evaluation

Portfolio

+ Narrative Self-Evaluation (Summative)

Holistic Assessment **+** Teacher's Evaluation of the
Student's Self-Evaluation

"assessment" and look critically at themselves as learners, answering the questions "How am I doing?" and "Where do I go from here?"

The next logical step is for the teacher to review the portfolios to validate or, if necessary, challenge students' self-evaluations. The teacher reads the reflections and comments on the students' assessment of their learning. Sometimes the comments are simple notations in the margins of the reflection; other times teachers write a paragraph or two at the conclusion of the reflection. Whatever format the teacher chooses, it is an important component of the portfolio, for it provides feedback to the students. The teacher's feedback lets students know whether their perceptions about their learning are accurate and insightful, and it coaches them on areas in which they might improve. Further, if the portfolio is to become part of a schoolwide or districtwide program of performance-based learning, the teacher's commentary helps the receiving teacher understand the strengths and weaknesses of incoming students. Thus, the reflections written by the students and teachers provide continuity as students progress from grade to grade and from school to school.

Self-Assessment Is the Basis for a Successful Portfolio

Information about the specific elements of quality of the work and information about the process of producing quality work gained through self-assessment are key to successful performance-based learning and assessment. Portfolios help the learner see the "big picture" of their work and see themselves as learners. Performance task assessment lists and models (benchmarks) of excellence are the specific tools that make self-assessment honest. The assessment lists and benchmarks also make perceptive self-reflection and goal setting possible.

WHAT INFORMATION ABOUT STUDENT PERFORMANCE IS COMMUNICATED? WHY? HOW? AND TO WHOM?

The first two questions we should ask when communicating information about student performance are, "For whom is the information intended?" and "What is the purpose of communicating this information?" This chapter attempts to answer these questions. It also explores the benefits of data collection and the differences between fixed-standard and individualized evaluations and grading practices.

PURPOSES FOR ASSESSMENT

Why are we assessing, and how will the assessment information be used? The answers include:

- to diagnose content knowledge and discrete process skills ("Do you know it?")
- to diagnose the application of these skills ("Can you use what you know?")
- to diagnose student strengths, needs, and patterns of change
- to provide feedback on self-assessment ("How honest and perceptive is your self-assessment?") and on regulating their own learning
- to provide feedback on goal setting ("To what degree have you set and accomplished goals for self-improvement?")
- to provide a basis for instructional placement
- to provide a basis for promotion or graduation

- to inform and guide instruction ("What shall I do to improve student performance?")
- to communicate learning expectations
- to motivate; to focus student attention and effort
- to provide practice in applying knowledge, skills, and work habits
- to provide a basis for student evaluation (e.g., grading)
- to provide a basis for comparing students
- to obtain data for site-based management
- to obtain data for district-level or state-level decision making
- to gauge program effectiveness

AUDIENCES FOR ASSESSMENT

For whom are the assessment results intended? The answers include:

- student
- teacher/mentor
- parents
- grade level, team, or department
- other faculty, such as the school improvement team
- school administrators
- district administrators, such as curriculum supervisors
- board of education
- state department of education
- general public
- higher education
- business

Once you have determined the purposes and audiences, then you can select the type of assess-

ment you plan to use. Figure 15 shows a chart created by McTighe and Ferrara to provide a framework of assessment approaches and methods.

ASSESSMENT IS A BALANCE OF STRATEGIES

Because literacy is a set of complex attributes of the learner, teachers should employ many assessment strategies to get a full picture. Spelling tests and persuasive essays, computation activities and open-ended math problems, and phonetics and reading for comprehension are all important; and each is assessed in a different way. This book is about assessing how well students use content, process skills, and work habits. The rest of this chapter discusses how information from these types of assessment is used and communicated.

INFORMATION AVAILABLE FROM ASSESSMENT LISTS

During the design of performance tasks and assessment lists, teachers become more conscious of the specific elements of student work that they can judge in assessing student performance. Teachers become more aware of the specific elements of how well students are learning to use content, process skills, and work habits to create quality work. As a result, in time, performance tasks become better connected to the curriculums, and assessment lists become more explicit. The assessment lists serve as the communication link among students, educators, and parents.

FIGURE 15. Framework of Assessment Approaches

How might we assess student learning in the classroom?

Selected Response Items	Performance-Based Assessments			
	Constructed Responses	Products	Performances	Process-Focused

❏ multiple-choice
❏ true-false
❏ matching
	❏ fill in the blank
	  • word(s)
	  • phrase(s)
	❏ short answer
	  • sentence(s)
	  • paragraphs
	❏ label a diagram
	❏ "show your work"
	❏ visual representation
	  • web
	  • concept map
	  • flow chart
	  • graph/table
	  • matrix
	  • illustration
		❏ essay
		❏ research paper
		❏ log/journal
		❏ story/play
		❏ poem
		❏ portfolio
		❏ art exhibit
		❏ science project
		❏ model
		❏ video/audiotape
		❏ spreadsheet
			❏ oral presentation
			❏ dance/movement
			❏ science lab demonstration
			❏ athletic competition
			❏ dramatic reading
			❏ enactment
			❏ debate
			❏ musical recital
				❏ oral questioning
				❏ observation ("kid watching")
				❏ interview
				❏ conference
				❏ process description
				❏ "think aloud"
				❏ learning log

Source: McTighe and Ferrara (1994). Used by permission.

Teachers can use data from the performance task assessment lists to answer the following questions about individual students or groups of students:

1. On which elements is performance best?
2. On which elements is performance least developed?
3. On which elements has there been the most improvement?
4. On which elements has there been the least improvement?
5. On which elements is there the most agreement between student self-assessment and the teacher's assessment?
6. On which elements is there the least agreement between the student self-assessment and the teacher's assessment?

The analytical nature of the data empowers teachers to adjust one or more of the components of instruction and study its impact on student performance. The data also allow the learner to set and carry out well-focused goals for personal improvement and to study the effect of subsequent work.

When teachers or teams of teachers study the data from groups of students, they can make inferences about the overall impact of instruction on student performance. The data can show how well a classroom or a grade level of students uses a concept, how well they know when and how to use a skill, or the quality of their work habits. The data can demonstrate how well a group students used the concepts of how energy moves in the food web, how well they know when and how to use bar graphs, and how well they set up and carry out a task management plan. When instructional decisions are based on such individual or group data, teachers can make much more efficient and effective decisions about how to improve student performance.

RELATING INFORMATION FROM ASSESSMENT LISTS TO THE DIMENSIONS OF A TYPE OF STUDENT WORK

Following are the dimensions of persuasive writing:

Opening Statement of Position
Structure of the Argument
Content (Concepts, Main Ideas)
Supporting Details
Closure
Information Sources
Sense of Audience
Language Mechanics and Presentation

When teachers build assessment lists for specific tasks requiring persuasive writing with this framework in mind, information from those lists can be keyed back to the dimensions of persuasive writing; and generalizations about the assessment of those dimensions can begin. Not only can the teachers talk about performance on a specific piece of persuasive writing, but they can also begin to discuss the strengths and weaknesses of students' persuasive writing in general and make plans to adapt instruction to strengthen weak elements of student performance.

Figure 16 shows a data management chart used to identify the weakest areas of each student's persuasive writing. From the aggregated data in this chart, the teacher can plan subsequent instruction to address those weaknesses. Similar data management charts can be constructed for all kinds of student products and performances, such as graphs, math problem solving, short stories, scientific experiments, and oral presentations. The use of the dimensions allows a consistent framework through which teachers can collaborate to improve student performance from assignment to assignment, from class to class, and from year to year. Analytical assessment lists provide the detail information needed to efficiently adapt instruction to improve student performance.

LINKING EVALUATION TO ASSESSMENT

Assessment is the act of collecting data about student performance. Analytical assessment, using an assessment list, provides analytical data; assessment, using rubrics, provides holistic data. An analytical assessment list for a graph will indicate specific areas of strength and weakness, whereas a rubric score defines the general level of quality of the graph. In each case, however, benchmarks of excellent graphs are used as the standard by which to assess the student's graph.

An assessor can describe the quality of the learners' work without knowing the learners. All characteristics about the learners, except the quality of their work, are irrelevant to the assessment process. Special needs status, tenure in the

FIGURE 16. Assessment of Nonfiction Writing in Science

Check the Dimensions of Relative Weakness for Each Student

Writing Assignment Title: _____

_____ Date: _____

Dimensions of Nonfiction Writing in Science

Student Names	Content, Main Idea	Supporting Details	Vocabulary Used	Vocabulary Explained	Diagrams, Drawings	Extensions	Connections	Organization	English Mechanics	Neat, Presentable

school, race, gender, and all other such learner characteristics are not important in the assessment process. Assessment is impersonal and reasonably objective if it is based on "fixed standards," as defined by benchmarks of quality and analytical lists or rubrics. Assessment lays the foundation for evaluation.

Evaluation is the act of using the data from assessment to make decisions and judgments regarding the quality, value, or work of a response, product, or performance. Once an assessment list is completed or a rubric score has been assigned to the student's graph, a judgment about the meaning of that data can be made. Questions such as the following can be answered:

- Does this graph represent this student's best work?
- How does this graph compare to the previous graphs made by this student?
- How does this graph compare to the graphs made by other students?
- What grade should this graph receive?

Evaluation can use a "fixed standard" or an "individualized" approach. Fixed-standard evaluation judges the quality of student performance against a preset, fixed standard of quality, as exemplified by a benchmark. Fixed-standard evaluation could also be called "criterion referenced evaluation." A level of quality that defines excellence is preset, and a judgment of the quality of the student's work is made only in reference to this fixed standard. For individualized evaluation, characteristics such as special needs status, tenure in the school, past performance, and perceived potential can contribute to the judgment as to the quality of the student's work.

Two students may have received the same assessment rating; but for one, the work is the best to date, and for the other, the work is uncharacteristically poor. The assessment story is the same for both students. But for one student, the individualized evaluation story is positive; for the other, the individualized evaluation story is negative. Individualized evaluation compares a student to her past work and her individualized goals for improvement. Fixed-standard and individualized evaluation are both important, and each has its place in communicating the overall picture of a student's literacy. It is important to know to what degree a student has reached the fixed, high standards for quality, and to what degree she has improved her own work.

VALUING BOTH QUALITY PERFORMANCE AND IMPROVEMENT

Story "A" describes the quality of the student's performance according to fixed standards. It is an objective, honest description of how well the student reads, writes, makes graphs, conducts scientific experiments, finds creative solutions to problems, and speaks. The good news here is that the performance is strong. Story "B" describes the quality of the student's performance, as compared to her past performance. The good news here is that her performance has improved. Both stories are important, but they are different and should be told separately. When they are "mushed" into one story, the meaning in both is lost. Value and celebrate both stories, but keep them separate.

GIVING GRADES ACCORDING TO FIXED OR INDIVIDUALIZED STANDARDS

Grades can be an act of fixed-standard evaluation or individualized evaluation. A grade given by fixed-standard strategies describes the quality of the student's work according to fixed standards and all students receiving that grade would have equivalent levels of performance. Fixed-standard grades are blind to student differences except for the quality of their work. A grade given by individualized-standard strategies describes the quality of the student's work according to that student's past performance and her goals for improvement. In this case, two students could get the same grade, but the quality of their work could be very different. Individual-

ized evaluation is often subjective and has the potential for being unfair. Individualized evaluation can also lead to inaccurate communication about student performance, especially when the audience for that communication thinks they are getting fixed standard evaluation.

Teachers in Connecticut's Region 15 Public Schools report that the use of analytical assessment lists and benchmarks of excellence has provided them with strategies to use fixed-standard evaluation (and fixed-standard grading) to present a more accurate picture of student performance. This information, gained through the use of these analytical approaches, provides a more objective basis for giving a grade and allows students and teachers to make better decisions about how to improve performance.

WHAT IS THE IMPACT OF PERFORMANCE-BASED LEARNING AND ASSESSMENT ON THE LEARNER?

WHAT DO I DO? (NO GUESSES AND NO EXCUSES!)

The format of the performance-based learning task and its accompanying assessment list provides students with built-in organization and precise expectations. The "no guesses, no excuses" layout enables students of all abilities to take charge of the task as active learners, moving at their own pace through the Cycle of Learning (see Exhibit 9 in Chapter 1) with a clearly written guideline. The task format provides a statement of the task, a description of the audience, and the purpose of the students' work. To perform the task, students access and acquire information that they process and use to perform or produce a product. They disseminate the product and then assess, evaluate, and regulate their

work (set goals for improvement) at their own level to reenter the Cycle of Learning. To the learners, the performance-based learning task becomes a problem to solve, complete with a sequenced plan of action on how to solve it. As the cycle continues, the students' confidence increases as they realize academic achievement. Performance improves; and as a result, students feel capable, needed, and influential.

IT'S ALL UP-FRONT (NO SURPRISES AND NO EXCUSES!)

Communication is a fundamental part of the Cycle of Learning and a component of all performance-based learning tasks. Because the product of each task includes a visual, written, or spoken element (illustrations, graph, chart, letter, dramatic performance, etc.) and an explanation of conclusions (oral, graphic, or written), the students engage in a multilevel presentation of ideas. After drafts, conferences, and revisions, students experience the creative process at the highest level. As part of the task, students internalize the "benchmarks" of excellence as ideals on which to model their performances. Further, tasks clearly define the audience with whom the students must communicate. The assessment lists provide clear boundaries by which students measure the success of their communication. The assessment list lays out all the criteria upfront. There are no surprises and no excuses. The performance-based learning task is a precise, accurate way to practice communication, an essential skill in today's world.

IMPACT ON SPECIAL NEEDS STUDENTS

Teachers of special needs students are among the most enthusiastic supporters of performance-based learning and assessment because of the positive impact it has on the performance of these students. Assessment lists and models of excellent work provide the structure especially needed by many of these students. Sometimes the assessment list is modified to meet the special need of the student. Assessment lists can be made more detailed and specific, or they can be simplified to focus on just a few elements of the work. The assessment lists and models of excellent work provide a clearer

communication link among the students, regular classroom teachers, and special needs teachers. Special needs students report feeling much more confident and capable to do the work. They work harder, persist longer, and take more pride in their work. They may not be the best writers or graphers in the class, but they know they are making progress, and they know how to improve.

STUDENT MOBILITY

Each year, many students move into and out of the school and school system. How do new students learn to do performance tasks and use assessment lists and benchmarks? Teachers need to spend time with these students teaching them the new system. But the good news is that, with the help of their peers in cooperative learning groups, new students in Region 15 are "brought up to speed" quickly. Performance tasks are interesting, and the assessment tools are easy to use. New students observe their peers using assessment lists to guide their work and check it when it is complete. These peers "coach" the new students through the process and can even check the new students' work through peer assessment.

Students also move from one school to another within the school system. When these strategies of performance-based learning and assessment are used widely in the school district, and when assessment lists for a type of work such as graphing are all based on an agreed-to set of dimensions for that performance, students can more easily adjust to their new class.

A common framework for performance-based learning and assessment in an entire school system promotes communication and continuity for student, teachers, and parents.

HOW DID I DO? (SELF-ASSESSMENT, NO GUESSES!)

Self-assessment is another essential step in the Cycle of Learning and the foundation of any student's success. Performance-based learning incorporates self-assessment at each step of the way. Teachers must model and teach honest self-reflection and common goal-setting skills—and allow students to practice them. Through the performance task process, students use self-assessment lists as directives for measuring the quality of their work. The students practice self-assessment with a "written escort"—the list—under a teacher's leadership. Regardless of ability, students can witness personal growth through comparison with their own previous work. They measure their work by assessment lists and by the development of their work over time. The long-term goal is for students to practice enough self-assessment under the teacher's guidance to be able to create their own lists of expectations and to measure their own performance independently. Such independence bolsters selfconfidence and improves self-awareness; in turn, students develop heightened capabilities for self-reflection and self-assessment. Students develop lifelong skills in setting personal goals, measuring their own achievement toward those goals, adjusting work accordingly, and eventually fulfilling the goals.

WRITING SELF-REFLECTIONS ABOUT THE PROCESS AND PRODUCTS OF THEIR WORK IS AN IMPORTANT PART OF PERFORMANCE-BASED LEARNING AND ASSESSMENT

For each performance task such as a writing assignment, students learn to use assessment lists, given to them by the teacher or ones they make themselves, and examples of excellent work to assess and evaluate their own work. Teachers have found a number of ways to help students use these data from self-assessment and the student's conclusions through self-evaluation to set goals to improve their writing. Exhibits 119–123 emphasize self-description (e.g., "Entry Slip: I'm Proud of This Work!") and goal setting (e.g., "Progress on Personal Goals for Writing").

Self-reflection uses data from self-assessment and judgments about these data from self-evaluation to *self-regulate*—to set goals for improvement. Students in Connecticut's Region 15 schools have been using these strategies, especially in writing across the curriculum, for 10 years; and the quality of their self-reflections shows the impact of this hard work. Exhibits 124–129 show samples of student self-reflection, from "A Letter to Yourself" to "A Letter to Next Year's Teachers" and "A Letter to Your Parents." These self-reflection samples also include pieces placed in student portfolios at different grade levels.

The samples of student self-reflection shown here represent the work done by all students in the Region 15 Public Schools. These self-reflective pieces are, themselves, examples of student writing, and have replaced other writing assignments. Self-reflective writing is not "in competition with" teaching writing. It is *part* of teaching writing. The high school English teachers at Pomperaug High School value the self-reflective "end piece" for the student's portfolio so much that half of the final exam grade in English is earned by this piece of writing.

Self-reflection improves student performance because the learner becomes more conscious of the strengths and weaknesses of his work and gains more control over improving it. Chapter 14 of this book presents a variety of data on student performance, and the information on writing shows that performance to be the most advanced in Region 15.

The examples shown in this chapter are used in performance tasks involving writing. Similar strategies are used in other curriculum areas for a variety of student work. Independent learning requires the learner to be an honest, perceptive, and reflective thinker who sets personal goals for improvement. Performance improves to the degree that the learners take responsibility for the quality of their work by looking at it critically in respect to specified standards of quality and by setting and carrying out goals for improvement. Region 15 students are well on their way to becoming independent learners capable of self-assessment, self-evaluation, and self-regulation—necessary attributes for the 21st century.

Exhibit 119. Entry Slip
I'm Proud of This Work

The title of the work is_____

I finished it on (date) _____

This is a work of (CIRCLE ONE):

Fiction   Non-Fiction   Timed   Writing   Other _____

Here's what I did to write this work:

	I did it	I attached evidence
Brainstorming	_____	_____
Rough draft/sloppy copy	_____	_____
Revisions on my draft	_____	_____
Made a new copy	_____	_____
Edited and/or revised again	_____	_____
Made a final draft	_____	_____

This is why I'm proud of this work:_____
_____
_____
_____
_____
_____

The sentence or phrase I really like in this piece is_____
_____
_____

I like it because _____
_____
_____
_____
_____

If I could revise again, I would change _____
because_____
_____
_____

Exhibit 120. Entry Slip

Your Name _____ Date _____

Description or Title of Work _____

About how much time did you spend on this work? _____

Where was it done?
mostly in school   mostly out of school   about half and half

Did anyone help you on this work? yes   no

Who helped and how did he/she help you? _____
_____
_____
_____

What is one thing that you think you did well in this work? _____
_____
_____
_____

What made that part of the work so good? _____
_____
_____
_____

If you could change one thing about the work, what would you change? _____
_____
_____
_____

Why would you change this? _____
_____
_____
_____

Did you like doing this work? yes   no   somewhat
Why did you like it? _____
_____
_____
_____

Exhibit 121. My Goals for Improving My Writing

Student Name _____

Date _____ Quarter _____

What is your **first** writing goal for the coming quarter? _____
_____
_____

Give **two** specific strategies you plan to use when you write to help you work on this goals.

#1. _____
_____
_____

#2. _____
_____
_____

What is your **second** writing goal for the coming quarter? _____
_____
_____

Give **two** specific strategies you plan to use when you write to help you work on this goal.

#1. _____
_____
_____

#2. _____
_____
_____

Exhibit 122. Progress on Personal Goals for Writing

Student Name _____

Date_____Quarter_____

Goal #1 _____
_____
_____

Goal #2 _____
_____
_____

Progress Made:

Date   What I did to work on my goals:

Date	What I did to work on my goals:
_____	_____
_____	_____
_____	_____
_____	_____
_____	_____
_____	_____
_____	_____
_____	_____
_____	_____
_____	_____
_____	_____
_____	_____
_____	_____
_____	_____
_____	_____
_____	_____
_____	_____
_____	_____
_____	_____
_____	_____
_____	_____
_____	_____
_____	_____

Exhibit 123. Assessing the Student's Self-Assessment Reflection

	Extensive Evidence	Significant Evidence	Some Evidence	Little Evidence	No Evidence
SELF-ASSESSMENT/REFLECTION					
1. Has the student described his/her use of the writing process accurately?	_____	_____	_____	_____	_____
2. Has the student described his/her writing strengths accurately?	_____	_____	_____	_____	_____
3. Has the student described his/her writing weaknesses accurately?	_____	_____	_____	_____	_____
4. Has the student used specific examples to discuss strengths and weaknesses?	_____	_____	_____	_____	_____
5. Has the student explained completely and clearly why he/she made the selection for his/her portfolio?	_____	_____	_____	_____	_____
6. Has the student used specific examples from the he/she made the selections for his/her portfolio?	_____	_____	_____	_____	_____
7. Has the student accurately and eloquently expressed his/her feelings about his/her writing progress this year?	_____	_____	_____	_____	_____
8. Has the student set appropiate and realistic goals for the coming year?	_____	_____	_____	_____	_____
9. Has the student explained clearly and completely why he/she selected these goals?	_____	_____	_____	_____	_____
10. Has the student conveyed an overall sense of who he/she is as a writer?	_____	_____	_____	_____	_____
11. .... and as a reader?	_____	_____	_____	_____	_____

Comments:

Exhibit 124. Sample of Self-Reflection in the Form of a "Letter to Yourself"
Middlebury Elementary School, Grade 4
Region 15 Public Schools, Connecticut

June 20, 1994

Dear Caitlin,

Improvements I have made being a writer is rewriting my whole story over like in my Dear Diary story. I rewrote my story 3 times to make it more interesting and make more sense. In the end the story came out much better. In all stories I reread them many times and corrected any mistakes I saw.

In my stories, things I still need to improve on are in my "Dear Diary" story a character did something without really having it happen, or told about in the story. I also need to have a point or reason to my story "The Lucky Pennies." Here's the part of the story I think it shows most, "Anyway," my mother said, "We really need to go buy decorations for her party and I was wondering if you would come with me?" "Okay, but where are we going?" "We are going to Maestos in Naugatuck," my mother replied. You see where the child asks her mother where are we going, like she wants something almost. I really don't think I need that sentence or to add where they were going, it was extra detail. Do you also notice where I said anyway at the beginning, it was because I got a bit off topic by talking about a party and the story.

In the beginning of the year I thought writing was fun and it was something I was good at, but in April writing become extremely important to me and I enjoyed it because it made me feel good. In the beginning of the year I did most of my writing in school and I still do that today. In September my most favorite type of writing was stories where a character told the story and what happened to them. In April my feelings changed. It changed to historic realistic fiction. I like writing about made up people and realistic problems they went through. In September my least favorite writing was letters. I found them boring, but now my least favorite is fiction, because it is boring and I have to make it all up. In the beginning I would have liked to have brainstormed more and gotten better ideas before I started to write. Now I would more time to write, and not get frustrated while I'm writing. As you can see my feelings have changed in a school year.

The pieces I put in my portfolio are special and especially selected in each category. Now I will tell you about the categories and the stories I have selected and why. For best fiction I chose my story, "The Perfect Shell." I chose this piece because I had a lot of details about the shells I found. For example vivid, swirly and peachy. I stayed more on topic talking about the shells, and using interesting words like glistening instead of shining. For the best non-fiction piece I chose my "I-Search" on Jackie Robinson. I chose it because it told about his life and gave good detail. My favorite piece is "Summary Of Chapter 5" from the book *In The Year Of The Boar And Jackie Robinson*. I chose it because it had a good beginning, middle, and end. I also chose it because it was fun to write. I chose my "Persuasive Piece" for the piece with all it's parts. I choose it because I thought it was a good example. For my best timed piece I chose "The Empty Cage" because I liked the story and I use interesting words. I also thought it was fun to write.

My plans and goals for writing next year are plenty. I plan to write in my spare time. I will try to make creative stories and original ideas. I plan to make an animation movie and write a script for it. And those are my plans and goals for next year.

(Except for word processing for publishing purposes, the student's writing was not changed.)

Exhibit 125. Self-Reflection in the Format of a Letter to Next Year's Teachers
Middlebury Elementary School, Grade 4
Region 15 Public School, Connecticut

Dear Fifth Grade Teachers,

I love to write. It is very important to me. In writing I can express my ideas and opinions. I can create characters and I can set examples in life. My feelings about writing have not changed a lot since the beginning of my fourth grade year. I still enjoy writing and using my imagination. I enjoy using words to express my feelings and thoughts. I have always loved to write and that is why my opinion about writing has really not changed. Writing and using good words has always fascinated me. I have always enjoyed looking at life and describing what I see. The colors or the texture of an object have always been fun for me to describe. I have always really enjoyed to write and my opinion has not changed a lot.

As a writer I have made many improvements. In the beginning of my 4th grade year I had trouble finishing my timed writing. In my first timed writing piece "Civil War" I wrote about a girl who went back to the 1800's, the time of the Civil War. I did not finish this piece, so it had no ending. Therefore it was not as interesting a piece as it could have been. In my last timed writing piece, "Imaginary Games," I wrote all about my experience with imaginary games, I finished this piece with a great deal of details and therefore it was a piece that was much more interesting and fun. I have also improved on my description of objects and places. In my story "The Lucky Seed," I described Maine as a beautiful place with tall mountains and deep blue ocean. Now at the end of my 4th grade year I would have described Maine as a breathtakingly beautiful place with tall thundering gray mountains and deep glistening aquamarine oceans sparkling with beauty. This adds to my story and makes it more interesting, I have also improved in my area of details. In my piece, "Clara and Me," which I wrote in the beginning of the year, I described Clara as curious. But in my picture book story, "The First Winter Snow," I described the main character in the story, a snowman, as a perfectly sculpted figure and I wrote that his large foot prints padded into the snow looked like giant polar bear prints. In this way my reader will get a better sense of what things look like in my story and they will feel more involved in the story. I have also improved on writing feelings in my story. In the beginning of the year, in my piece "Clara and Me," I did not add many actions or feelings. In the end of my 4th grade year, in my piece "The First Winter Snow," I wrote that I felt I could fly. I think adding feelings into stories are important. They help to link stories to real life. These are some of the major improvements I have made as a writer.

Although I have made many improvements as a writer I still need to improve many things about my writing. I still need to improve on organizing my stories. In my last writing piece of the year "The First Winter Snow," I had a long story but it was not divided into paragraphs very well. I think organizing writing pieces will help readers to understand and to get a clearer picture of my story. I also need to improve on the endings of my stories. I often have trouble finishing and balancing details in my stories because I put so much thought into my stories therefore the end of my stories are often overlooked. I am going to improve on balancing my stories with details and writing the end of my stories well. Also I must try to improve my spelling and my puncuation. For example, in my last draft of "The First Winter Snow" I had many spelling errors. In my timed writing I also had many spelling errors. I hope to get much better in this area. Spell-

(Exhibit continues on the following page.)

Exhibit 125 (continued)

ing words correctly can improve your presentation of a writing piece. Puncuation is also something I must improve. When I write timed writing or a short essay I often make many puncuation errors, I am going to work on making fewer puncuation errors. I think puncuation is important because it makes your work more presentable and easier to read. These are some things I still need to improve on in my writing.

I have 3 goals in writing for next year. One of my goals is to organize my writing paragraphs. I plan to accomplish this goal by practicing everyday to make my writing interesting, but organized. I will keep that writing in a small journal and I will bring it everywhere I go. Another goal I have is to balance the details in my story. To do this I will keep a separate journal. Here I will practice balancing my beginning, middle, and end so my story is interesting. My third goal is to work on my spelling and puncuation to accomplish this goal I will take my time to write the words I know correctly. But for the words I cannot spell, I will carry a small pocket dictionary with me. To improve my puncuation I will take my time on writing and when I read I will pay attention to how the story is punctuated. In that way I will learn more. These are my goals and plans in writing for next year. I love to write and it means a lot to me. I am very excited about next year and I hope I will always love to write.

(Except for word processing and publishing purposes, the student's writing was not changed.)

Exhibit 126. Self-Reflection in the Format of a "Letter to Parents" as Part of the Teacher's Progress Report to Parents

Directions to Students for Writing Progress Report

Dear Students,

The time has come for us to sit back and assess what we have done, what we have learned, and how well we have learned in language arts. In addition to my writing to your parents and letting them know how you are doing, you will be writing to your parents to tell them what and how you are doing in this class. To help you organize your thoughts and ideas, please use the format below:

Paragraph #1—Introduction
Explain your purpose for writing. Remember to create a proper paragraph (topic sentence, body sentences, closing sentence).

Paragraph #2—What have we studied together and worked on in class?
Describe the work that we have done so far—both in writing and in literature study. Refer to your notebook if you are unsure.

Paragraph #3—What progress have you made in writing?
Discuss your progress in writing.
- What are your goals?
- What have you done to try to improve in the goal areas?
- Do you think you want to adjust your goals? Why/why not?
- What progress have you made toward your goals and/or in improving your writing in general?

Paragraph #4—What grades have you earned?
Look over your grade page and tell your parents what your test and quiz averages are. What can you conclude about your performance on tests and quizzes? What do you think you need to work on? What do you plan to continue to work on? How are you doing on homework? Are you doing your best every night? Why/why not? What goals do you have in the area of improving (or maintaining) your grades?

Paragraph #5—Conclusion
Sum up your progress so far and let your parents know what your goals are for the second half of the marking period in language arts class. Ask them for feedback/ideas/help.

(Exhibit continues on the following page.)

Exhibit 126 (continued)

Cover Letter to Parents
(Sent home with student's progress report letters)

Dear Parents,

Attached is your child's progress report for the first marking period. As you can see, I have asked your son or daughter to write to you about his/her own learning. After all, you are a key member of the student-teacher-parent "triad."

I will be asking students to write to you several times this year assessing their own performance in language arts. My primary purpose for asking the students to make these "self-assessments" is to encourage them to take a more active role in their own learning. So often students appear to be unaware and disconnected when it comes to learning. This activity encourages the students to look carefully at their individual learning and performance. It requires them to look carefully at their grades and calculate their averages, so that they might see the connection between one or two low quiz/test scores and their final marking period grade.

In addition to reporting on their grades, I have also asked the students to discuss what they have learned this quarter. There should be a general commentary about the topics we have covered in class so far. The students also should explain what their first quarter writing goals are and how they are progressing on those writing goals. Although we have not had as much time for writing (due to the Connecticut Mastery Tests) as I would have liked, a number of students have had the opportunity to work on their goals through our weekly vocabulary work and on short pieces that they have been creating during our Monday/Friday writing workshops.

Finally, I have asked the students to "sum up" their first quarter performance and to ask you for feedback, guidance, and help. I encourage you to write a brief response to your child. It need not take long, but I am certain that he/she would truly appreciate your feedback. You might choose to comment on his/her writing goals (if these are not entirely clear to you, please ask your child to explain what he/she is trying to accomplish), or you might merely comment on the child's test and quiz performance. You might choose to give this feedback to your child privately, but I do encourage you to attach it to your child's letter so that he/she may include it in his/her writing folder—as a constant reminder of your ideas, concerns, and/or thoughts.

For the most part, the letters represent a good "first start" in the area of self-assessment. To be certain, they are far from perfect, and we will be learning how to become better at self-assessment. I have not edited these letters, and you will find errors in spelling and punctuation—particularly if your child has set those two areas as goals for the first quarter. At the bottom of each letter, you will find a comment about how well the student evaluated his/her progress. We have also given you an indication of your child's current grade average.

Please attach any comment you care to make to the child's hand-written progress report, sign it, and have your child return it to me by Tuesday, October 26th. I want to keep these progress reports in your child's writing folder. If you would like a copy of his/her letter to you, please let me know.

If you have any questions at all about your son/daughter's performance in language arts, please do not hesitate to call me. The best times to reach me are from 9:45–10:30 or after school until 4:30 p.m.

Sincerely,

The Teacher

(Exhibit continues on the following page.)

Exhibit 126 (continued)

Sample of Self-Reflection in the Format of Student's Letter to Parent Included in the Teacher's Progress Report Sent to Parents
Rochambeau Middle School, Grade 6
Region 15 Public Schools, Connecticut

Dear Mom and Dad,

We have been working on writing a progress report about ourselves. I am writing this progress report to tell you what I have done, what I have learned, and how well I have learned it in language arts. Through the marking period I have done a lot of different things. I have written different kinds of paper each marking period, I've made a lot progress in writing by working on the goals that I have, and my spelling has improved.

In class I have accomplished many different types of writing. The first thing I did was a "Bio Poem" that told different things about myself. Then I wrote about the different roles that I have to play in my life were I explained the jobs that I had to do and which role was my favorite. After reading the book *Mrs. Frisby* and *The Rats of N.I.M.H.* and then watching the movie, I wrote a paper on how the book and the movie was the same and different. I then wrote a paper which explained the goals that I try to accomplish through the marking period. Along with the spelling tests that I had I wrote short stories which included ten different spelling words. Also in class we were assigned a topic to write about in a forty minute time period. This type of writing is called Timed Writing. The last thing that I wrote was persuasive paper which was about letting a boy with muscle dystrophy bring his trained dog to help him around school. I think that I have done a lot of writing last marking period.

So far this marking period we have written a lot of poetry. I've written couplets which are poems that have two lines. Quatrains are a type of poem that has four lines and I wrote those. I have also written a ballad, a poem that has four quatrains. Another kind of poem that I wrote was a sonnet which has three quatrains and one couplet. Then the last kind of poem that I wrote was a cinquin which has five lines and each line has a certain amount of syllables. Another type of writing that I have written is a persuasive letter, which was timed. We wrote a letter to Mrs. Nelson which explained why the class shouldn't have homework. I hope that the paper has her think about not giving us any homework. The last thing that we are doing is this progress report, which will include what, and how I'm doing in language arts.

In writing I've progressed a lot. I had goals to accomplish which helped me progress. One of my goals is to make my writing clearer by using more adjectives, verbs, adverbs, and nouns. I also am trying to make to describe my main ideas better by making webs, brainstorming, and listing details. My last goal was to organize my thoughts better by brainstorming, making webs, and to conference with others. I have improved a lot in writing. With those ideas that I have in making me to be able to accomplish my goals, my writing has become more interesting and clearer. In the beginning of the year my sentences and writing was hard to picture and very boring. I'm still working on my goals because I haven't fully accomplished them. I want to be sure that I have done everything so that my sentences are perfect.

In order to have a good paper, you should know how to spell. In spelling so far this year I have done very well. My grades are very high. I usually get one hundreds and maybe sometimes ninety-five's or nineties so my average should be very high. I feel that my spelling has improved through the year. I am very pleased with it. I can now spell more chal-

(Exhibit continues on the following page.)

Exhibit 126 (continued)

lenging words with no problem. Since I'm getting better at spelling my grades are consistently high and sometimes improving. I think that my grades are very high because of how I study. After my mom or dad tests me they will check the paper and then mark down any words that I got wrong and then I have to spell them five times.

That concludes my progress report. I am still doing very well in language arts but I'm still trying to progress. My goals are still the same which are making my sentences clearer, describing my main ideas better, and organizing my thoughts better. I'm still working on accomplishing them and I'm almost there.

Sincerely,

Adam

(Except for word processing and publishing purposes, the student's writing was not changed.)

Parent's Response

January 2, 1995

Dear Adam,

I found it very interesting to read your progress report, as well as all of your poems and the other projects in your folder. I am **very** impressed with the structure of your paragraphs and sentences, not to mention your vocabulary and spelling abilities. In reading some of your earlier writings, I would say that you have made significant improvements in all areas of this subject since the beginning of the year. **You should be very proud of your achievements and excellent grades!**

I think that your three "goals" are well thought out, appropriate, and good objectives to focus on between now and the end of the school term. I would agree with your teacher that you now need to establish a detailed "action plan" to help you achieve those objectives. You might try to think of three or four specific things that you can do to help meet each one of the goals that you set for yourself (i.e., for your first goal, you might want to think about reviewing the use of adjectives, nouns, etc., and then checking all of your writings **before** they are finalized to ensure that they have been properly and adequately used).

Keep up the good work, Adam, and as you go through the next six months, always keep your goals in mind and I **know** that you will be successful in achieving them.

Love,

Dad

P.S. Let Mom and me know if we can help you.

Exhibit 127. Sample of Self-Reflection
Reading and Writing
Memorial Middle School, Grade 8
Region 15 Public Schools, Connecticut
Looking into the Mirror of Language Arts

With every year that I mature, my writing does as well. When I write, I let words flow out like a river into the ocean, which describe how I feel and what I am like as an individual. There are certain techniques that have been expressed to us to help us improve the way we write. These techniques allow us to let our colors shine through and flaunt what we have learned. The words a person uses and the way that they express these words can tell you almost everything about them. This is what I feel makes writing so special for me.

The best way to learn every one of these numerous techniques is from reading work of other people. There are three levels at which you can read. The first one is just reading and enjoying what you read, only comprehending the words you have read. The second level is reading between the lines to get an idea of what the author was trying to say, which allows you to make inferences within the story. The third level is analyzing the story inside and out and comprehending the theme of the book, maybe even finding a moral to it. *The Old Man and the Sea* is a perfect example of the three levels which a book can be interpreted. It can just be a book about a man who got lucky and caught a big fish, or it can demonstrate a struggle that occurs in everyone's life which has morels to follow and learn. It wasn't until this past year that I have learned to read at the third level. By reading at the third level, I have learned to appreciate reading more than I did in the past. As a result of this appreciation, I learned techniques like alliteration, for example, which taught me how I can stress key points in a story. Another technique is symbolism in my sequel *Timmy*. I used color and weather to symbolize situations and characters. For example, on page three, third paragraph, I wrote, "Betty Lee was short and full figured. Her hair was always pulled back in a white bandana and wore a white apron with a blue dress. Her eyes are what fascinated Laura most. They were like dark little pools of ink that brilliantly sparkled."

I used the white to symbolize her purity, the blue to symbolize her wisdom, and the black to show that even she had a dark side to her. I learned how to do this by reading *The Hobbit*. Tolken uses color to represent his characters. We discussed what each color meant in our Language Arts. For example, we learned that blue could represent wisdom or sadness, red represents danger, yellow can mean cowardliness, etc. These are only some techniques that I have learned this past year, and each of them have helped me improve my writing by learning to write on a mature level. Also, I have grown to appreciate reading far more than I ever have and will only benefit from continuing to read a vast variety of books.

There is another factor that is important to me when I write. The tools for writing a successful paper are a key factor but what is just as important is the atmosphere in which I write in. I need to have a quiet and relaxing place where I can forget everything for the moment and create a story that I am able to feel as if I am each of the characters in order to produce a strong paper. My get away from everything is in a small room with a desk that only as four objects on it. A sheet of paper, a pen, a bright desk lamp, and a computer. I keep the desk uncluttered because I write to my fullest

(Exhibit continues on the following page.)

Exhibit 127 (continued)

potential when my thoughts are the same way. Last year in my reflective letter, I set goals for myself which is essential to become a successful writer. One of my goals which I feel is most important was to use the writing process completely, which I have successfully achieved. First I make a list of whatever comes to my mind. Then I organize my list, and write a first draft. After that, I continue to make more drafts until I am satisfied with my paper. Next, I ask for a second opinion from my father, who I consider as my personal editor, before typing my final draft. *Timmy* was the piece that I feel I made the most drafts, which successfully models the writing process. I rewrote the whole paper until I was satisfied with it, making sure that it was as perfect as I could possibly get it to be and this is what the writing process is about.

Timmy was also my favorite piece, because I put all of my effort into it and felt as I myself was a character in it. I used color and weather to symbolize the characters personality and mood of the setting. I developed the characters through dialog, which was a first for me. I had never used dialog in any of my stories before. *Timmy* strongly demonstrates my strengths as a writer successfully so I choose this as my best piece of fiction as well. I chose *The Holocaust* as my best nonfiction, because it too demonstrates my strengths. I pride myself in my effective vocabulary and my ability to weave metaphors and similes into my writing pieces. In the first paragraph in *Timmy*, the fifth sentence is an excellent example of this, "The memories came rushing over Laura like ocean waves on a drowning victim during a stormy night as she peered through the curtains of her bedroom bay window." I also feel I have engaging opening and closing sentences which I deliberately try to do. *Timmy* by far was the most creative fictional piece which made all of my strengths clearly evident.

Another goal has been to become stronger writer when I am writing a timed piece. For one of our tests in Language Arts, we had to write a timed essay for a test. We were allowed to choose the topic we wished to write about. I always am looking for a challenge, so wrote about the hardest topic which is how war was a symbol in the book, *The Miracle Worker*. I feel this was a strong persuasive paper despite the fact that it was timed. I had no problem choosing my best timed writing piece. My essay had a strong beginning and closing statement and I feel I clearly expressed my ideas. I began with "In the 1880's the war wasn't only between North and South America, it was also between Anne Sullivan and Helen Keller."

The last goal I set for myself was to improve my spelling and grammar. I have improved on my punctuation, but as far as spelling and run on sentences go, well let's just say that's still my goal for ninth grade. A new goal I would like to set for myself is to use more writing techniques such as alliteration and symbolism in all of my writing pieces. By using these writing techniques I feel I will become a mature and strong writer who can express ideas more effectively and efficiently and become a successful young writer.

Between reading and practicing writing in this manner, I will hopefully become a powerful writer and will be able to prove the saying that the pen is mightier than the sword correct. I do not want to become a writer as my profession, but that does not mean that I don't have to sound like I am. I am hoping that my writing will mature as I do and as I continue to read more novels that range in categories.

(Except for word processing for publishing services, no changes were made in this student's writing.)

Exhibit 128. Sample of Self-Reflection in the Format of a Portfolio Reflective Piece

Instructions to Students

This is the time for you to look back over the writing you've done this year. Follow these directions:

Read through all your work and choose...

1. Your best nonfiction (not poetry).
2. Your best fiction (not poetry).
3. Your best response to literature.
4. Your best timed writing.
5. Your favorite piece (if it is different from 1–4). This can be poetry.
6. One piece of writing that has all the prewriting. This can be one of your selections from above.

Now that you have chosen your pieces for your portfolio, it's time to write a reflective paper about your feelings concerning your writing.

Use the Following Form as a Guideline

Paragraph 1: Introduction

Begin by discussing how you feel about writing. Tell what kind of things do you like to write about and why. Comment on how you use the writing process. For example, do you brainstorm, create a web, outline, or write groups of ideas? How many drafts do you write? Tell about the process and how it works for you.

Paragraph 2: Process used in creating your portfolio

Explain why you chose each piece and what they show about you as a writer. Make sure you identify each piece by title and by the six categories above.

Refer to the suggestions below when writing about your strengths and weaknesses in paragraphs 3 and 4.

Paragraph 3: Strengths

Suggestions for Strengths and Weaknesses

Consider the following examples:

- Planning
- Elaborating
- Organizing

- Developing Ideas
- Showing Personal Voice
- Paragraphing
- Using Transitions

- Organizing Sentence Structure
- Focus
- Using descriptive words
- Using Descriptive Words

What are your three (3) strongest points as a writer as shown by the papers you have chosen? Use the suggestions above to help you decide or write your own on the lines below. **Be sure to support at least three (3) strengths with specific examples from the papers you've chosen!!

Strengths: _____

_____

Paragraph 4: Weaknesses

What are your weak points as a writer? What skills do you feel need improvement? How would using the writing process more effectively help your writing? Use the above suggestions to help you decide or write your own on the lines below. Use specific examples to explain.

Weaknesses: _____

_____

(Exhibit continues on the following page.)

Exhibit 128 (continued)

Paragraph 5: How have your feelings about writing changed?

Do you feel differently about your writing now than you did in the beginning of the year? Reread your progress reports and your goals. Did you accomplish any of them? Explain and give evidence of your success. Now set 2 goals you would like to work on next year to continue improving your writing. Be sure to reread the paragraph on your weaknesses to help set your goals.

Self-Reflection
Portfolio Reflective Piece
Rochambeau Middle School, Grade 6
Region 15 Public Schools, Connecticut

How do you feel about writing? Do you enjoy it, or do you dread the time when your teacher tells you that she is giving you a writing assignment? Well, for me, I'll have to say that I lean more toward liking it than disliking it. I can sit down and just write about anything that comes to my mind. My favorite type of writing is fiction because then I can use my imagination without doing research to find out information for my report. I'll have to say that there are some areas in writing that I don't like to write about, but working on these areas is one of my personal goals. I especially don't like to write about things in our environment including bugs, plants, and trips outdoors because I have never actually thought about these areas or really experienced them. I use the writing process the way that I was taught to. First, I brainstorm, forming a web, then I jot down main ideas and details, next I write my drafts, and finally I proof read it and have a peer proof read it. Usually, I write three drafts. Rough, middle, and final. My rough draft is normally messy with scribbles, cross outs and carrots that I use to add in more detail. My middle draft is neat and has everything correct as if it were the final draft. I use this draft to make sure that nothing is done differently than was suppose to. My final draft has no mistakes and is very organized. This draft is handed into the teacher with an assessment list attached. Overall, I feel that writing is enjoyable and a learning experience as well.

In sixth grade this year I have learned how to write a good paper with rich description and details. Most of the topics I have written about were enjoyable and showed how much I cared about making my paper a superior paper. Although I have received high grades on everything I have written this year, I can narrow these pieces down to my favorites. My favorite non-fiction piece was a persuasive essay that I wrote about a child named Michael with a disease that made him very weak. He had lived with a trained dog named Ashley for about a year, and decided that he wanted to take her to school with him to help him out. The school did not like this idea and decided to fight with this problem. Mrs. _____ class picked their opinion of whether or not they thought that Ashley should attend school with Michael, and then tried to persuade the school or Ashley's parents about their opinion. I decided to say that Ashley should not go to school with Michael because of all the consequences it would cause. For example: one of the consequences would be about how Ashley would act toward other students. What if she were to all of a sudden start getting nervous from being around too many people, and bite one of the children? This would cause many more problems and hurt many people. This piece showed me that I was capable of supporting my opinion. I chose this piece because it showed me that I did not have to feel the same way everyone else felt; just think about my opinion. (Everyone else in my class thought that

(Exhibit continues on the following page.)

Exhibit 128 (continued)

Ashley should accompany Michael to school.) My favorite fiction piece was my folk tale. This was my favorite piece and was about a girl named Velneritta who was mistreated by her parents. She had two friends that helped her find a magic crystal in the ocean.

They showed her how much they cared about her by giving her the crystal to keep for herself. The crystal gave her three wishes, and Velneritta used them. I chose this piece because my sentence flowed, I used figures of speech, and I had good graphics. One example of a figure of speech I used was: "...as fair as a star that is shining in the sky." I used this to describe not only Velneritta's looks, but her feelings to other people as well. This piece showed me as a writer that I can make things up off of the top of my head using my imagination and creativity. A Natural Disaster Strikes article that I wrote about my country was my best response to literature. I pretended that I was a newspaper writer and an earthquake hit my country. My job was to try to relate this earthquake to how it effected geography, culture, economy, technology, education, government, and history. I chose this article because it showed me that I can write about things that could happen in the real world; not just about fiction things that I use my imagination for. Timed writings are difficult for me because I like to take my time to think about what I am going to write about. My favorite timed writing this year was my story about "The T.V. Repair Man." This was about a T.V. addict named Karen who was obsessed with the T.V. She did everything with the T.V. on including eating, sleeping, and going to the bathroom. In fact, she had a toilet build into the couch just so that she didn't have to get up and miss a minute of television. One day, a big storm hit her town, and the T.V. went off. This caused a major problem and got Karen very upset, therefore she called Bob, the T.V. repair man. Soon, the T.V. was fixed, but in the meantime strange things went on. I am not good with time limits, so this was not too well written, but I like the topic that I chose. I chose this piece because it showed me that I can be proud of a story I have written, even though it isn't as good as some of the pieces that have taken my time on. My favorite poem that I wrote was a sonnet about Easter. I wrote this to a women that was very sick to help cheer her up. It showed me that I can write for someone else; not just for myself. My best pre-writing is my progress report to my mother. I gave this to my mother to update her on everything that I had done since the beginning of the year. She wrote back giving me some feedback or ideas that would help me become a better writer. I chose this piece because it included all of my rough, middle and final drafts. This piece showed me how to keep all of my drafts in order and be very organized. So, as you can see I have a lot of favorite pieces all of them in different categories.

Everyone has at least a few strong points in writing. Actually, I have three. Making figures of speech is one. In my folk tale, "Velneritta and the Magic Crystal," I used many figures of speech, including the one I mentioned in the previous paragraph. Another one from this particular piece is, "...as cool as a cucumber." I used this to describe the temperature of the water that Velneritta was swimming in. As you probably know already, figures of speech can be funny as well as serious and down to the point. An example of this is, "we're as ready as cows waiting to be milked." I used this to try to give the readers a picture of how ready the Flounder Twins were to start looking for the crystal. Many people would like to read a funny figure of speech in between all of the others. My second strong point is focusing. Usually, I have a focus sentence. An example of a focus sentence that I have used in the past is, "The time has come for me to sit back and assess what I have done, what I have learned, and how well I have learned in Language Arts." This particular focus sentence came from the progress report that I wrote to my mom. If you were the reader of my progress report, then you would know that I was going to explain about everything that I had done since the beginning of the year up until then. My final strong point is proof reading my drafts. Before I bring one of my drafts to school, I always check to make sure that it sounds right. I read my paper out loud to myself just in case I find a mistake. I do this because I know that

(Exhibit continues on the following page.)

Exhibit 128 (continued)

there is a chance that I will have to read my paper out loud to the class, and I don't want to sound like I don't know what I am talking about. For example, "The killer quake caused about 600 aftershocks and damage widespread." Do you know what is wrong with this piece? Of course. First of all, this is a newspaper article and I don't think that the readers want to know "about" how many aftershocks there were. They probably want to know the exact amount of aftershocks. And second of all, it is not supposed to be "damage widespread", it is supposed to be "widespread damage." The final sentence after fixing these mistakes would be, "The killer quake caused 600 aftershocks and widespread damage." Overall, I feel that I have many strong points that affect my writing a lot.

As everyone knows already, a writer must have some weak points as well as strong points. Three weaknesses that I have are: planning, transition sentences, and getting down to the point. Planning does not come naturally to me. Most of the time I don't plan things out, I just make them up as I go along. This does not affect me a lot because I always proof-read my work to make sure that my sentences flow, I stay on topic , and I follow a criteria. An example of a time that I didn't plan was on T.V. Repair Man timed writing. I didn't really have a main idea or details, I just worked my way through it. My second weakness is making transitions sentences. I am not good at writing these especially when I am trying to connect my introduction to my all of the rest of my paragraphs. An example of me trying to do this is, "I'm writing this letter to analyze my performance on the different types of writings I've worked on this year, my spelling test grades, and If I've succeeded in accomplishing my goals or not." This transition sentence came from my progress report to my mom. Though out the whole sentence I listed; not trying to intertwine my sentences. When I say that one of my weaknesses is getting down to the point, I mean that sometimes I write too much. For example; one time I wrote a bigger summary than the article itself. Now how does this summarize the piece? You may recognize this example from the "Ashley" story. My teacher gave me a low grade explaining to me that I was supposed to summarize, not write a one hundred page report. So even though I have some pretty strong strengths, weaknesses do exist.

Writing is something to value. I have felt the same way about writing since the beginning of the year up until now. To me writing is something to be proud of; and throughout my life I have been proud of my writing. Every year my strengths get stronger; and I get prouder. It is like climbing everlasting steps. You get prouder after every step, and just can't wait to move up again. If you ever feel like one step is taking too long and too much work, just remind yourself that there is no pressure or stopping point. As for my goals, I have accomplished most of them including using descriptive words. Just take a look at my folk tale. The whole story is filled with descriptive works. I know that many people would like to see an example, but for me to even write the smallest bit would take too long. But along with the descriptive words my vocabulary has increased, so using descriptive words was a big step forward and a great success. Two goals that I want to continue working on next year are, thinking of good ideas quickly and planning. These two goals kind of work together as a team. What I mean by this that if I can become a good planner, then the ideas will come to my head. So, I believe that this year helped me climb about five steps instead of one, and showed me as a writer that if I put all of my ideas together, I can come up with something very creative.

(Except for word processing for publishing purposes, no other changes were made in this student's writing.)

Exhibit 129. Sample of Self-Reflection End Piece for the Writing Portfolio
Pomperaug High School
Region 15 Public Schools, Connecticut

Sophomore English Reflective Piece   by_____

> "Pondering his own fate, Macbeth fails to realize that things begun unnaturally can only get worse if not remedied in a positive, honest, natural way. Macbeth is portrayed or depicted to be a strong, stable, loyal and effective leader at the beginning of this work. However, it quickly becomes apparent that his trust in the predictions of the witches has left him a overconfident, impulsive, young fool."

This piece was derived from a paper entitled "Reversal of Intention" which was written as an expository essay about Shakespeare's Macbeth. Of all the papers that I have written this year, I am most proud of this one. It is an example of what I can do when I work at editing and restructuring until I get a combination that is pleasing to the ear as well as the mind. This writing reflective is designed to outline and analyze my best work and to highlight my strengths and weaknesses as a writer.

To begin, as emphasized above, my Macbeth paper is an example of my best expository work. It is structurally sound and my ideas are conveyed in a precise, concise manner. I feel that it demonstrates my ability to narrow a topic and to provide adequate textual support to prove my thesis statement. I am very proud of it because for the first time this year, I was able to write a strong introduction and conclusion that tie together in a meaningful way. My introduction was descriptive enough to predicate a format for the paper, but vague enough so that it didn't give away the entire focus. In addition, my conclusion summarized the thesis in a succinct manner and did not stray from the main ideas brought forth throughout the paper.

Personally, I have always found it difficult to write descriptive, effective narratives. Thus when I completed my Christmas paper, I was pleasantly surprised by the outcomes. Since I am a strong expository writer, I was especially pleased that I had successfully created a narrative I could be proud of. It was through this paper that I learned how to transform thoughts into words, so that my audience could feel part of the story. In addition, this paper demonstrates my proficiency in incorporating vocabulary that creates an informal and casual tone. Here I was able to use dialogue as an effective way to portray events. This paper exemplifies my abilities to write fluently and descriptively. Perhaps the most interesting and challenging of all of the papers that I have had the pleasure of writing in, sophomore honors English class was my Modest Proposal entitled "Oil Our Unspoken Enemy." This paper allowed me the liberty to explore several different subjects and I was allowed to choose my own topic. Maybe that is why I enjoyed writing it. As a writer, I feel that a good prompt is an essential part of any paper. In addition to enjoying this paper, I think it demonstrates my ability as a writer to adapt to diverse forms of expression. In this case, it was "Modest Proposal." This piece exemplifies the many hours of writing, rewriting and revising that go into each one of my papers. The rough draft contains countless numbers of additions, cross outs and word changes. All of these things aid me in my attempts to create a final product that I can be proud of. In addition, one might notice that my rough draft is handwritten. I find it difficult to sit down and type a paper, it is too impersonal for me, thus, I write out all my papers and then type them.

(Exhibit continues on the following page.)

Exhibit 129 (continued)

This past year, I have had extreme difficulty with timed writing in English class. My writing is not fluent when I'm timed and my pieces lack a completeness that make them difficult to understand. I usually have no problems with the subject matter and the degree of difficulty does not create a conflict for me. As demonstrated in my CAPT test, my problem lies in my ability to satisfactorily structure an effective essay in a short period of time. For the most part, I am happy with the content of my essays, but not the topic. The lack of time does not allow me the luxury of editing my work.

Also included in my portfolio is a piece that I wrote outside of English class. For my free choice, I chose a history essay that I wrote in response to a question regarding the atomic bomb. I feel that this piece demonstrates my ability to make practical applications to realistic concepts. Since the format of this paper is different from others that I have previously used, I feel that it spotlights my ability to be flexible in the interest of adequately accommodating and highlighting a given topic. It is essential to formulate each paper based upon the reaction one hopes to receive. This paper is a persuasive essay, written to convey my own personal opinion and to explain my point of view based on historical knowledge.

To emphasize my strengths and to focus on the progress that I have made this past year, I feel that my best work is generated when I have time to organize my ideas and when I have a prompt that induces enthusiasm on my part. My strengths lie in my ability to present an argument and to back it up logically with facts. I can organize ideas so that they flow sequentially and my strong vocabulary makes my writing more powerful. In addition, my sentence structure is smooth, which allows my papers to flow freely.

In the future, I would like to better my abilities by emphasizing a need for improvement in consistency and developing a method that incorporates words which will compliment each other. In addition, I must learn to write a satisfactory essay even when the subject does not stimulate personal interest. I am most proud of my accomplishments up to this point, but I know that my writing is far from perfect. I will continue to work to eliminate my flaws and will always strive to be the best. Communications is vital in our world today and the demand for people who have superior writing capabilities is growing. My goal is to be one of those people with outstanding writing skills.

Finally, I think that as a writer, I admire my mother the most. She has her own individual style, one which is completely unique. It took years for her to foster it but it was well worth it. She creates a chemistry among words without thinking twice. This chemistry gives her an exciting flair that continually flows throughout her work. Here is an excerpt from an article she wrote entitled, "From Housework to Homework":

> "The most amazing transformation took place during my decade at home with the children. In just a few short years, I managed to change from a well-informed, competent professional to an indecisive introvert wracked with insecurities. Along with my waist-line, I had lost my confidence, my initiative, and my perspective."

In closing, I feel that excellent writing requires not only effort, but time, discipline and a good prompt.

(Except for word processing, no changes were made in this student's writing.)

WHAT IS THE IMPACT OF PERFORMANCE LEARNING AND ASSESSMENT ON THE TEACHER?

In developing and using a performance task and its corresponding assessment lists, teachers, like students, advance through the Cycle of Learning (see Exhibit 9 in Chapter 1). The educator moves through the eight steps of the cycle to improve overall performance as an instructor and assessor. In crafting the elements of the task, teachers identify the content and skills needed to successfully complete the product. This enables teachers to better measure their own and the students' knowledge of content taught. If gaps are found, teachers can identify these gaps and fill them accordingly, thereby enhancing their own knowledge base.

ADVANCING THROUGH THE STAGES OF COMPETENCE

In addition to experiencing the Cycle of Learning, teachers progress through professional steps of development. Throughout a career—and during various moments within that career—teachers move through stages of competency, as follows:

• In the initial stages of experience, teachers will be in a state of *Unconscious Noncompetency*, whereby they have not yet mastered a skill, yet they are unaware of this lack of competency.

• After experience and training, teachers move to a stage of *Unconscious Competency*. During this stage, teachers have developed a level of mastery, yet they are still unaware of the transition of their abilities.

• After more practice and training, the teachers become aware of professional strengths and success in a stage called *Conscious Competency*.

• Ironically, this competency is followed by the point of understanding and identification of weaknesses called *Conscious Noncompetency*. Once teachers understand their own strengths and weaknesses, they are then able to set goals for improvement to reenter the cycle, which becomes a spiral of professional growth.

Are you feeling competent to assess the quality of a student-made graph? The following table may help you decide what state of consciousness and competence you inhabit:

The Stages of Consciousness

Unconscious Noncompetency	"I don't know that I don't know how to assess the quality of a graph" (In fact, this thought would not occur to you.)
Unconscious Competency	"I know a good graph when I see one, but I can't explain exactly how I make that judgment."
Conscious Competency	"I know a good graph when I see one, and I can write an explicit list of criteria for assessing graphs."
Conscious Noncompetency	"I realize that I am not always sure when a line graph is appropriate."
Goal Setting	"My goal is to learn what types of graphs are appropriate for which kinds of data."

While using performance-based learning tasks, educators move through these stages of competency at an accelerated rate. The assessment lists provide an intense focus on student work and teacher knowledge. This focus helps teachers analyze their own performance, as well as that of the students, to better see their strengths and weaknesses and set new goals.

PERFORMANCE TASKS: FRONT-LOADING YOUR PLANNING

Once comfortable using performance-based learning tasks, teachers find that a great advantage in classroom planning time is the comprehensive nature of the task. Teachers "front load" the planning for the task—they write the task and make a plan for assessment ahead of time. Because everything is organized and presented, students may work more independently. Students look to the written assignment for guidance and reassurance. The accompanying assessment lists function as a guidebook, enabling students to consult the lists instead of the teacher. Thus the role of the teacher changes to facilitator, with more freedom to address specific needs as they arise.

STUDENTS SPEND MORE TIME ON TASK

Students spend more "time on task" doing their assignments, self-assessing, and revising their work. The structure provided by the task, the assessment list, and the models of excellence helps the students get started more efficiently, sustain independent work, and reach closure knowing that they have completed the assignment. Thus, teachers spend less of their time "managing" the class and more of their time teaching individuals and small groups.

COMMUNICATION TO PARENTS: "NO MYSTERY"

The written performance task functions as a communications tool among teachers, students, and parents. Clearly written steps and expectations explicitly communicate the teacher's objectives. Parents recognize this "no guesses, no excuses" format of the task. The mystery of student work is solved for the parent, and the teacher encounters less conflict in interpretation of assignments. The comprehensive layout of the task contributes to the teacher's self-confidence as an instructor and communicator.

We must recognize, however, that the assessment lists are links, or correlations, between where the learner is and where the teacher would like the learner to go. We must not think of any assessment list as a static thing. It must be a dynamic and ever-changing tool that enables students to continue to grow as learners and helps teachers target and communicate long-term goals.

PERFORMANCE TASKS: FLEXIBILITY IS THE KEY

The challenge of using performance-based learning tasks lies in the amount of time needed to create the task and assessment lists, to collect resources and materials, to teach each step of the task, and to afford students time to complete each stage of the project. The teacher must rearrange the classroom schedule to balance the time needed for the task with time needed to teach content material. Initially, the teacher must be prepared to reapportion classroom time to meet the task schedule. After teachers and students have successfully used several tasks, however, this challenge will become easier to meet.

Because student abilities differ, the teacher must practice flexible scheduling and must be able to accommodate the various needs of each student. For example, students with special needs may require help in reading and organizing a task of any magnitude. In these cases, the teacher may need to schedule special resource teachers, arrange for volunteers to work in the classroom, or help those students who may need assistance. Performance-based tasks are designed to authentically assess each student's performance; therefore, the teacher may need to adjust the task and its assessment lists for some students or allow these students to adapt the lists themselves.

STRUCTURES GUARANTEE SUCCESS FOR SPECIAL NEEDS STUDENTS (NO CONFUSION, NO FRUSTRATION)

Special education teachers have always understood the importance of highly structured activities that are carefully broken down into small, more manageable pieces for students who have organizational, processing, and time-management difficulties. For this reason alone, special education teachers find it helpful to use performance learning tasks (which break each task down into a step-by-step procedure), coupled with the performance task assessment lists (which break the assessment components down into easily understood "elements of excellence"). These teachers have found that performance tasks and assessment lists maximize each student's performance and enable all students to meet with success.

These tools become especially powerful for students with special needs when the regular classroom teacher and the special education teacher collaborate on designing and implementing performance learning tasks and assessment lists. In fact, the extra collaboration often helps the teachers clarify expectations and anticipate areas of potential confusion and frustration for students. This process results in an improved task and assessment list for *all* students. Another possible result of such collaborations is the modification of either the task or the assessment list for students with differing needs.

The special education teacher then uses the task and the assessment list to facilitate completion of the activity by the students. As the students work at the task, the teacher may ask

them to highlight parts of their rough drafts to show evidence of a given element of excellence. By changing the color of the highlighter for each element, students can see exactly which elements they have done particularly well on, and which ones need work. In this strategy, the "rough draft" becomes more than merely words on paper; it becomes a colorful "painting" that shows the student what she needs to do to improve her work. For visual learners, the strategy helps them to cut through the cycle of confusion and frustration that they often feel when confronted with a page full of words and are asked to "revise this and make it better."

As special and regular education teachers continue to collaborate on developing tasks and assessment lists, the lines between special and regular education inevitably become more and more "smudged" until the two begin to realize that they are both pursuing the same goals, and that strategies that work well for students with special needs also work for their nonidentified "regular ed" peers. When this understanding and blending of strategies occurs, the confusion and frustration often felt by both the special education students and their mainstream classroom teachers will diminish; and the inclusion and mainstreaming of special education students will be more successful for everyone involved—students, classroom teachers, and special education teachers.

WHAT IS THE IMPACT OF PERFORMANCE-BASED LEARNING AND ASSESSMENT ON PARENTS?

Parents are important in the learning process, and their support is crucial to the success of students. To gain parents' support, we must explain and communicate the goals and procedures of performance-based learning and assessment. During open house or in a letter home, teachers should explain what tasks and assessments are and how they are used. Models of excellent work can be shown and explained. Teachers can emphasize the goal of performance-based learning: to help students become motivated, independent learners who know and use essential concepts, information, learning skills, and work habits. Overall, in Connecticut's Region 15, this method of instruction has had an extremely positive impact on parents.

Performance assessment tasks can either be completed in the classroom or done as homework. If students do the work in school and take their final products home, showing parents the assessment list and task helps students to clearly explain what they accomplished and why they received a particular grade or rating. This process increases communication between students and parents and provides a framework for discussion when parents confer with teachers.

PARENT SUPPORT—AND PARENT COMMENDATIONS

If a task is to be completed at home, the structure of the task itself and the assessment list will not only help students complete the assignment, but will also assist those parents who wish to be part of the learning process. For parents who make it a point to schedule homework time and make themselves available to provide support and guidance for their children, performance tasks and assessment lists give a clear indication of what students must do. One parent wrote:

> The assessment sheets and tasks are invaluable. They help parents know exactly what is expected.

Even when parents are not actively involved, aside from the benefits to the students, performance tasks and assessments can keep parents informed of expectations.

Assessment tasks and lists help parents in other ways. The task is clearly stated, the assessment list provides detailed criteria, and the models provide students with ideas. As a result, the students aren't as apt to ask parents for assistance and help. One father wrote:

> My daughter really enjoyed this program and worked independently on it. The assessment lists are a great way of letting students know exactly what is expected of them.

Authentic performance tasks add a new dimension to the classroom. More students are actively engaged in the learning process and can show what they can do with what they know. One mother wrote:

> What I liked about this unit was the chance for the students to use their imaginations to create a product which was uniquely theirs.

Performance-based learning and assessment also improve communication between parents and teachers. When conferencing with individual parents, teachers find it beneficial to show parents their child's work and the task and assessment that goes with it, rather than simply saying: "Jane received a '60' on her report." With a task and list, the teacher can point out specific areas that need work. The teacher is able to effectively discuss the areas that need improvement, and the parent then understands the grade.

TAKING THE MYSTERY OUT OF HOMEWORK

Parents also appreciate "check-point" dates, a time table for long-term tasks and units, and some helpful hints so they can support and encourage their children without doing the work for them.

As noted in Chapter 11, performance tasks and assessment lists take the "mystery" out of classroom assignments and grades for parents.

Exhibit 130 shows a performance task written as an interdisciplinary assignment by a pair of 8th grade science and English teachers. Exhibits 131 and 132 show the rubric and assessment list that were used to guide and assess this performance task. The science content was the responsibility of the science teacher, whereas the English teacher worked with the students on writing in the format of a "letter to the editor." Both teachers and the media center staff worked with the students on their research skills. The science teacher assessed the science content, and the English teacher assessed the quality of the writing. Before the students began the assignment, this pair of teachers sent a letter home to the parents of all their students (see Exhibit 133). In the letter, the teachers provided suggestions to parents about how to help their sons and daughters with the performance task without doing the work for them. The assessment lists have provided a way for parents to know what is expected by the teacher and have provided support for quality work at home.

Exhibit 130. Performance Task
"To the Editor": Our Atmosphere Is in Danger

Background

As a student sitting in your earth science classroom for the past few weeks, you have learned about the possibility of global warming, the loss of the ozone shield, and other changes that people have brought about in the atmosphere. Now that you are aware of the potential problems and dangers that we face, you have made up your mind not to sit around any longer and just let things happen to you and your world. You decide that you as one person can make a difference. You decide that if each one of us takes a small step, large results can follow, but somebody has to start the whole thing moving. That person is you!!!

Your Task

Write either an editorial or a letter to the editor of the local newspaper on the topic of either "global warming" or the depletion of the ozone layer.

Your Audience

Readers of the newspaper are the audience for your letter/editorial.

Your Purpose

The primary purpose of your work is to inform the readers of a situation that threatens the atmosphere and our quality of life, and to send out a call for action by others who feel the same way that you feel.

Materials

You will need your class notes, as well as additional research data to help you prepare your letter/editorial.

Procedure

1. Review the assessment list for a letter to the editor/editorial.
2. Review the models discussed in class.
3. Conduct your research and gather your facts.
4. Brainstorm ideas.
5. Share your ideas with a classmate.
6. Draft your editorial/letter using the models as your guide.
7. Use the assessment list to help you assess your draft.
8. Revise your draft.
9. Create a second draft of your work.
10. Check the assessment list a second time or have a peer check it.
11. Redraft your editorial/letter.
12. Proofread your editorial/letter.
13. If necessary, make a third draft.
14. Complete the "final" self-assessment.
15. Submit your paper to your teacher and to the newspaper.

Exhibit 131. "To the Editor" : Scoring Rubric

S:

The editorial or letter meets all the requirements of a **T** paper. In addition, the work is so well crafted that it could be published. The whole transcends the sum of the parts in producing a work that is as artful as it is scientific. The writer has insights into the problem that go beyond the material read and discussed in class.

T:

The letter or editorial is well crafted in the style called for. The student has demonstrated a thorough knowledge of the structure of the atmosphere, as well as the problem chosen as the focus of the writing. The writing is well organized around a central issue connected to the problem. The main idea is clearly stated. Data are included to support ideas, and credit is given to the sources of the data to lend an air of creditability to the position taken by the writer. The writer further anticipates the opposing viewpoint and possible arguments that may be raised to refute the position of the writing and meets them with sound reasoning to further establish his/her position. The writer is able to gain the attention of the audience and is effective in establishing a position through the use of facts and logic. The paper is well edited with no more than one or two errors left in the final draft.

U:

Very similar to the **T** above but without the argument being as clearly presented. This will not have as much detail or be as well organized. Errors in editing will be more prevalent. The writer still has a clear concept of style, audience, and purpose but has not demonstrated as great a skill level in working with logic and persuasion.

V:

Like **W** in many ways, but there are moments of clear, logical argument and style. On the whole, the writer shows an understanding of the topic and process that could be transformed into a solid letter or editorial. The writing suffers more from lack of revision and polish than a lack of ability on the part of the author.

W:

Writer has not mastered or used one or more of the elements of a good editorial or letter to the editor. The work contains generalizations that are not supported. No attempt is make to give the science behind the issues of the way the structure of the atmosphere interacts with the issue. There are multiple editing errors and flaws in organization. The paper is not successful in advancing an opinion in light of possible counter arguments. The writer does not have a grasp of the issue or does not have a clear position to offer. He/she cannot use writing to further their cause.

X:

Like **W** in many ways. Paper is replete with errors to the point of being unintelligible. Misinformation abounds.

Exhibit 132. Performance Task Assessment List
Letter "To the Editor"

| | | ASSESSMENT POINTS | |
| | Points | Earned Assessment: | |
Element	Possible	Self	Teacher
1. Knowledge of the atmosphere displayed through facts and information used.	10	_____	_____
2. Knowledge of the issue shown by facts and information used.	10	_____	_____
3. Balance is maintained (avoids the "Chicken Little" syndrome).	5	_____	_____
4. Anticipates and responds to the other side of the issue.	10	_____	_____
5. Research beyond the scope of the classroom activities.	5	_____	_____
6. Main idea clearly stated.	10	_____	_____
7. Supporting details and information are accurate and forceful.	15	_____	_____
8. References to source of information given for added emphasis and effect.	5	_____	_____
9. Tone of the letter is rational and logical.	5	_____	_____
10. Letter style is maintained throughout.	5	_____	_____
11. Effectiveness in getting the attention of audience.	5	_____	_____
12. Mechanics of writing are followed (punctuation, spelling, grammar).	5	_____	_____
13. Paper is well organized.	10	_____	_____
Total	100	_____	_____

Exhibit 133. Letter from Teachers to Parents

January 22 1994

Dear Parents:

As you may recall from previous letters, newsletter articles, and our comments at Open House, we believe that our students should be given multiple opportunities to demonstrate their learning in a "real world" setting. Because we all share a concern for our atmosphere, we have decided to have the students write letters to the editor explaining their positions on global warming or the thinning of our ozone layer.

This activity was introduced in both science and language arts class today, and your child has been given the task and the assessment list that will be used to evaluate his/her work. You may be wondering how you might help your child be successful with this task. Therefore, we hope that the following suggestions will be helpful.

1. We encourage you to review the assignment and the assessment list with your child so that you will be aware of the scope of the activity.
2. Your child will need to got to the public library during the course of the activity. We have contacted both libraries to let them know about the project, and books have been placed on reserve so that the students may be assured of finding materials.
3. Encourage your child to work steadily on the project and not leave it to the last minute. Help your child make and follow a time-management schedule of getting each part of this project done.
4. Ask to see your child's rough draft and encourage him/her to compare the draft to the assessment list. For each item on the assessment list, ask you child to show you the part of his or her work that fulfills that element. For example, item 6 is, "Main idea clearly stated." Ask your child to point out the clearly stated main idea in his or her work.
5. Help your child with revision by pointing out areas of weakness (but please do not make changes *for* him/her).
6. Call us if your child is not making progress on the project *or* it your child seems overwhelmed, confused, or distraught by this assignment.

Once again we thank you for your support and assistance. If you have any questions, please give us a call. The best times to reach us are from 9:45–10:30 a.m. or after school until 4:00 p.m.

Sincerely, [Teachers]

Please detach, sign and return to Mrs. Van Wagenen before January 28.

We have reviewed the information about the "letter to the editor" performance task and understand that the final letter must be handed in to Mrs. Van Wagenen on Friday, February 16 1994.

Student's Name

Parent Signature

_____   _____

IMPLEMENTING PERFORMANCE-BASED LEARNING AND ASSESSMENT IN THE SCHOOL AND SCHOOL DISTRICT

13

Seen through the framework of student performance improvement, lasting educational change occurs one classroom at a time, one school at a time. Directed efforts to implement any educational strategy (in this case, performance-based learning and assessment) by classroom teachers, by schools, and by school districts necessarily result in change; and this transformation may be felt in both the processes of implementation and the resulting effects of that effort.

IMPACT OF PERFORMANCE-BASED LEARNING AND ASSESSMENT AT THE SCHOOL LEVEL

At the school level, when teachers first begin to use performance tasks, assessment lists, rubrics, and models, they feel both excited and tense. On one hand, trying something new can be energizing; on the other hand, newness is fraught with risk. As a result, when performance assessment techniques are first used within a school, teachers tend to increase their communication and support activities among their colleagues, especially those who are trying similar strategies. Teaming, sharing ideas and materials, and using common vocabulary gradually become evident in a school that is beginning to implement performance learning methods.

Another aspect of team planning comes in the form of a schedule for performance tasks. When several teachers in a departmentalized or team-teaching structure begin using performance tasks, they must be careful not to have too many projects going at once so that students and their parents will not be overwhelmed. Figure 17 shows a strategy for mapping when performance tasks are scheduled. Some teachers send such a timetable to parents each marking period.

The use of assessment lists and models of excellence focuses teachers' attention on student performance. The "input" of curriculum development and lesson planning becomes a means to an end, rather than an end in itself. Teachers also gain content knowledge and add to their repertoire of the "most appropriate" instructional methods as they begin to write performance

tasks, assessment lists, and rubrics aligned with their curriculums.

Figure 18 uses a frontier metaphor to show how teachers gain strength and knowledge over time, as they work together. As staff members who are initially involved in the first efforts to use performance assessment (the scouts) share their successes and challenges, other teachers (the pioneers), who have observed the process from a distance, may feel increasingly more interested in trying similar techniques in their own

FIGURE 17. Time Mapping Performance Tasks

Teacher(s): _____

Grade Level: _____ Marking Period: _____

Performance Task Title	Subject(s)	Format of Product and/or Performance (I = Intermediate Work) (F = Final Work)	Time Line: Use an Arrow to Show When the Task Begins and When It Ends			
			Month:	Month:	Month:	Month:

FIGURE 18. Working Together to Improve Student Performance

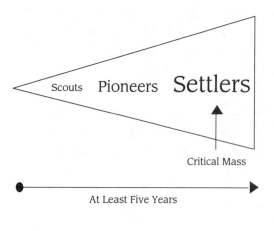

Scouts   Pioneers   Settlers

Critical Mass

At Least Five Years

writing led to the use of various forms of writing in performance-based learning and assessment tasks in many disciplines. In turn, this training led to the student writing portfolio for all students in grades 1–12. Figure 19, "Timeline of Region 15 Initiatives—Portfolio Implementation," shows the steps along the long path (again using frontier terminology), from the early writing emphasis through the scout, pioneer, and settler stages of implementing writing portfolios.

BEYOND MECHANICAL USE TO CRITICAL MASS AT THE INTEGRATION LEVEL

As educators begin to learn about an innovation such as performance-based learning and assessment, they go through a series of stages of concern about its adoption. Figure 20 shows those stages, as described by the Concerns-Based Adoption Model (CBAM). Concerns begin with the need to learn the "basics" and how the teacher's day-to-day work will be affected. As teachers implement the innovation more fully, they progress through a stage of concern about managing the new procedures; concerns about the impact on students; concerns about coordinating efforts with others; and, finally, concerns about "reconstructing" the innovation to integrate it with other strategies.

classes. Requests for professional development often reflect this growing interest in the "need to know" about performance assessment. Eventually, as the number of involved staff increases (the settlers join in), and they become more comfortable with and competent in performance assessment, a "critical mass" emerges within the school. The arrival of settlers is a real signal that a shift in the instructional paradigm for that school has occurred.

EXAMPLE OF LONG-TERM CHANGE IN A DISTRICT: STUDENT WRITING PORTFOLIO

Improving student performance in writing has been a goal in Connecticut's Region 15 Public Schools for many years. Training in process

Figure 21 describes the concerns teachers have in learning to make and use performance tasks such as those in the Responding to Literature collection in Chapter 5 of this book. Professional development must be matched to the level of concerns of the teachers. For example,

FIGURE 19. Timeline of Region 15 Initiatives—Portfolio Implementation

1994–95 **Full Implementation (Settlers)**
All students in grades 1 through 12 were engaged in creating a portfolio of their writing. In-Service Courses were offered at each school (Beginner and Advanced) to assist teachers with the process. During the summer of 1995, the three manuals were revised.

1993–94 **Expanded Pilot (Pioneers)**
In-Service Course was taught at each school as a "critical mass" of teachers became involved in performance-based assessment and the creation of portfolios. The Region Portfolio Team wrote manuals on the portfolio process at the elementary, middle and high school levels. Some models of portfolios were selected to be used as models for each grade level.

1992–93 Pre-Pilot (Scouts)
Performance-based learning using assessment lists became more common. Professional development at the school level focused on using performance tasks and assessment lists. The Portfolio Leadership Team planned the model that the Region would use. Other teachers joined in the experimentation.

1991–92 **Research and Experimentation (Scouts)**
The Assistant Superintendent formed the Portfolio Leadership team, composed of volunteer teachers from each school, the English Department Chairperson from the high school, a middle school and an elementary school principal, to learn more about portfolios and formulate a list of criteria for a successful portfolio plan and coordinate analysis and use of data from the Connecticut Mastery Test. Experimentation with portfolios by individual teachers began.

1990–91 **Research and Experimentation (Early Scouts)**
Performance tasks using various forms of writing were beginning to be used across the grade levels and disciplines. Teachers were learning how to use assessment lists and coach students to be more honest and perceptive self-assessors. Teachers attended conferences and workshops to learn about portfolio development and use. Pre/1990 Ten +/– years of study, in-service, and practice in process writing. From 1980 to 1985 improving writing across the curriculum through utilization of the writing process was a Region-wide goal. Staff members were trained; a Regionwide holistic writing sample was taken in the fall and spring of each year and scored by staff; an analytical scoring process was developed and implemented.

Pre-1990 **Ten +/- Years of Study, Inservice, and Practice in Process Writing**
From 1980 to 1985, improving writing across the curriculum through use of the writing process was a Regionwide goal. Staff members were trained; a Regionwide holistic writing sample was taken in the fall and spring of each year and scored by staff; and an analytical scoring process was developed and implemented.

FIGURE 20. Concerns-Based Adoption Model (CBAM)

Stages of Concern: Typical Expressions of Concern about the Innovation

		Stages of Concern	Expressions of Concern
I			
M			
P		6 Refocusing	I have some ideas about something that would work even better.
A			
C		5 Collaboration	I am concerned about relating what I am doing with what other instructors are doing.
T			
Time **T**		4 Consequence	How is my use affecting students?
A			
S		3 Management	I seem to be spending all my time getting material ready.
K			
	S	2 Personal	How will using it affect me?
	E		
	L	1 Informational	I would like to know more about it.
	F	0 Awareness	I am not concerned about (the innovation)

Source: CBAM Model developed by Hord, Rutherford, Huling-Austin, and Hall (1987).

teachers at the *orientation* level are interested in what these performance tasks and assessment lists look like. Those at the *preparation* stage want to "make and take," whereas teachers at the *mechanical* use level are establishing a routine of using these performance-based learning and assessment materials in their classrooms. Critical mass at this stage would look like a schoolwide or districtwide adoption; but without further professional development, the innovation will quickly fade.

With continuing support and networking, teachers move from the *mechanical* level through the *routine* level to the *refinement* level. Teachers at this level need to be involved with other educators in studying student performance and making adaptations to instructional materials and strategies. If an innovation is to change the culture of a school or school district, it must reach critical mass at the *integration* level, where teachers are integrating performance-based learning materials with other strategies, such as multiple-intelligence strategies, issue controversy, cooperative learning, Dimensions of Learning, and the scientific method. Finally, the scouts and pioneers move on to *renewal*, where the whole model is reconstructed.

In Region 15, professional development for the scouts and pioneers, who have worked for years on creating and implementing performance-based learning and assessment, includes leadership on the school and regionwide curriculum and professional development projects. It also includes such activities as teacher-designed research projects, portfolios for educators, writing and presenting for professional organization,

FIGURE 21. Concerns-Based Adoption Model (CBAM) Applied to Performance-Based Learning and Assessment (PBLA) and the Responding to Literature Tasks in Chapter 5

Level 0—Non-use
State in which the individual has little or no knowledge of PBLA, no involvement with it, and is doing nothing toward becoming involved.

Decision Point A—Takes action to learn more detailed information about the innovation.
Level I—Orientation
State in which the individual has acquired information about PBLA and the Responding To Literature Tasks and/or has explored its value orientation and what it will require.

Decision Point B—Makes a decision to use the innovation by establishing a time to begin.
Level II—Preparation
State in which the user is preparing for first use of a classroom performance task (e.g., a Responding to Literature task)

Decision Point C—Begins first use of the innovation.
Level III—Mechanical use
State in which the user focuses most effort on the short-term, day-to-day use of performance-based learning and assessment strategies with little time for reflection. Changes in use are made more to meet user needs than needs of students and others. The user is primarily engaged in an attempt to master tasks required to use PBLA strategies. These attempts often result in disjointed and superficial use.

Time

Decision Point D—A routine pattern of use is established.
Level IVA—Routine
Use of PBLA strategies is stabilized. Few if any changes are being made in ongoing use. Little preparation or thought is being given to improve innovation use or its consequences.

Level IVB—Refinement
State in which the user varies the use of PBLA strategies to increase the impact on students. Variations in use of PBLA strategies is based on knowledge of both short- and long-term consequences for students.

Decision Point E—Initiates changes in use of the innovation based on input from and in coordination with colleagues for benefit of clients.
Level V—Integration
State in which the user is combining own efforts to use PBLA strategies with related activities of colleagues to achieve a collective impact on students.

Decision Point F—Begins exploring alternatives to or major modifications of the innovation presently in use.
Level VI—Renewal
State in which the user reevaluates the quality of PBLA strategies, seeks modifications of, or alternatives to, present innovation to achieve increased impact on students, examines new developments in the field, and explores new goals for self and the organization.

consultation and professional development for other school systems, and writing books such as this.

Professional development often stops well short of providing the support educators need to move to and through the integration level of change. Too often, people see change as a product that can be accomplished in a year or two. Change is a continuous process—and if the journey is stopped, the change will evaporate.

THE "IMPLEMENTATION EVENT" FOR A SCHOOL OR DISTRICT

A general exposure to performance-based learning and assessment, even with a rich set of examples, is usually not nearly enough of a "stimulus" to get this innovation started. State-level performance assessments can act as the powerful motivator for school districts to move into classroom-level use of these strategies. Other "implementation events" can be programs such as a super science fair, a push on persuasive writing, a mammoth math problem-solving initiative, or a convention of cultural diversity in social studies and art. Through proper professional development and the use of performance tasks, assessment lists, and models of excellence, students, teachers, and parents would step into the use of these strategies. These "implementation events" are a beginning, a "toehold" on a long-term effort to make performance-based learning and assessment a part of the education of every student.

LEADERSHIP IS ESSENTIAL FOR CHANGE TO BEGIN AND BE SUSTAINED

A new program of performance-based learning and assessment must have a leader who is a "champion of the cause." That person must be well informed about performance-based learning and assessment, able to communicate and build support, creative in finding time and resources, and committed to many years of collaborative work. The leader usually requires "position power" as well as "expert power" and "personal power" to carry out all the functions to lead, facilitate, and manage the long-term efforts to change the culture of the school system. Position power helps to overcome barriers and establish policies, expert power helps to build credibility and allows the leader to take part in creating materials and strategies, and personal power helps to form the personal relationships essential for collaborative decision making. The leader balances a top-down approach with a bottom-up approach so that the best of both approaches work together over the many years of work to create and implement performance-based learning and assessment.

FOCUS ON STUDENT PERFORMANCE IS ESSENTIAL

Student performance is the essential focus of educators. Not only must educators study data from assessment lists and other sources, but they must make sure that clear targets for student performance have been set. Leaders must keep the attention of administrators and teachers on the five questions shown in the central part of Figure 22. We must answer Questions 1 and 2 before it is reasonable to even ask Questions 3, 4, and 5. Educators too often find themselves working on curriculum and instructional materials and engaging in staff development before they have clearly decided what students should know and how they should use their content knowledge, process skills, and work habits.

Figure 22 shows an interactive cycle that is, in reality, much more complex than the graphic shows. Leaders must continually challenge themselves to be more and more explicit and articulate in working with their fellow educators to answer all five questions. Following is a restatement of those questions in terms of performance-based learning and assessment:

Question 1: What content, process skills, and work habits are the priorities?

- What are performance tasks like that would require students to use this content and these process skills and work habits in an authentic way?

Question 2: What would excellent performance be like when students engaged in these performance tasks?

- What are the assessment tools and the models of excellence we will use to define quality work?

Question 3: What performance tasks shall we use for learning and assessment?

Question 4: When students engaged in these performance tasks, what was the actual quality of their work?

Question 5: What will we do to improve student performance?

- How will we adapt curriculum, instruction, allocation of time and other resources, and assessment to improve student performance?

- What professional development is needed?

- What leadership needs to be expressed?

We need to address Questions 1–4 so that the work to answer Question 5 is "on target." Maintaining a focus on all five of these questions is a "habit of mind" to be nurtured in educators.

HORIZONTAL AND VERTICAL NETWORKING WITHIN AND AMONG SCHOOLS

Continuity and communication are essential if a new program is to move through the school and school district. One of the important roles for leaders is to form and facilitate network meetings within and among schools, especially for the scouts and pioneers, for the purpose of discussing the dynamics of the new program. Educators must celebrate and share successes; and networking educators find that they can solve problems collaboratively. A feeling of "team ownership" is essential for educators to continue their hard work to create and implement change. The network meetings should include "horizon-

FIGURE 22. School Improvement Based on Improving Student Performance

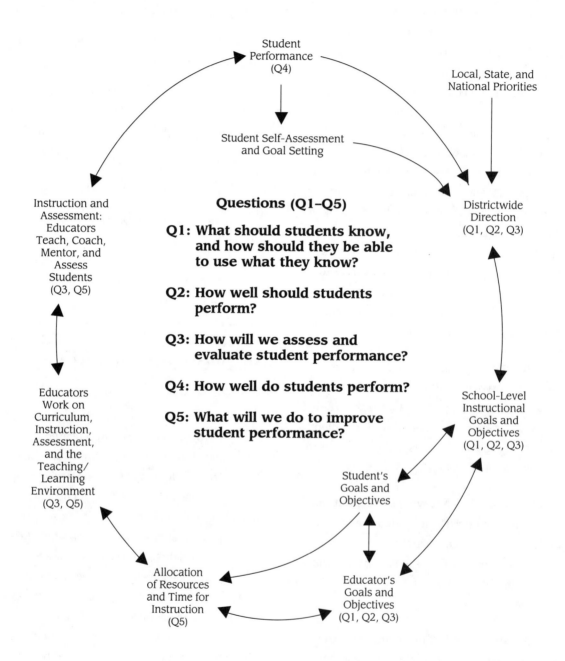

Student Performance (Q4)

Local, State, and National Priorities

Student Self-Assessment and Goal Setting

Instruction and Assessment: Educators Teach, Coach, Mentor, and Assess Students (Q3, Q5)

Districtwide Direction (Q1, Q2, Q3)

Questions (Q1–Q5)

Q1: What should students know, and how should they be able to use what they know?

Q2: How well should students perform?

Q3: How will we assess and evaluate student performance?

Q4: How well do students perform?

Q5: What will we do to improve student performance?

Educators Work on Curriculum, Instruction, Assessment, and the Teaching/ Learning Environment (Q3, Q5)

School-Level Instructional Goals and Objectives (Q1, Q2, Q3)

Student's Goals and Objectives

Allocation of Resources and Time for Instruction (Q5)

Educator's Goals and Objectives (Q1, Q2, Q3)

tal" interactions of educators at the same grade level, and "vertical" interactions of educators at different grade levels. Communication and coordination within and between grade levels is essential for the implementation of performance-based learning and assessment in the school and school district. The network meetings help the scouts and pioneers to feel that they are capable of moving ahead with their work, that they are needed by others, and that the work they are doing is important.

Settlers also benefit greatly from networking with educators from their own school and other schools. When the settlers are at the mechanical use level or beyond, network meetings among teachers at that grade level or in that discipline help to pull them out of isolation and into the teamwork of implementing the change. Knowing that they will be expected to share some successes with performance-based learning and assessment motivates them to do the work in the classroom to be ready for the network meeting. Knowing that problems are permissible and even expected makes the environment safe for addressing barriers and finding ways to overcome them. Communication and continuity are enhanced by the networking of all educators.

A COMPASS KEEPS THE CHANGE PROCESS "ON COURSE"

Educators must make thousands of small decisions along the way to long-term change. Especially in the beginning when the "vision" is not too clear, the leaders and their collaborators may worry that their work to construct performance-based learning and assessment in their own school or school district may run "off course." A compass is needed to keep all those day-to-day decisions working in a common direction to accomplish the goal of improving student performance. The educators in the Region 15 Public Schools constructed their own statement of the principles of cognitive learning theory shown in Figure 23. Cognitive learning theory describes the student as a "constructor of meaning," rather than a sponge to "soak up information." Curriculum, instruction, and assessment that follow the principles of cognitive learning theory value both the process and products of this "constructive" act of learning. Figure 24 shows another compass to guide their work: the list of essential characteristics of performance-based learning and assessment. This brief overview of the Region 15 model can help administrators and teachers keep the change process on track.

As the administrators and teachers in Region 15 worked for many years to invent and implement their version of performance-based learning and assessment, these two compasses helped keep each "next" level of the innovation on track so that each element of the overall change built a "whole that is greater than the sum of its parts." Figure 25 shows the "waves of change" that have rippled through all of the Region 15 public schools. Each "wave" is still active in Region 15. The culture here is that change is long term, and efforts to implement it are sustained. The first program identified with this long-term effort was process writing, which began in 1978. Each subsequent change has been influenced by each wave before it and, in turn, influ-

FIGURE 23. Cognitive Learning Theory: A Compass for Performance-Based Learning and Assessment

1. Learning is the active process of using content, process skills, and work habits to build new knowledge.

2. Meaningful learning connects what the learner already knows to the new information and skills.

3. Themes, essential questions, and big ideas serve as the "wooly velcro" on which the specific information—"hooky velcro"—stick.

4. Problem solving within and among many disciplines, helps new learning "stick."

5. Successful learners consciously select from a repertoire of learning strategies, depending on the situation.

6. Hard work and persistence are two of the most important attributes of successful learning.

7. Motivation and the learner's perception of his or her "capability" influence learning.

8. Learners differ greatly in learning styles, attention spans, memory, developmental paces, and intelligences.

9. Learners do better when they know the goal, see models, and know how their performance compares to the standards of excellence.

10. Learning benefits from collaboration with others. Group work and individual responsibility can be complementary.

11. Honest and perceptive self-assessment improves learning.

12. Both holistic and analytical evaluation serve to provide information needed to improve student performance.

ences each element of the change that comes after it. Continual feedback occurs among these waves, and an innovation such as interdisciplinary instruction, which was evident in 1980, has been "reconstructed" by all the other changes that came after it. Science and the Arts are the latest two waves, and each is benefiting from 18 years of work that preceded them. Process writing and cooperative learning are improved because of the innovations in social studies and performance-based learning and assessment. An essential element in Region 15 is that important initiatives are kept alive and integrated in ways that improve student performance.

FIGURE 24. Essential Characteristics of the Region 15 Model of Performance-Based Learning and Assessment, "How Are We Doing?"

1. Assessment task are opportunities for both learning and assessment.

2. Assessment tasks are embedded within curriculum rather than added on at the end.

3. Assessment tasks connect content, process skills, and work habits.

4. Assessment tools are analytical (lists) rather than holistic (rubrics).

5. Assessment tools allow student self-assessment (a must).

6. Assessment tools allow for assessment and grading.

7. Process elements in lists (such as for nonfiction writing) are derived from a common set of dimensions for that process.

8. Specific content expectations must be evident in the tasks and assessment lists for all but the most mature learners.

9. Learners are "weaned away" from lists as they mature. One step in this process is to have students make their own lists.

10. Lists provide a communication link among teachers, with students, and with parents.

11. Lists provide students and teachers with the details they need to plan for improvements.

12. Models must be shown to the learner. Models of excellent work and models with flaws are both useful.

13. Performance assessment follows the principles of cognitive learning theory (see Figure 23).

14. Portfolios are a strategy to focus the learner on the big picture. Portfolios should be implemented after a foundation of performance-based learning and assessment is in place.

FIGURE 25. Waves of Change in the Region 15 Public Schools

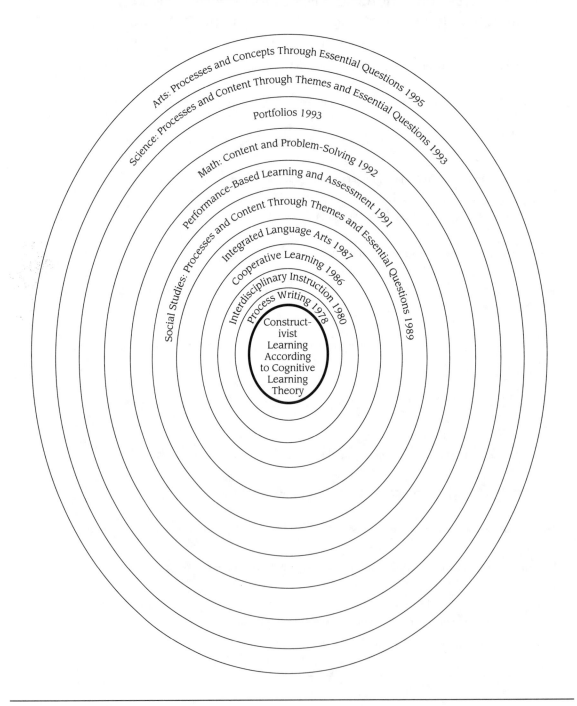

Arts: Processes and Concepts Through Essential Questions 1995

Science: Processes and Content Through Themes and Essential Questions 1993

Portfolios 1993

Math: Content and Problem-Solving 1992

Performance-Based Learning and Assessment 1991

Social Studies: Processes and Content Through Themes and Essential Questions 1989

Integrated Language Arts 1987

Cooperative Learning 1986

Interdisciplinary Instruction 1980

Process Writing 1978

Constructivist Learning According to Cognitive Learning Theory

SYMBOLS COMMUNICATE THE VISION FOR YOUR VERSION OF PERFORMANCE-BASED LEARNING AND ASSESSMENT

A clear statement of vision is an important strategy in implementing change. Elements of the vision will come from leaders and those whom they are leading. It is the leader's responsibility to state and communicate that collaborative vision so that it acts like a beacon drawing all participants to it. Direct statement, actions, models, and graphics all communicate the vision. The graphics and models in this book have been used to communicate the vision to all educators in Region 15. Figure 26 presents the "big picture" of how all the pieces fit into the whole of performance-based learning and assessment in Region 15.

Figure 26 shows how all the pieces come together to create the culture of performance-based learning and assessment in Region 15. Curriculum is defined. Performance tasks and basic instruction are balanced and feed into a system that makes instruction and assessment a continuous cycle. The quality of student performance is assessed and evaluated with the help of assessment lists, rubrics, and models of excellence. Student self-assessment, self-evaluation, and self-regulation (goal setting) are at the heart of what education is all about. Information from learning and assessment is communicated clearly to various audiences. All the "pieces" fit into a "whole that is greater that the sum of its parts." When a visitor walks into a Region 15

classroom, observes students and teachers, and asks, "Is this the teaching day or the assessment day?" the answer is, "ABSOLUTELY!"

DISTRICTWIDE FRAMEWORKS FOR PERFORMANCE-BASED LEARNING AND ASSESSMENT: BALANCING CENTRALIZED AND DECENTRALIZED DECISION MAKING

Innovation that systematically builds toward a common vision requires a balance of district-level structure and classroom-level creativity and implementation. Curriculum frameworks and common structures for performance tasks and assessment lists have provided the foundation for this balance in Region 15. Exhibit 134 (at the end of this chapter) shows the themes for science and social studies that teachers and administrators collaboratively selected to serve as a curriculum framework for grades 1–12. These themes not only provide a valid framework for the content of coursework, but they also give students lenses through which they can view the world for the rest of their lives. Some of the themes also act as bridges into other disciplines and thus promote an "interdisciplinary" way of learning. Science Theme 4, which includes the statement "Humans use science to invent technologies to meet their wants and needs; and for every change in technology there are 'gains' and 'losses,'" is such a bridge into social studies. Social Studies Theme 2, which includes the statement "The environment influences the lives of

FIGURE 26. Performance-Based Learning and Assessment: Pomperaug Regional School District 15

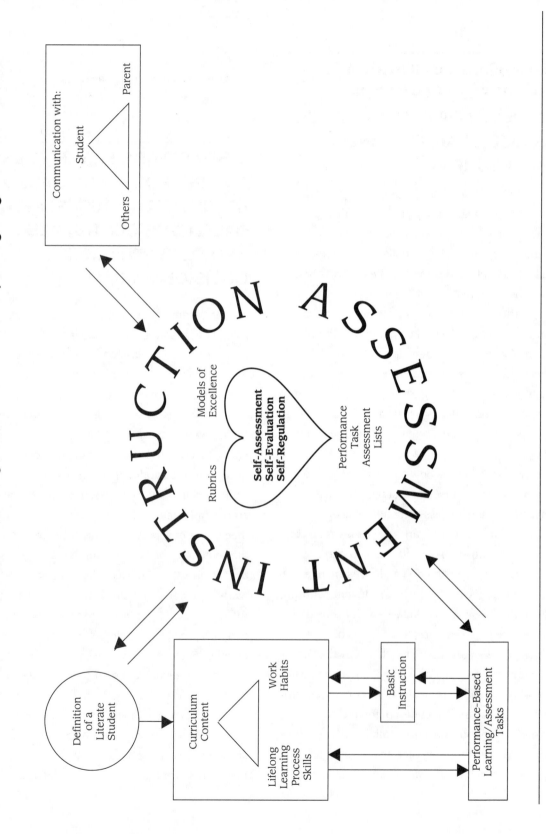

people (and cultures); and the people influence their environment," is such a bridge into science. Themes provide a districtwide framework for classroom creativity.

Themes organize the "content" of the disciplines they serve. Chapter 3 contains an example of how two themes (one from science and one from social studies) were used as the basis for essential questions, focus questions for topics, and performance tasks. Exhibit 135 provides another example of that flow. American history is the topic of social studies for grades 7 and 8 in Region 15. Exhibit 135 shows the five essential questions that provide the foundation for the information learned about American history during those two years. Classroom instruction is a balance of basic instruction and performance tasks. Teacher-directed work, cooperative group tasks, and individual study are mixed in the instruction planned by the teacher teams at each of these grade levels.

Although the topics and essential questions are the same for all classes at these grade levels, instruction varies greatly. All teachers work toward the same district-level goals that they helped set, but they have much professional freedom in the classroom. The extensive menu of performance tasks, created over the years, offers these teachers many options because regular performance-based learning and assessment tasks may be shaped by the classroom teachers. What remains constant among all teachers at a grade level is the anchor performance tasks they have agreed to do. Anchor tasks, as described in Chapter 3, are performance tasks that are the most engaging to students and the most well connected to the content, process skills, and

work habits of the curriculum. Anchor tasks have been selected out of the menu of performance tasks by teachers at those grade levels to be the "common experiences" of all students at those grade levels. The anchor tasks for 7th and 8th grade social studies are listed in Exhibit 135 and represent only some of the performance tasks in which students at those grade levels engage. The mix of regular performance tasks and anchor tasks provides a districtwide framework for classroom creativity.

For each anchor task, there is an assessment list for the final product. This assessment list connects the student work to the content of the essential question and its corresponding theme, the process skills such as persuasive writing, and work habits such as organization and presentation. There may also be assessment lists for intermediate products and processes, such as research notes, graphic organizers, group work, and first drafts. The use of assessment lists for intermediate and final products provides continuity for students as they move from teacher to teacher and from grade to grade.

Besides curriculum themes and essential questions and anchor tasks, the structure of the performance tasks and assessment tools provides a district-level foundation for classroom work. Exhibits 136–138 are the common forms used throughout Region 15 for the creation of performance tasks and assessment tools.

Exhibit 136 is the outline for the dozens of performance tasks provided in this book. Hundreds of additional performance tasks have been created by teachers in Region 15 using this outline. Exhibit 137 is an outline of a teacher's guide that accompanies performance tasks. These guides have not been included in this book. Exhibit 138 is an assessment list used to structure the work of both making and assessing classroom materials for performance-based learning and assessment. This assessment list establishes the framework, but allows much creativity on the part of teachers.

AVOID THE "DE-CAPACITATORS" OF CHANGE

Over the years, through direct experience and through observing many other schools and districts work on performance assessment, we

FIGURE 27. De-Capacitators of Change

1. No Clear Targets for Improving Student Performance

2. Too Many "Side Trips" Divert Energy from Improving Student Performance

3. Administrators Bounce from One New Idea to Another and Teachers "Hold Their Breath" Waiting for This New Idea to Pass

4. High Stakes Too Fast

5. Too Fast, Too Fast

6. Change Seen as Bureaucratic

7. Administrator Seen as Not Caring and/or Unskilled Regarding the "New Program"

8. Wrong Paradigm: Teacher as Provider, Student as Receiver

9. Changes Seen as Discrete Events Rather Than Connected to an Over-All Structure (Model, Paradigm, Vision, or Strategic Plan)

10. Lost the "Meat": Process Overshadows Content In Performance Tasks

11. "Add to" Rather Than "Reshape" Mentality

12. "Pulled In Many Directions" Rather Than "Pulling Together"

13. Too Little or Too Much Structure (Regulations)

14. The Wrong Teachers and Administrators Asked (Pushed) to Begin the Change. Did Not Follow the Sequence of Scouts, Pioneers, and Settlers

15. Professional Development Depends on "Outside" Help for Too Long

16. Professional Development Not Site-Based and Not Embedded in the Jobs of All

17. Risk Not Valued and Risk-Takers Not Protected

18. Resources, Including Time, Insufficient to Support Change

19. Poor Conflict Resolution Skills Among Adults

20. Mistakes Made In Communication of the Changes to Parents and Other Members of the Community

have identified a set of problems to avoid, called "De-Capacitators." De-capacitation means that the "human energy" is drawn out of the initiative. This list provides a *warning of what not to do*. It takes many years and hard work to create and implement a change. It takes a relatively little "mistake" to destroy all those efforts. Once "drained of its energy," an initiative is difficult to get started again. Figure 27 lists these de-capacitators.

NURTURE POSITIVE CONDITIONS AND CLIMATES FOR A SAFE, HEALTHY, MUTUALLY RESPECTFUL, AND SUPPORTIVE COMMUNITY OF LEARNERS

Creating and implementing a sequence of interacting changes over a period of many years to establish performance-based learning and assessment in the culture of the Region 15 school system has been greatly facilitated by an environment of positive conditions and a climate for a safe, healthy, mutually respectful, and supportive community of learners. Figure 28 shows the Cycle of Learning and its three gears of competencies within a frame.

The work done to create performance-based learning and assessment is the authentic Cycle of Learning work done by Region 15 educators. Their discipline-based competencies, their interpersonal skills, and their intrapersonal skills are all important to this work. But all this work takes place in an "environment" created by other elements of the education community, such as the

Board of Education, the parents, and other members of the community. This frame can either project a supportive influence, or it can be hostile and exude a grit that clogs the gears and impedes the work that is necessary to improve student performance. The "frame" for the work of administrators and teachers in Region 15 has been positive, thanks to the work of the Superintendent and Board of Education. Parent support has been increasingly strong. The accomplishments of the Region 15 educators to improve student performance have, in term, influenced the "frame" to continue and magnify its support.

Together, all stakeholders in education in Region 15 are working together to improve the performance of our students. We are proud of our accomplishments. We have a long way to go, and the journey is exciting.

LARGER IMPACT OF PERFORMANCE-BASED LEARNING

Performance-based learning has far-reaching effects on schools and districts that commit themselves to performance learning as an essential instructional and assessment strategy. The following represents an indicative, although not exhaustive, summary of these effects:

1. Increased expectations for student performance and the development of processes and tools to assist students in accomplishing high-quality work.

2. A dynamic and growing culture for viewing student work through the strategies of performance assessment.

FIGURE 28. A Supportive Environment for the Cycle of Learning: Positive Conditions and Climate for a Safe, Healthy, Mutually Respectful, and Supportive Community of Learners

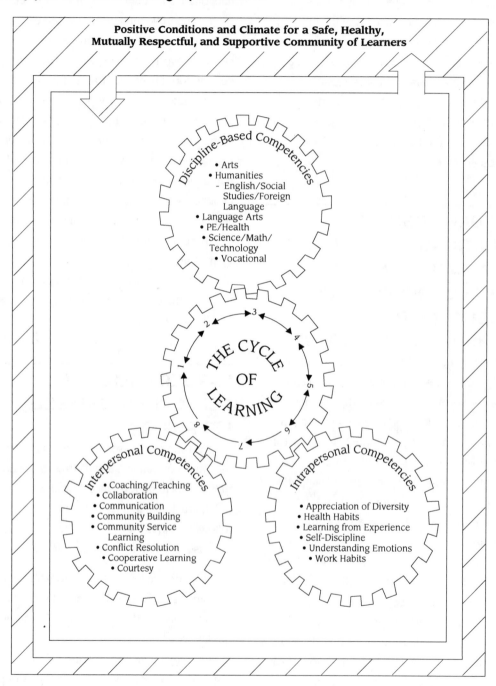

3. A more common vision and focus for curriculum, instruction, and assessment.

4. Establishment of a common conceptual framework and professional vocabulary for school and district staff.

5. Focused professional development activities related to performance assessment.

6. Stronger communication and collaboration among teachers. Performance assessment brings together staff members throughout the school and across the district, including those who are members of different formal or informal organizational structures, such as teams.

7. Identification of and commitment to elements of quality within a performance or product. Performance learning asks teachers to decide what quality looks like in student work and to communicate this to the student early in the task or assignment. As rubrics or assessment lists for products and performance are shared and shaped through collegial communication, the elements of quality become better standardized for the school and school district.

8. More direct student instruction in self-assessment, an activity emerging as a necessary consequence of having students use assessment tools to review and revise their work before submission.

9. Thoughtful collection of quality "benchmarks" or "models of excellence" that communicate both elements of quality and level of sophistication in a product or performance. Many times, these model are gathered from previous student work, "real life" resources (such as magazines, journals, and newspaper), or teacher-generated samples.

10. The ability to communicate student performance to parents in ways that are more specific and meaningful, and to include parents in a collaborative dialogue about setting learning goals for their children.

Schools and school districts embarking on their journey toward performance assessment will experience significant changes in the way they do business. Both the process and long-term impact of this journey engage us in discussions that continually seek to improve student performance and the quality of instruction in our schools.

Exhibit 134. Region 15 Science, Social Studies, and Geography Themes for Grades 1 Through 12

Science (Sci.)

All Phenomena Will Be Viewed Through a Systems Framework.

A System Can Be Studied Through One or More of the Following Themes:

I.   Learning about a system through studying its attributes of size, scale, diversity, distribution, and normality.

II. Learning about a system through studying about the relationship between its function and structure.

III. Learning about a system through studying the patterns of changes of its matter and energy.

IV. Learning about the special system of society, science, and technology.

V.   Learning about systems through experimenting, modeling, and inventing.

Social Studies (SS)

Studying Peoples and Cultures Through:

I.   Learning about how civilization developed through innovation and cultural diffusion.

II. Learning about how humans interact with their environment.

III. Learning about how a people define their values, beliefs, political ideas, and institutions.

IV. Learning about the patterns of social and political interaction.

V.   Learning about the rules of conflict and cooperation.

VI. Learning about history through comparing major events in history.

Geography (G)

Studying Places and People Through:

I.   Location: Use of maps to locate places, regions, and paths of movement.

II. Place: Physical and cultural characteristics of a location.

III. Interaction: Patterns of interaction between humans and their environment.

IV. Movement: Patterns of movement of humans and their products from place to place.

V.   Region: How areas are defined as "regions" by common characteristics and how "regions" are continuously "redefined."

Exhibit 135. Region 15 Social Studies
Connections Among Themes, Topics, Essential Questions, and
Performance Anchor Tasks for Grades 7 and 8

Topic: American History

Grade 7: Native Americans and the Land, Exploration, Colonization, Revolution, Framing the American Government, National Expansion, Civil War and Reconstruction

Grade 8: Snapshot of America at our 100th Birthday, Settlement of the West, Expansion of Industry, Immigration, Conflict and Reform, Imperialism, Between the Two Wars, World War II, America 1945–1960, Protest and Changes 1961–1975, 1975–Present

Essential Questions for Grades 7 and 8:

1. What is an American? (SS, I)
2. How have the people of the United States interacted with their environment and technology? (Sci., IV, and SS, II)
3. What values, beliefs, political ideas, and institutions have the people of the United States developed? (SS, III and IV)
4. How have conflict, cooperation, and compromise influenced the way of life of the diverse groups and individuals who make up the United States? (SS, V and IV)
5. How have past events, inventions, innovations, ideas, and individuals influenced my life and my world? (SS, VI)

Performance Anchor Tasks for Grade 7

- **Book on Native Americans for Third Graders** (geography influences people's lives, EQ 2)
- **Comparison Chart: Life in the Colonies** (geography influences people's lives, EQ 2)
- **Exploration News Article** (exploration is a part of change, EQ 2, EQ 5)
- **Civil War Diary** (a person's attitudes, values, and beliefs shape their live, conflict influences people, EQ 3, EQ 4)
- **Manifest Destiny Diary** (interaction with environment, conflict and cooperation, values and beliefs, EQ 2, EQ 3)
- **Pilgrim's Diary** (values and beliefs, conflicts causing immigration, adaptation to environment, EQ 2, EQ 4)
- **Native American Class Museum** (What is an American; interaction with environment and technology; values, beliefs, political ideas and institutions, EQ 1, EQ 2, EQ 3)
- **A Revolutionary War Newspaper** (values, beliefs, political ideas, and institutions, EQ 3)
- **Issue Controversy** (issue varies, EQ to be selected)
- **Student Developed Assignments For Other Students** (literal understanding level assignment/test/quiz, EQ to be selected)

Key: SS = Social Studies Theme Reference; Sci = Science Theme Reference; EQ = Essential Question Reference.

(Exhibit continues on the following page.)

Exhibit 135 (continued)

Performance Anchor Tasks for Grade 8

- **V-Mail During WOW (Simulated V-Mail)** (man, science, and technology, EQ 2)
- **Those Crazy, Mixed-Up Kids (Interview and Venn Diagram)** (values, beliefs, ideas, EQ 3)
- **The Indomitable Theodore Roosevelt (Portfolio, scrapbook)** (past events, inventions, innovations, ideas, and individuals influence the culture, EQ 5)
- **Perfectly Suited (Drawing)** (values and custom interact, EQ 3, EQ 4)
- **Go West, Young Man (Speech)** (past events, inventions, innovations, ideas, and individuals influence the culture, EQ 5)
- **Issue Controversy** (the specific issue will be selected by the teacher and students, EQ to be selected)
- **Museum Display** (contributions of immigrants to America, EQ 1, EQ 5)
- **Research Report** (the particular topic will be selected by the teacher and students, EQ to be selected)
- **Oral Presentation (What Is an American?** EQ 1)
- **Student-Developed Assignments for Other Students** (literal understanding level assignment/test/quiz, EQ to be selected)

Key: SS = Social Studies Theme Reference; Sci = Science Theme Reference; EQ = Essential Question Reference.

Exhibit 136. Framework for Making a Performance Task (What the Student Sees)

Task Title

Background: (setting the stage and "grabbing" the student's attention)

Task: (specifying the format for the products and/or performances)

Audience: (specifying the audience for those products and/or performances)

Purpose: (explaining the reason that this task is being done for this audience)

Procedure: (description of the steps are appropriate to the "developmental maturity" of the students)

Exhibit 137. Framework for Making a Performance Task: Teacher's Guide

Task Title: _____

Grade Level: _____ Subject(s): _____

Author(s):_____

Curriculum Connections

Content Objectives:

Process Skills Objectives:

Work Habit Objectives:

Managing the Performance Task

Materials Needed:

Advance Preparation:

Allocation of Time:
   School Time:

   Notes on Use of Homework Time:

Safety Precautions:

Notes on Managing the Performance Task and Communicating with Parents:

Exhibit 138. Performance Assessment List for Creating Performance Tasks and Assessment Lists

Scoring Key: S = Superb E = Excellent W = Needs Work

	ASSESSMENT	
Element	*Self*	*Other*
The Performance Task		
1. The content relevant to the task is of high priority in your curriculum.	_____	_____
2. The process skills relevant to the task are of high priority in your curriculum.	_____	_____
3. The work habits relevant to the task are of high priority in your curriculum.	_____	_____
4. The task is engaging (nifty) to the students.	_____	_____
5. The structure provided in the task is appropriate to the "performance maturity" of the students.	_____	_____
6. The task, through the selection of audience and final product or performance, is either actually or virtually authentic.	_____	_____
7. The task is safe.	_____	_____
8. The task is organized to efficiently use the time available.	_____	_____
9. The graphic layout or format of the task is attractive and well organized.	_____	_____
10. Mechanics of English are correct.	_____	_____
The Performance Task Assessment List		
11. The list provides for both self-assessment and teacher's assessment.	_____	_____
12. Elements connected to content are clearly present.	_____	_____
13. The degree to which content called for is explicit is appropriate to the "performance maturity" of the students.	_____	_____
14. Elements connected to process skills are clearly present.	_____	_____
15. Process skill elements are well connected to the appropriate dimensions of student work.	_____	_____
16. Process skill elements specify the thinking skill required.	_____	_____
17. Elements connected to work habits are clearly present.	_____	_____
18. The degree to which process skills and work habits are "spelled out" is appropriate to the "performance maturity" of the students.	_____	_____
19. The list is graphically well organized.	_____	_____
20. Mechanics of English are correct.	_____	_____
Models of Student Work		
21. Models of student work from similar tasks are provided to identify the standards of excellence.	_____	_____

LOOKING AT STUDENT PERFORMANCE FROM MANY POINTS OF VIEW: EVIDENCE FOR THE IMPACT OF PERFORMANCE-BASED LEARNING AND ASSESSMENT

14

Student literacy has many facets. All sorts of assessment strategies are needed to study the "whole picture" of how the learner is growing. Performance-based learning and assessment are strategies to help educators, students, and parents improve student performance. As a school or school district works to implement its own version of performance-based learning and assessment, it can continue to use other measures, such as the Scholastic Achievement Test (SAT) (formerly called the Scholastic Aptitude Test), Advanced Placement (AP) tests, and state-level and locally generated tests and assessments. The public wants to see that student performance, as measured by all these instruments, is improving.

This chapter presents data from various sources about student performance in Connecticut's Region 15, which serves the towns of Middlebury and Southbury. These performance data demonstrate the influence of a district-wide implementation of performance-based learning and assessment on the overall "academic environment" for students in the Region. A timeline of significant events that have been a part of creating and implementing performance-based learning and assessment has been included to show connections between those events and changes in the quality of student performance.

The following data sources provide information about student performance in Region 15:

1. Timeline of events important to the creation and implementation of performance-based learning and assessment in Region 15

2. Scholastic Achievement Test (SAT)

3. Advanced Placement Tests (AP)

4. Connecticut Academic Performance Test (CAPT), state-mandated tests for all high school sophomores

5. Connecticut Mastery Test (CMT), state-mandated tests for grades four, six, and eight

6. Survey of graduates of Pomperaug High School (Region 15's only high school)

7. Survey of townspeople as to their opinion of the quality of education in Region 15

TIMELINE FOR CREATING AND IMPLEMENTING PERFORMANCE-BASED LEARNING AND ASSESSMENT IN REGION 15

The timeline in Figure 29 shows the important events in the process of creating and implementing performance-based learning and assessment from kindergarten through grade 12 and across all disciplines in the Region 15 Public Schools serving the towns of Middlebury and Southbury, Connecticut. This long-term systemic change has resulted in improved student performance.

FIGURE 29. Creating and Implementing Performance-Based Learning and Assessment in Region 15

1987	1988	1989	1990	1991	1992	1993	1994	1995	1996

National Standardized Test, Grades 3, 5, and 7

SAT

AP Tests

CMT, Grades 4, 6, and 8

CAPT, Grade 10

Process Writing

Cooperative Learning, Including Issue Controversies in Social Studies

Integrated Language Arts

Performance-Based Learning Strategies Across the Disciplines and Grade Levels

Writing Portfolio for All Students

Social Studies, Themes, and Essential Questions

Math, Content and Problem Solving

Science, Content and Process

Computer Technology to Support Learning

Note: Dotted lines indicate small-scale pilot projects.

MEASURES OF STUDENT PERFORMANCE

Region 15 assesses student performance in many ways, including spelling tests, essay questions, integrated tasks requiring the application of content and process skills from several disciplines, and writing portfolios for all students. Whereas these "internal" measures of student performance are telling us that student performance is improving, "external" measures of student performance are also important to parents and educators because they give an "unbiased" view of student performance in Region 15. The most important external measures are shown on the timeline.

For many years, Region 15 had used one national standardized test, the Iowa Test of Basic Skills (ITBS), in grades three, five, and seven. In 1994, the ITBS was replaced by the Metropolitan Achievement Test (MAT). After one year, Region 15 stopped using the MAT, because the data on student performance provided by the Connecticut Mastery Test (CMT) were more useful in making decisions to improve performance.

Two other national standardized tests provide important scores. First, students are encouraged to take the SAT. In 1981, about 65 percent of the students took this test. By 1994–95, 88 percent were taking it. The SAT is seen by the public as one valid measure of student performance. Second, in Region 15, AP tests are given in nine subjects. Performance on the AP exams provides another source of valid and unbiased data on student performance.

The information provided by the Connecticut Mastery Test (CMT) on individual students and on overall performance of each school and the region provides a valid and unbiased data of student performance that teachers could use to improve student performance. The CMT is administered to students in grades four, six, and eight and is scored by the Psychological Corporation. An "off-year" version of the CMT for students in grades three, five, and seven is available to be used and scored by the individual school.

In 1994, the region began administering the Connecticut Academic Performance Test (CAPT), an excellent performance assessment experience for all grade 10 students. The content and process frameworks of the CAPT in literature, math, science, and an integrated task focus attention on the most important elements of student performance. Rubric scores are available for each student on each section of the CAPT. Although these data help "take the temperature" of student performance in Region 15, the test does not provide the specific information needed to make decisions to improve student performance.

Later sections of this chapter present information on the performance of Region 15 students on these standardized tests. First, it's important to focus on our performance-based strategies, because these had a strong effect on students' scores on the standardized exams.

INITIATIVES IN CREATING AND IMPLEMENTING STRATEGIES OF PERFORMANCE-BASED LEARNING AND ASSESSMENT THROUGHOUT REGION 15

The timeline in Figure 29 shows the gradual integration of various strategies that helped provide concrete indicators of student progress, from the long-term emphasis on process writing to the more recent use of computer technology:

- *Process writing* provided Region 15 teachers with their original experience in using performance tasks, assessment tools such as rubrics and analytical lists, and benchmarks to improve student performance.

- Long-term, sustained professional development saw *cooperative learning* implemented throughout Region 15. The social studies department adopted a cooperative learning strategy, developed by David and Roger Johnson, called "issue controversy" (also called "creative controversy"), as a core type of performance embedded in instruction. The experiences students have had with issue controversy—along with their skills in reading and writing gained through process writing, integrated language arts, and self-assessment—are responsible for their exceptional performance on the integrated task on the CAPT.

- *Integrating the language arts* led to performance tasks that connected reading comprehension and writing within the content areas, including literature, social studies, science, and math. The assessment tools used in process writing were adapted to fit performance tasks that integrated the language arts. A debate occurred as to whether holistic rubrics or analytical assessment lists were most functional in the classroom. Reading comprehension and writing performances are exceptionally strong in Region 15, as measured by the CAPT and CMT.

- *Performance-based learning and assessment* strategies included the invention of the performance-task assessment lists presented in this book. As a result of our debates over rubrics, we decided that rubrics were not "user-friendly" enough, and we found the analytical assessment lists much more useful as teaching and learning tools. We developed strategies to include *self-assessment* as the goal of using assessment lists, to enable students to be more active in the learning process. Self-assessment provided such a boost to student performance that self-assessment spread quickly throughout the grades and disciplines.

- Teachers and administrators experimented with *writing portfolios* for three years before they were made a required part of performance learning and assessment in Region 15 in 1994. The writing portfolios were built on a foundation of analytical assessment of the many forms of writing being used in language arts and the content areas. Writing portfolios continued to develop the students' skills of self-assessment, self-evaluation, and self-regulation (goal setting).

- Six years of work have gone into organizing the entire *social studies* curriculum around *themes, big ideas,* and *essential questions.* All strategies we learned through process writing, cooperative learning, integrated language arts, and performance-based learning and assessment have merged in a program that balances "Do you know it?" and "Can you use it?" Assessment includes tests, quizzes, and performance-based projects from grades 1 through 12. Student performance is strong.

- *Science* and *math* are following the patterns established by social studies. It will take several more years before the performance-based learning and assessment will be fully developed in these two curriculum areas. Improvements in student performance are already being seen.

• The application of *computer technology* has developed slowly, primarily because of the lack of funds for the acquisition of hardware and the wiring to support networking. In the past two years, significant progress has been made; and computer technology is more commonly used by students for their work on performance projects.

• Strategies of performance-based learning and assessment are being applied with success to work on the *visual and performance arts*. These strategies have recently been developed in Region 15 (not shown on Figure 29).

STUDENT PERFORMANCE IN REGION 15

Student performance indicators for Region 15 include percentages and scores of students taking the SAT, AP exams, and other tests. Other indicators are results of student and community surveys. Let's look first at Region 15 SAT scores.

SCHOLASTIC ACHIEVEMENT TEST (SAT)

All students can improve their performance. In Region 15, all students are encouraged to improve by taking challenging courses. Approximately 80 percent of the graduates of Pomperaug High School continue their education immediately after graduation. All students are encouraged to take the SAT.

Figures 30 and 31 show the performance of Region 15 students on the verbal and mathematics sections of the SAT. In 1981–82, approximately 65 percent of the students at Pomperaug High School in Region 15 took the SAT test. Their scores were well below the state and national averages. By 1994–95, approximately 88 percent of the students took the test, and their

FIGURE 30. SAT Scores on the Math Component

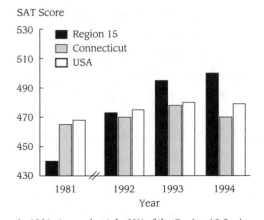

In 1981, Approximately 65% of the Region 15 Seniors Took the SAT
In 1994, Approximately 88% of the Region 15 Seniors Took the SAT

FIGURE 31. SAT Scores on the Verbal Component

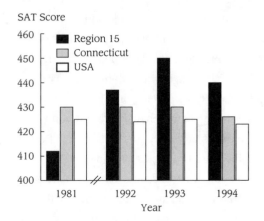

In 1981, Approximately 65% of the Region 15 Seniors Took the SAT
In 1994, Approximately 88% of the Region 15 Seniors Took the SAT

scores had improved dramatically to be well above the state and national averages. In 1994–95, the girls' average math score exceeded the boys' score for the first time. Our task is to continue to improve the performance of all students.

Note: We offer *no special SAT preparation courses* as part of the curriculum at Pomperaug High School in Region 15. Also note that Region 15 has few minority students, so no breakdowns for ethnic or racial groups are available.

ADVANCED PLACEMENT COURSES (AP)

Many high school juniors and seniors take AP courses, which are equivalent to freshman college courses. Each course follows the national guidelines established by the College Board. A national test, including multiple-choice and written responses, is given for each course. Scores range from a low of 1 to a high of 5. Scores of 3 or better are considered excellent and allow students various options of credit or academic placement in many colleges and universities in the United States.

In Region 15, students are encouraged to challenge themselves by taking AP courses. Although they are encouraged to take the AP test, they are not required to do so. Pomperaug High School in Region 15 offers AP courses in U.S. History, European History, English Literature, English Composition, Biology, Physics, Chemistry, Calculus, Computer Science, Studio Drawing, French, and Spanish. Figure 32 shows the number of AP tests taken and the percentage of test scores of 3 or better over the years 1989 through 1994. Not only have many more tests been taken, but students' performance on these tests has improved dramatically over the past five years.

FIGURE 32. The Percentage of AP Scores Over Scores of 3, 4, or 5

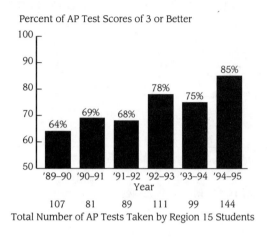

Total Number of AP Tests Taken by Region 15 Students

SURVEY OF GRADUATING SENIORS

In 1994, a survey was conducted of the graduating classes of 1989, 1991, and 1993 of Pomperaug High School in Region 15, Connecticut. Approximately 41 percent of the graduates in each of the three classes responded to the survey. Figure 33 shows the perception of these graduates of their preparation at Pomperaug High School.

The more recent graduates feel better prepared and more competitive. Their perceptions correspond to the level of performance-based learning and assessment they encountered in Region 15.

Figure 34 shows the graduates' responses to a question about the quality of learning skills they developed in high school. On a scale of 1 to 5, the 1993 graduates ranked six learning skills as exceptionally or very strong (see scores in boldface), as opposed to only two learning skills for the class of 1989. The highest ratings, for

---

FIGURE 33. The Opinion of Region 15 Graduates as to Their Academic Preparation to Be a College Freshman, as Compared to Their Fellow Students at That Institution of Higher Education

| | | *Percent Continuing* | *QUALITY OF PREPARATION* | | |
Graduating Class	*Class Size*	*Their Education*	*Better Prepared*	*About the Same*	*Not as Well*
Class of 1989	159	75%	**42.9%**	42.9%	14.3%
Class of 1991	135	84%	**34.0%**	58.0%	7.5%
Class of 1993	158	82%	**50.0%**	44.6%	5.4%

---

both 1991 and 1993 classes, were for writing, reading, mathematics, thinking, problem-solving, and science skills (the 1991 graduates also ranked listening skills as very strong). *Writing and reading skills received the highest rankings.* The skills marked with an asterisk were ranked neutral or below. By 1993, only three skills were ranked neutral or below.

Performance-based learning and assessment in Region 15 have a foundation in integrated language arts. Writing, especially nonfiction writing, has become a part of most performance tasks embedded in all curriculum areas. Reading comprehension, especially of nonfiction, has also become a part of many performance tasks across the disciplines.

CONNECTICUT ACADEMIC PERFORMANCE TEST (CAPT)

Beginning in 1993–94, all high school sophomores in Connecticut are required to take the CAPT in the spring. This test is a balance of literal understanding and performance assessment. The test consists of five sections with six goal areas, as follows:

- **Responding to Literature.** The students read a short story and write responses to questions that require literal understanding, analysis, connections to their lives and other literature, and evaluation of the quality of the short story. Students are given one holistic score for their overall written responses.
- **Editing.** Students are given written passages to edit and receive one editing score.
- **Total Language Arts.** A combination of the Responding to Literature and Editing subtests.
- **Mathematics.** Students solve "one correct answer" math problems and show their work on many open-ended problems. Algebra is prominent on this test.
- **Science.** Students perform an actual laboratory activity, answer questions about the scientific process, respond to multiple-choice questions on content, and write responses to questions requiring the use of concepts from earth science, biology, physics, and chemistry. Students get a laboratory score, a content score, and an overall score.
- **Integrated Test.** In this test, students are given an issue such as "Should cigarette compa-

FIGURE 34. Rating of Learning Skills Developed at Pomperaug High School by the Graduates of 1989, 1991, and 1993

| | QUALITY OF SKILL DEVELOPMENT | | |
| | Rating by the Graduating Class of | | |
Learning Skill	1989	1991	1993
Writing Skills	3.77	**3.92**	**4.13**
Reading Skills	**3.92**	**4.13**	**3.95**
Mathematics Skills	3.77	**3.78**	**3.91**
Thinking Skills	**3.83**	3.67	**3.88**
Problem-Solving Skills	3.77	**3.80**	**3.82**
Science Skills	3.54	**3.83**	**3.80**
Study Skills	3.43*	3.19*	3.78
Listening Skills	3.72	**3.81**	3.77
Research Skills	3.57*	3.56*	3.73
Grammar Skills	3.52*	3.53*	3.63
Computer/Tech. Skills	2.75*	2.63*	3.10*
Public Speaking Skill	3.12*	3.02*	2.97*
Appreciation of Art/Music	3.42*	3.28*	3.26*

Rating Guidelines

Rating	Interpretation
4.00–5.00	Exceptionally Strong
3.80–3.99	Very Strong
3.60–3.79	Strong
3.30–3.59	Neutral
3.00–3.29	Relative Weak
2.50–2.99	Very Weak
Below 2.50	Exceptionally Weak

Note: Ratings in the Very Strong and Exceptionally Strong ranges are in bold. Skills marked with an asterisk were ranked neutral or below

nies be allowed to advertise freely?" and a packet of readings on both sides of the issue. After reading the packet, the students perform a critical analysis of each side and write a persuasive letter of their informed opinion to a specific audience. Students are given a holistic score for their persuasive letter.

The first CAPT, administered in 1994, was considered a "pilot"; and the cutoff scores for achieving the "high goal" in each of the six areas had not been set. The second CAPT, given in the spring of 1995, had the goal levels in place. Students receive a seal on their high school transcripts for each goal achieved. Students who do not achieve one or more goals may retake one or more sections of the CAPT during the junior or senior year in an attempt to gain those seals. (The CAPT test may not be used, according to state statute, as the sole criterion for graduation.)

The goals for each area of the CAPT are considered to be high goals, similar to receiving a grade of *B+* or *A* or a top rubric rating on a performance task.

Figure 35 shows the performance of Region 15 sophomores in 1995, as compared to the scores of sophomores in school districts socioeconomically similar to Region 15 in Connecticut and to the average scores in Connecticut. In all cases, Region 15 students received higher ratings.

The score for the integrated task was in the top 5 percent, and the score for total language arts was in the top 8 percent in Connecticut. Scores for math and science surpassed both the state average and the score of school districts similar to Region 15. This pattern of performance matches the pattern of implementation of per-

FIGURE 35. Connecticut Academic Performance Test (CAPT) 1994–95: Percentage of 10th Graders Reaching or Exceeding the High Goals in Each of Four Content Areas

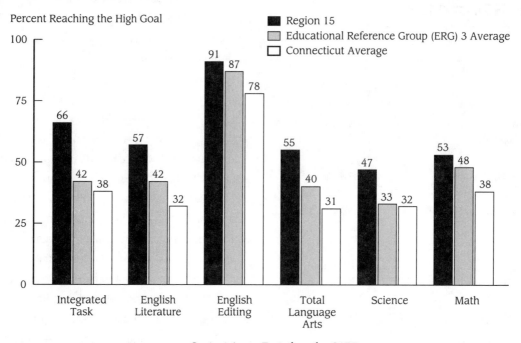

formance-based learning and assessment in the various program areas in Region 15. Integrated language arts and social studies (where performance tasks like the CAPT integrated task have been used for several years) have a longer history of using performance-based learning and assessment than do science and math.

In Region 15, 24 percent of the sophomores received the goal (a grade of *B*+ or *A*) in all six areas. The Connecticut average was 12 percent.

Note: Region 15 encourages all students to improve their performance. No students were exempted from the CAPT in Region 15. (Exemptions must be made formally by a special education pupil planning team.) One student was absent long enough not to be retested. In Connecticut, an average of 5 percent of students are exempted; and another 5 percent are not tested due to absence. Region 15 scores look even better when this 99 percent rate of test completion is compared to the 90 percent test-completion average in Connecticut.

CONNECTICUT MASTERY TEST (CMT)

The CMT was first administered to 4th graders in 1985–86 and expanded to include 6th and 8th graders in 1996–87. These tests, which were administered in the fall, were continued through

1992–93, then revised to become the second-generation CMT. The revised CMT is now the basis for school improvement planning in all Connecticut public schools.

The CMT consists of a language arts section including a Degree of Reading Power test, a multiple-choice section on reading comprehension and English mechanics, a listening test using a taped dialogue with follow-up multiple-choice questions, and a writing sample. The mathematics section includes multiple-choice and constructed-responses tasks. Writing, reading, and math are scored as follows:

• Student performance in *writing* is shown by the percentage of students scoring at or

above the high state goal on the holistic writing scores.

• Performance in *reading* is shown by the percentage of students scoring at or above the high state goal on the Degree of Reading Power test.

• Performance in *mathematics* is shown by the average number of math objectives mastered.

Figures 36–38 show the data on writing, reading, and math from the CMT for Region 15 students in grades 4, 6, and 8 and their counterparts in school systems similar to Region 15 (Educational Reference Group 3 in Connecticut). By 1993–94, the first data shown on these graphs, the CMT had been in use for five years,

---

FIGURE 36. Percentage of Students Reaching the High Goal in Reading Comprehension, as Measured by a Degree of Reading Power (DRP) Test on the Connecticut Mastery Test (CMT)

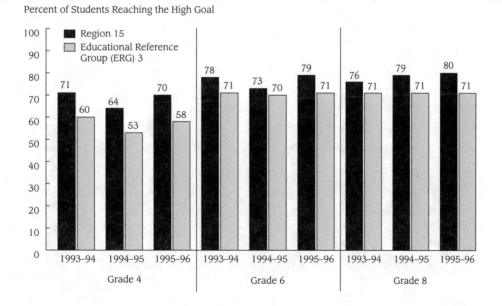

FIGURE 37. Percentage of Students Reaching the High Goal in Writing, as Measured by a Holistically Scored Writing Sample on the Connecticut Mastery Test (CMT)

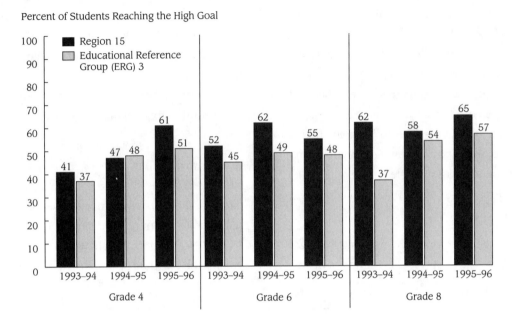

FIGURE 38. Percentage of Students Reaching the High Goal in Math, as Measured by a Math Test, Including Forced-Choice and Constructed-Response Tasks, on the Connecticut Mastery Test (CMT)

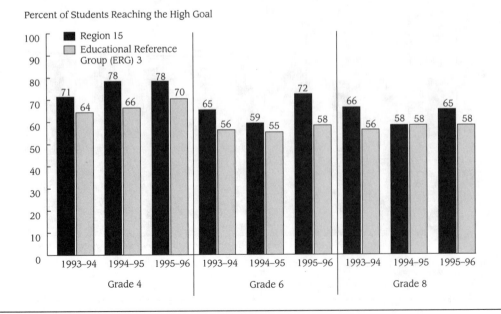

and Connecticut educators have been shaping performance-based learning and assessment in their classrooms accordingly. Student performance in Region 15 began the second generation of the CMT (1993–94) in a high position and has generally stayed high or improved over the past three years. These trends of strong and improving performance are seen again on the 10th grade CAPT.

SURVEY OF THE CITIZENS OF SOUTHBURY, CONNECTICUT

In the fall of 1995, the Democratic Town Committee mailed a survey to a random sampling of residents within each of three categories of political registration—Democrats, Republicans, and Independents. The survey included the residents of Heritage Village (a large retirement community in Southbury) and the town in general. The survey asked questions about town government, the public schools, the police department, and general youth services. The response rate was approximately 18 percent.

One question asked how the residents of Southbury felt about the quality of education the children of Southbury were receiving. Figure 39 shows the opinions of the various subgroups. All groups responded overwhelmingly that the qual-

FIGURE 39. Does Region 15 Do a Good Job of Educating the Children of Southbury?

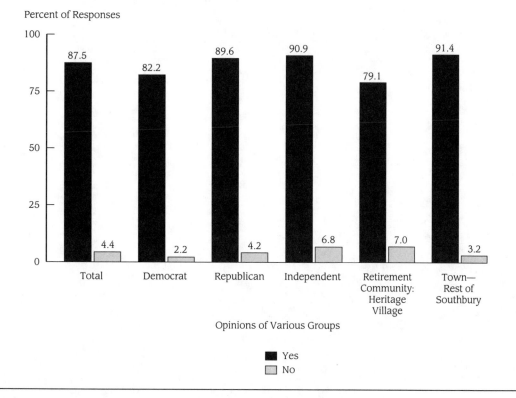

ity of education was excellent. A second question asked if the residents thought that the education budget was well spent. Although their responses were still positive, there were more "no" opinions. The reaction to the "money issue" is probably related to the perception of the level of teacher salaries in Connecticut. Although Region 15 salaries are below the average in Connecticut, the "money issue" is a concern to the residents of Southbury.

Note: Connecticut has 169 school districts. Region 15 is ranked, by the most recent state data, as 122 in overall per-pupil expenditure. That level of expenditure puts Region 15 well below the average. The Region 15 Board of Education, the Superintendent, and others have worked hard to keep costs for education down while improving student performance.

THE BOTTOM LINE: STUDENT PERFORMANCE

The teachers and administrators in Region 15 have worked for 10 years to create and implement strategies of performance-based learning and assessment within and among all disciplines at all grade levels. The goal has always been to improve the performance of students as measured by a variety of tests and assessments. Literacy is a complex set of learner characteristics, and we believe we must judge the success of our efforts from many points of view. The data presented in this chapter confirm that student performance is strong and improving—and the data point to areas in need of much more work. Performance-based learning and assessment do not constitute a "program to be implemented," but a process of teaching and learning that continually strives to set and reach higher goals. The journey is the message.

GLOSSARY

Accountability: Responsibility for general school processes and student achievement, including confirming that resources were effectively used and using assessment results to provide information to the public about what children have learned.

Analytical Assessment Lists: Lists of specific criteria by which the quality of a product or performance is judged.

Anchor Task: An anchor task is a performance task that, because of how successfully it engages students and how well it is connected to the content, process skills, and work habits of the curriculum, has been designated as a required performance task for that grade level and subject area. The task and its assessment list will be used in a standardized way by all teachers at that grade level or in that course.

AP Tests: Advanced Placement (AP) Tests are nationally standardized, college-level tests (usually including multiple-choice and essay questions) given to high school students completing college-level courses within the high school program. These tests are developed and scored by The College Board.

Assessment: Using various methods to obtain information about student learning that can be used to guide a variety of decisions and actions. Methods include observations, interviews, videos and audiotapes, projects, experiments, tests, performances, and portfolios.

Assessment, Authentic: See Performance Assessment, Authentic

Assessment, Analytical: Assessment of student work using a set of specific criteria, usually in a list format, and benchmarks of student work to define the performance standard.

Assessment, "Classroom Flexible": Assessment strategies (tasks, assessment lists, models of excellence, and the type or amount of support provided by the teacher and other students) that are adapted to meet the needs of the students and curriculums of individual classrooms.

Assessment, High Stakes: Assessments that are connected to important consequences such as final grades, promotion or graduation, college admittance, or employment. High-stakes assessments are summative assessments.

Assessment, Holistic: Assessment of student work that views the work as a whole and uses a rubric (rather than a detailed list of criteria) and benchmarks of student work to define the performance standard.

Assessment, Interdisciplinary or Integrated: Performance tasks that assess students' abilities to apply concepts, principles, and processes from two or more subject disciplines to a central question, theme, or problem.

Assessment, Low Stakes: Assessments that are not connected to important consequences. Low-stakes assessments are learning and assessment activities used in the day-to-day classroom. Low-stakes assessments are formative assessments.

Assessment, Standardized: An assessment with a set of consistent procedures for administering and scoring. The goal of standardization is to ensure that all students are assessed under uniform conditions so that interpretation of their performance is comparable and not influenced by differing conditions.

Benchmarks: An example of student work at a certain level of quality. For example, a benchmark for excellent persuasive writing at the 10th grade level is used by students, teachers, parents, and others to identify the goal of excellence for those students. (See performance standards.)

Bias: A lack of objectivity, fairness, or impartiality on the part of the assessor or evaluator, the assessment instrument or procedures, or in the interpretation and evaluation process, that leads to misinterpretation of student performance or knowledge.

CAPT: The Connecticut Academic Performance Test (CAPT) is given statewide in the spring to all 10th graders in the state. The test includes math, science, responding to literature, editing, and an integrated task. Data are provided at the student, class, school, school district, and state levels.

CBAM: The Concerns-Based Adoption Model is a set of client-centered strategies for change based on the following principles: Change is a process, not an event; change is accomplished by individuals; change is a highly personal experience; change involves professional growth; change is best understood in operational terms; and the focus of facilitation should be on individuals, innovations, and the context for the change.

CMT: The Connecticut Mastery Test (CMT) is given statewide in the fall to all students in grades four, six, and eight. The test includes math, writing, language mechanics, reading comprehension, and listening comprehension. Data are provided at the student, class, school, school district, and state levels.

Content Standards: Themes, big ideas, essential questions, and content objectives deemed to be important to an area of study.

Critical Friends: Individuals from outside the working group who give constructive feedback and advice to the working group.

Critical Mass: The condition when enough educators in an organization are effectively using strategies such as cooperative learning, process writing, interdisciplinary instruction, or performance-based learning and assessment so that these new strategies have a high probability of becoming a permanent part of the culture of that organization (school or school district).

Criterion Referenced: An approach for describing a student's performance according to established criteria; e.g., she typed 55 words per minute without errors.

Cycle of Learning: A sequence of events in authentic performance learning that includes making an assessment list to evaluate the quality of the work, and the steps of identifying task, audience, and purpose for the work to be done; assessing and acquiring information; processing information; producing a product; disseminating the product to the intended audience; and assessment, evaluation, and goal setting for the next cycle of learning.

Developmentally Appropriate: Practices based on what is known about how children and youth develop, learn, and manifest their learning at various age levels.

Dimensions of Learning: The Dimensions of Learning are descriptions of the five types of thinking that are essential to the learning process: (1) positive attitudes and perceptions about learning, (2) thinking involved in acquiring and integrating knowledge, (3) thinking involved in extending and refining knowledge, (4) thinking involved in using knowledge meaningfully, and (5) productive habits of mind. The Dimensions of Learning were the basis for the development of assessment standards developed by Marzano, Pickering, and McTighe (1993), linked to the declarative and procedural knowledge of the content areas, such as science, math, and English, and the Lifelong Learning Standards: (1) complex thinking, (2) information processing, (3) communication, (4) collaboration/cooperation, and (5) habits of mind. The Dimensions of Learning, Content Standards, and the Lifelong Learning Standards are similar to the steps in the Cycle of Learning used in the Region 15 Public Schools (see charts comparing these models, at the end of the glossary).

Dimensions of Student Work: The basic elements that are always part of a specific type of work, such as persuasive writing. These dimensions, to whatever degree of quality they are carried out, can be seen in any occurrence of this type of work. These dimensions are the foundation on which analytical assessment lists are based.

Discipline-Based Competencies: Competencies are learned proficiencies. Science content and the scientific processes are discipline-based competencies. Reading comprehension, interpreting themes in literature, and essay writing are other examples. Knowledge of algebra and math problem-solving skills are further examples.

Elementary: The grades between the primary and middle school grades, usually grades three through five.

Essential Question: A question that is "essential" when it helps to improve the understanding of basic concepts of a discipline. "How have organisms developed structures to accomplish the function of protection within their environment?" is an essential question within the content of biology. This question flows from the science theme of Form Follows Function.

Evaluation: The process of interpretation and use of information to make decisions; judgment regarding the quality, value, or worth of a response, product, or performance.

Evaluation, Fixed Standards: Using the same benchmarks of performance for all learners being evaluated (in contrast to Evaluation: Holistic Standards).

Evaluation, Individualized Standards: Using different standards of performance to evaluate different students. For example, sometimes students are evaluated based on their own past performance rather than against fixed standards. Individualized standards are most often employed with low- or high-performing students.

Exhibition: An extended, multipart project resulting in tangible products or presentations; often used to describe major performances or activities in a student's school career or a culmination of work in a class.

Exit-Level Performance: A performance expected of a student at the end of a segment of schooling, such as the end of a course or the end of the last grade level at the school.

FAST Plants: A type of plant (*Brassica rapa*) related to wild mustard and broccoli, used as a classroom organism because of how easy it is to grow and because it goes through its life cycle from seed to mature plant with seeds that can be planted in about 40 days. The use of this plant as a classroom organism is promoted by the Plant Pathology Department of the University of Wisconsin and is sold through Carolina Biological Supply (see Resources).

Focus Question: A topic-specific version of the essential question used in the classroom. The focus question, "What structures have spiders developed to protect themselves?" flows from the essential question, "How are the structures of animals related to their function?" which in turn flows from the theme, Form Follows Function.

Formative Assessment: Assessment occurring during the process of a unit or a course.

Guidelines for Geographic Education: Curriculum standards for geography developed by the National Council for Geographic Education and the American Geographers.

High Stakes: Assessment is high-stakes when the performance on it has a strong consequence for the student. High-stakes decisions can impact moving from grade to grade, can influence graduation, or can provide information used by college admission officers and employers.

Important Learning: Central concepts, essential skills, and critical ways of thinking within or across a subject/discipline.

Interpersonal Competencies: Competencies "among" people, such as communication, conflict resolution, and courtesy.

Intrapersonal Competencies: Competencies "internal" to the person, such as health habits, self-control, reaction to diversity, and work habits.

Issue Controversy: (also called Constructive Controversy) A process of using a critical decision-making process to examine both sides of an issue to reach an informed personal opinion. Group work is often a part of the process, which usually ends in individual persuasive writing.

Knowledge, Declarative: Otherwise known as content knowledge, including themes, big ideas, essential questions, content standards, and information.

Knowledge, Procedural: Knowledge of process skills, such as nonfiction writing, computation, oral presentation, critical decision making, group work, self-assessment, or creative problem solving.

Learning Styles: Characteristic cognitive, affective, and physiological behaviors that serve as relatively stable indicators of how individual learners perceive, interact with, and respond to the learning environment.

Low Stakes: The consequences for a level of performance that will have a low level of impact on a student. For example, the consequences to the student for his or her performance on a short, embedded performance task on spiders in science class may be no greater than a grade in the grade book. (See Performance Assessment: Embedded)

Norm Referenced: An approach for describing a student's performance by comparison to a normed group; e.g., he typed better than 80 percent of his classmates.

Opportunity to Learn: Giving students the means to acquire a high level of knowledge and skills; providing equitable and adequate learning resources, including capable teachers; rich curriculum; high-quality facilities, equipment, and materials; and essential support services.

Performance: A presentation of one's work before an audience, which may include classmates, parents, or members of the community, in addition to scorers.

Performance Assessment: General term for an assessment activity in which students construct responses, create products, or perform demonstrations to provide evidence of their knowledge and skills.

Performance Assessment, Authentic: The products or performances which are assessed are like products and performances that occur in the "real world."

Performance Assessment, Embedded: A performance task that is placed into the sequence of classroom instruction where it is a powerful opportunity for students to learn by "putting it all together—content, process skills, and work habits."

Performance Assessment, on Demand: A performance task administered on a specific date regardless of whether or not it fits into the curriculum at that time, such as a statewide test or the Advanced Placement tests.

Performance-Based Learning and Assessment: An approach to teaching and learning that embedded performance tasks within day-to-day instruction serves both as opportunities to learn and opportunities to measure the competencies of the learner.

Performance Maturity: The degree to which a learner can use discipline-based competencies, intrapersonal competencies, and interpersonal competencies "independently" to do authentic work.

Performance Standard: An established level of achievement, quality of performance, or degree of proficiency. Performance standards specify what a student is expected to achieve or perform to show that the student has substantially met content standards. A performance standard is sometime called a benchmark.

Performance Task Assessment List: A list of the criteria to be used to judge the quality of a product or performance from a performance assessment task. The items in the list can be highly detailed or more general. This type of assessment tool usually provides a more analytical approach than rubrics provide.

Performance Task Assessment List, Generic: An assessment list composed of criteria related to the dimensions of a specific type of work such as graphing, but not specific to the particular content of a specific graph done as a performance task.

Performance Task Assessment List, Tailored: An assessment list composed of criteria related to the dimensions of a specific type of work such as graphing and worded to identify the specific content of the graphing assignment.

Pioneers: The educators who are in the second round (after the scouts) of the innovation. Pioneers help to create the innovation and make it "user-friendly."

Portfolio: A purposeful or systematic collection of selected student work and student self-assessments developed over time, gathered to demonstrate and evaluate progress and achievement in learning. A *portfolio assessment* is the process of developing, reviewing, and evaluating student portfolios.

Primary: Kindergarten through grade two.

Process Creep: The condition where performance assessment becomes more and more orientated to processes, such as nonfiction writing, oral presentation, drawing, or graphing, and less and less connected to the content of the curriculums. (While processes are essential, content must not be neglected!)

Professional Development: Continued learning by educators to improve their knowledge and skills.

Project: An extended work, such as a research report in history or a science investigation.

Reliability: The degree to which an assessment measures consistently or the degree to which assessment scores are free from errors of measurement.

Rubric: A series of narrative statements describing the levels of quality of a product or a performance. The rubric can be a list of narrative statements or a matrix of narrative statements. Rubrics can be holistic or analytical. This type of assessment tool usually provides a more holistic approach than that of assessment lists.

Sampling: A way to collect information about a group by examining only a part of the group (the sample), or by dividing a test into sections and giving each member of the group or the sample only one part of the test (matrix sampling).

SAT: Scholastic Achievement Test (SAT—formerly the Scholastic Aptitude Test) consisting of verbal and math sections created and scored by The College Board.

Scouts: The educators who get in on the first stages of inventing a strategy to improve student performance. Scouts have a high tolerance for uncertainty, are risk-takers, and can withstand mistakes and setbacks.

Self-Assessment: The learner uses an assessment list or rubric and benchmarks to assess his or her own work.

Self-Evaluation: The learner interprets information from the assessment of his or her own work.

Self-Regulation: The learner makes plans for improvement based on the assessment and evaluation of his or her own work.

Senior Exhibit: An exit-level performance for seniors.

Settlers: Settlers are the educators who make the innovation "work" in the entire school or school district. The efforts of settlers ensure that the innovation will become a part of the culture of the organization.

Stakeholder(s): Those individuals who have a substantial interest in schools and student learning. Stakeholders may include students, teachers, administrators, other school staff, parents, advocacy organizations, community members, higher education institutions, and employers.

Summative Assessment: The assessment done at the end of a unit, course, or sequence of courses or grade levels. Summative assessments are usually formative assessments within the "bigger picture." The test and performance assessment at the end of the chapter, a final exam, the final draft of the 8th grade writing portfolio, a senior exhibition—all are examples of summative assessments.

Task Planning, Cycle of Learning: Developing a task that requires a student to go through all the steps of the Cycle of Learning. The intermediate products, such as the information organized through the step of "accessing and acquiring information," and the final product, which is disseminated to an audience, can be assessed.

Task Planning, Inside-Out: Developing a performance task by starting with a task that has proven to be engaging to students and then improving the connections between the task and the assessment tool and the content, process skills, and work habits of the curriculum.

Task Planning, Outside-In: Developing a task by starting with specific content, process skills, and work habits and then finding a task that is engaging to students.

Task Planning, Partnership with High-Stakes Assessment: Developing a classroom performance task that is similar in content and format to a performance task that is part of a standardized, state-level or district-wide high stakes assessment. The high-stakes performance task most likely is scored with a holistic rubric. The classroom version is administered as a "classroom flexible" learning and assessment activity and is scored using an analytical assessment list in the Region 15 Public Schools.

Task Planning, Planning Backwards: The process educators use to envision the type of performance task students should be able to do (but presently cannot) and then plan backwards in time to provide content, process skills, and work habits that will build the "performance maturity" necessary for those students to be successful in reaching this level of performance.

Test: A set of questions or situations designed to permit an inference about what an examinee knows or can do in an area of interest.

Theme: A big idea or a higher-order conceptual category that can subsume vast quantities of specific information. An important science theme is the Form Follows Function in living and engineered systems. (See Essential Question and Focus question to see the relationship among themes, essential questions, and focus questions.)

Topic: A particular item to be studied. "Spiders" is a topic within a science course. (See theme, essential question, and focus question.)

T–O–W: Terrific–OK–Needs Work, the levels of quality used in some elementary assessment tools.

Upper Grades: Middle and high school grades, usually grades 6 through 12.

Validity: The extent to which an assessment measures what it is supposed to measure. More precisely, the degree to which evidence and judgment support or disprove the adequacy and appropriateness of inferences and actions based on specific assessment information. Validity indicates the degree of accuracy of predictions or inferences based on an assessment score.

Work Habits: A *Coalition of Essential Schools* summary term for various dispositions important for effective thinking and learning, including reading with curiosity; reflecting critically on one's own work; developing independence, clarity, and incisiveness of thought; willingness to work hard; an ability to manage time effectively; persistence; accuracy and precision; and working collaboratively.

Note: See the next two pages for comparisons of the Cycle of Learning with the Dimensions of Learning and the Lifelong Learning Standards.

A Comparison of the Cycle of Learning and the Dimensions of Learning*

Steps in the Cycle of Learning	*Connections to the Dimensions of Learning*
1. Stating the task (product format), audience, and purpose for the learner's work	(Not directly in the Dimensions of Learning)
2. Accessing and acquiring information	Dimension 2: Acquiring and Integrating knowledge
3. Processing Information	Dimension 3: Extending and refining knowledge
	Dimension 4: Using knowledge meaningfully
4. Producing a product	Dimensions 3 and 4
5. Disseminating the product	(Not directly in the Dimensions of Learning)
6. Self-Assessment	Dimension 5: Productive habits of mind
7. Self-Evaluation	Dimension 5
8. Self-Regulation (setting goals for improvement)	Dimension 5
Through individual work	Dimension 5
Through collaboration with others	(Not directly in the Dimensions of Learning)
Developing the perceptions** of:	
I am capable of this work	Dimension 1: Positive attitudes and perceptions
I am needed	Dimension 1 about learning
The work I do is important	Dimension 1

Assessing Student Outcomes: Performance Assessment Using the Dimensions of Learning Model, Robert J. Marzano, Debra Pickering, and Jay McTighe, 1993, ASCD.

**Perceptions used in the Cycle of Learning are from *Developing Capable Young People,* H. Stephen Glenn and Jane Nelson, 1991, Empowering People Books, Tapes, and Videos Inc.

A Comparison of the Cycle of Learning and the Lifelong Learning Standards*

Steps in the Cycle of Learning	Connections to the Lifelong Learning Standards
1. Stating the task (product format), audience, and purpose for the learner's work	Category 3: Communication standards
2. Accessing and acquiring information	Category 1: Complex thinking standards
	Category 2: Information processing standards
3. Processing Information	Categories 1 and 2
4. Producing a product	Category 3
5. Disseminating the product	Category 3: Communication standards
6. Self-Assessment	Category 5: Habits of mind standards
7. Self-Evaluation	Category 5
8. Self-Regulation (setting goals for improvement)	Category 5
Through individual work	Category 5
Through collaboration with others	Category 4: Collaboration /cooperation standards
Developing the perceptions** of:	
I am capable of this work	Related to category 5
I am needed	Related to category 5
The work I do is important	Related to category 5

Assessing Student Outcomes: Performance Assessment Using the Dimensions of Learning Model, Robert J. Marzano, Debra Pickering, and Jay McTighe, 1993, ASCD.

**Perceptions used in the Cycle of Learning are from *Developing Capable Young People,* H. Stephen Glenn and Jane Nelson, 1991, Empowering People Books, Tapes, and Videos Inc.

RESOURCES

BOOKS AND OTHER RESOURCES

Archbald, D., and F. Newmann. (1988). *Beyond Standardized Testing: Assessing Authentic Achievement in the Secondary School*. Reston, Va.: National Association of Secondary School Principals (NASSP). *Available from:* NASSP, 1904 Association Drive, Reston, VA 22314. Phone: 703-860-0200. Item # 210-8808

Armstrong, Karen. (1994). *Designing Assessment in Art*. Reston, Va.: National Art Education Association (NAEA). *Available from:* National Art Education Association, 1916 Association Drive, Reston, VA 22091.

Armstrong, Thomas. (1994). *Multiple Intelligences in the Classroom*. Alexandria, Va.: Association for Supervision and Curriculum Development (ASCD). *Available from:* ASCD, 1250 North Pitt Street, Alexandria, VA 22314. Phone: 703-549-9110. ISBN # 0-87120-230-1.

Assessment in the Mathematics Classroom. (1993). Reston, Va.: National Council of Teachers of Mathematics (NCTM). *Available from:* NCTM, 1906 Association Drive, Reston, VA 22091. Phone: 703-620-9840. ISBN # 0-87353-419-0.

Assessment Standards for School Mathematics. (1995). Reston, Va.: National Council of Teachers of Mathematics (NCTM). *Available from:* NCTM (See information listed previously). ISBN # 0-87353-419-0.

Benchmarks for Scientific Literacy: Project 2061. (1993). New York: American Association for the Advancement of Science (AAAS). *Available from:* Oxford Press, 200 Madison Avenue, New York, NY 10016. ISBN # 0-19-508986-3.

Bredekamp, S., and T. Rosegrant. (Eds.) (1992). *Reaching Potentials: Appropriate Curriculum and Assessment for Young Children*. Washington, D.C.: National Association for the Education of Young Children (NAEYC). *Available from:* NAEYC, 1509 16th Street, N.W., Washington, DC 20036-1426. Phone: 202-232-8777. ISBN # 0-935989-53-6.

Brandt, R. (Ed.). (1992). *Readings from Educational Leadership: Performance Assessment*. Alexandria, Va.: Association for Supervision and Curriculum (ASCD). *Available from:* ASCD (See information previously listed). ISBN # 0-87120-195-X.

Brooks, Jacqueline Grennon, and Martin G. Brooks. (1993). *The Case for Constructivist Classrooms*. Alexandria, Va.: Association for Supervision and Curriculum Development (ASCD). *Available from:* ASCD (See information previously listed). ISBN # 0-87120-211-5.

Burke, K. (1993). *How to Access Thoughtful Outcomes*. Palatine, Ill.: IRI/Skylight Publishing. *Available from:* IRI Skylight Publishing, Inc., 200 E. Wood Street, Suite 274, Palatine, IL 60067. Phone: 800-348-4474. ISBN # 0-932935-58-3.

Charting the Course Toward Instructionally Sound Assessment. (1993). San Francisco: California Assessment Collaborative (CAC). *Available from:* California Assessment Collaborative, 730 Harrison Street, San Francisco, CA 94107.

Connecticut Mastery Test (CMT) and the Connecticut Academic Performance Test (CAPT). Connecticut State Department of Education. *Available from:* The Connecticut State Department of Education, Student Assessment, P.O. Box 2219, Hartford, CT 06145. Phone: 860-566-1684.

Curriculum and Evaluation Standards for School Mathematics. (1989). Reston, Va.: National Council of Teachers of Mathematics (NCTM). *Available from:* NCTM (See information listed previously). ISBN # 0-87353-273-2.

Davidson, Neil, and Toni Worsham. (1992). *Enhancing Thinking Through Cooperative Learning*. New York: Teachers College Press. *Available from:* Teachers College Press, 1234 Amsterdam Avenue, New York, NY 10027. ISBN # 0-8077-3158-7.

Diez, M., L. Castenell, S. Wegener-Soled, G. Galluzzo, D. Hinkle, F. Murray, L. Trentham, and R. Kunkel. (1993). *Essays on Emerging Assessment Issues*. Washington, D.C.: American Association of Colleges for Teacher Education (AACTE). *Available from:* AACTE, One Dupont Circle, Suite 610, Washington, DC 20036. Phone: 202-293-2450. ISBN # 0-89333-113-9.

ERIC Review. (Winter 1994). *Performance-Based Assessment. Rockville, Md.: Educational Resources Information Center (ERIC)*. *Available from:* ACCESS ERIC, 1600 Research Boulevard, Rockville, MD 20850. Phone: 800-538-3742.

Gill, Kent. (1993). *Process and Portfolios in Writing Instruction*. Urbana, Ill.: National Council of Teachers of English (NCTE). *Available from:* NCTE, 1111 W. Kenyon Road, Urbana, IL 61801-1096. Phone: 800-369-NCTE.

Glenn, H. Stephen, and Jane Nelson. (1991). *Developing Capable Young People*. Provo, Utah: Empowering People Books, Tapes, and Videos Inc. *Available from:* Empowering People Books, Tapes, and Videos Inc., P.O. Box B., Provo, UT 84603. Phone: 800-456-2811. ISBN # 0-8141-3724-5.

Goodman, Kenneth S., Lois Bridges Bird, and Yetta M. Goodman. (1992). *The Whole Language Catalog: Supplement on Authentic Assessment*. New York: Macmillan/McGraw-Hill. *Available from:* American School Publishers, 1221 Farmers Lane, Suite C, Santa Rosa, CA 95405. Phone: 1-800-882-2502. ISBN # 0-383-03537-6.

Hammond, L.D., J. Ancess, and B. Falk. (1995). *Authentic Assessment in Action: Studies of Schools and Students at Work*. New York: Teachers College Press. *Available from:* Teachers College Press, 1234 Amsterdam Avenue, New York, NY 10027. Phone: 212-678-3992. ISBN # 0-8077-3439-1.

Handbook of Research on Improving Student Achievement. (1995). Arlington, Va.: Alliance for Curriculum Reform. *Available from:* Educational Research Service, 2000 Clarendon Boulevard, Arlington, VA 22201. Phone: 703-243-2100.

Hart, D. (1994). *Authentic Assessment: A Handbook for Educators*. Reading, Mass.: Addison-Wesley Publishers. *Available from:* Addison-Wesley Publishing Company, Jacob Way, Reading, MA 01867. Phone: 800-552-2259. ISBN # 0-201-81864-7.

Herman, J., P. Aschbacher, and L. Winters. (1992). *A Practical Guide to Alternative Assessment.* Alexandria, Va.: Association for Supervision and Curriculum Development (ASCD). *Available from:* ASCD (See information listed previously). ISBN # 0-87120-197-6.

Hibbard, K. Michael, and Mary Yakamoski. (1996). *A Partnership to Improve Student Performance: Connecting State-Level Assessment and Classroom Practices.* Hamden, Conn.: Connecticut Association for Supervision and Curriculum Development (CASCD). *Available from:* CASCD, c/o Richard Nabel, President CASCD, Principal, Hamden High School, 2040 Dixwell Avenue, Hamden, CT 06514. Phone: 203-248-9311.

Hord, Shirley M., William L. Rutherford, Leslie Huling-Austin, and Gene E. Hall. (1987). *Taking Charge of Change.* (Concerns Based Adoption Model, CBAM). Alexandria, Va.: Association for Supervision and Curriculum Development (ASCD). *Available from:* ASCD (See information listed previously). ISBN # 0-87120-144-5.

Jacobs, Heidi Hayes. (1989). *Interdisciplinary Curriculum: Design and Implementation.* Alexandria, Va.: Association for Supervision and Curriculum Development (ASCD). *Available from:* ASCD (See information listed previously). ISBN # 0-87120-165-8.

Johnson, W. David, and Roger T. Johnson. (1992). *Creative Controversy: Intellectual Challenge in the Classroom.* Edina, Minn.: Interaction Book Company. *Available from:* Interaction Book Company, 7208 Cornelia Drive, Edina, MN 55435. Phone: 612-831-9500. ISBN # 0-939603-18-7.

Johnson, David W., Roger T. Johnson, and Edythe Johnson Holubec. (1994). *The Nuts and Bolts of Cooperative Learning.* Edina, Minn.: Interaction Book Company. *Available from:* Interaction Book Company (See information listed previously). ISBN # 0-939603-21-7.

Kagan, Spencer. (1993). *Cooperative Learning: Resources for Teachers.* San Juan Capistrano, Calif.: Author. *Available from:* Spencer Kagan, Resources for Teachers, 27134 Paseo Espada # 202, San Juan Capistrano, CA 92675. Phone: 714-248-7757.

Maintaining a Substantive Focus: A Look at Performance Assessment for Art Education. (1994). Reston, Va.: National Art Education Association (NAEA). *Available from:* National Art Education Association (See information listed previously).

Mathematics Assessment: Myths, Models, Good Questions, and Practical Suggestions. (1991). Reston, Va.: National Council of Teachers of Mathematics (NCTM). *Available from:* NCTM (See information listed previously). ISBN # 0-87353-339-9.

Maryland Assessment Consortium. This consortium is a source of assessment tasks and rubrics. *Available from:* Maryland Assessment Consortium, c/o Jay McTighe, 115 East Church Street, Frederick, MD 21701. Phone: 301-694-1337.

Marzano, R., D. Pickering, and J. McTighe. (1993). *Assessing Student Outcomes: Performance Assessment Using the Dimensions of Learning Model.* Alexandria, Va.: Association for Supervision and Curriculum Development (ASCD). *Available from:* ASCD (See information listed previously). ISBN # 0-87120-225-5.

McDonald, J., E. Barton, S. Smith, D. Turner, and M. Finney. (1993). *Graduation by Exhibition: Assessing Genuine Achievement.* Alexandria, Va.: Association for Supervision and Curriculum Development (ASCD). *Available from:* ASCD (See information listed previously). ISBN # 0-87120-204-2.

McTighe, J., and S. Ferrara. (1994). *Assessing Learning in the Classroom.* Washington, D.C.: National Education Association (NEA). *Available from:* NEA Professional Standards and Practice, 1201 16th Street, N.W., Washington, DC 20036-3290. Phone: 202-822-7350.

Measuring What Counts: A Conceptual Guide For Mathematics Assessment. (1993). Washington, D.C.: Mathematical Sciences Educational Board National Research Council. *Available from:* National Academy Press, 2101 Constitution Avenue, N.W., Washington, DC 20418. Phone: 800-624-6242. ISBN # 0-309-04981-4.

Mitchell, Ruth. (1992). *Testing for Learning: How New Approaches to Evaluation Can Improve American's Schools.* New York: The Free Press. *Available from:* Council for Basic Education, 725 Fifteenth Street, N.W., Washington, DC 20005. Phone: 202-347-4171. ISBN # 0-02-921465-3.

Moving Into the Future: National Standards for Physical Education. (1995). Reston, Va.: National Association for Sport and Physical Education (NASPE). *Available from:* Mosby-Year Book, Inc., 11830 Westline Industrial Drive, St. Louis, MO 63146. ISBN # 0-1851-7338-5.

Murphy, Sandra, and Mary Ann Smith. (1992). *Writing Portfolios, A Bridge from Teaching to Assessment.* Markham, Ont., Canada: Pippin Publishing Limited. *Available from:* Pippin Publishing Limited, 380 Esna Park Drive, Markham, Ontario, Canada. ISBN # 0-88751-044-2.

National Geography Standards. (1994). Washington, D.C.: Geography Education Standards Project. *Available from:* National Geographic Research and Exploration, 1145 17th Street, N.W., Washington, D.C. 20036. ISBN # 0-7922-2775-1.

National Health Education Standards: Achieving Health Literacy. (1995). Washington, D.C.: Joint Committee on National Health Education Standards. *Available from:* American Cancer Society. Phone: 800-ACS-2345.

National Staff Development Council's Standards for Staff Development. Elementary Level Edition, Middle Grades Level Edition, and High School Level Edition. (1994, 1995). Oxford, Ohio: National Staff Development Council (NSDC). *Available from:* NSDC, P.O. Box 240, Oxford, OH 45056. Phone: 800-727-7288.

National Standards for the Arts. (1994). Consortium of Reston, Va.: National Arts Education Associations. *Available from:* Music Educators National Conference, 1806 Robert Fulton Drive, Reston, VA 22091. Phone: 703-860-4000. ISBN # 1-56545-036-1.

Neill, M., P. Bursh, C. Thall, M. Yohe, and P. Zappardino. (1995). *Implementing Performance Assessments: A Guide to Classroom, School and School Reform.* Cambridge: FAIRTEST: The National Center for Fair and Open Testing. *Available from:* FAIRTEST, 342 Broadway, Cambridge, MA 02139. Phone: 617-864-4810.

Perrone, V. (Ed.). (1991). *Expanding Student Assessment.* Alexandria, Va.: Association for Supervision and Curriculum Development (ASCD). *Available from:* ASCD (See information listed previously). ISBN # 0-87120-182-8.

Porter, Carol, and Janell Cleland. (1995) *The Portfolio as a Learning Strategy.* Boynton/Cook Publishing. *Available from:* Heinemann, 361 Hanover Street, Portsmouth, NH 03801. ISBN # 0-86709-348-x.

Region 15 Curriculum and Assessment Materials. Performance Tasks and Assessment Lists For Grades One Through Twelve, Across the Disciplines. Request Catalogue *Available from:* Region 15 Curriculum and Assessment Materials, c/o K. Michael Hibbard, Ph.D., Region 15 Public Schools, 286 Whittemore Road, Middlebury, CT 06762. Phone: 203-758-8250.

Rothman, R. (1995). *Measuring Up: Standards, Assessment, and School Reform.* San Francisco: Jossey-Bass. *Available from:* Jossey-Bass Publishers, 350 Sansome Street, San Francisco, CA 94104. Phone: 415-433-1740. ISBN # 0-7879-0055-9.

The Secretary's Commission on Achieving Necessary Skills (SCANS). (1992). Washington, D.C.: U.S. Department of Labor. *Available from:* Pelavin Associates, 2030 M Street, N.W., Suite 800, Washington, DC 20036.

Simon, Karen. (1994). *On Target with Authentic Assessment: Creating and Implementing Classroom Models.* An Appalachia Educational Laboratory (AEL) School Excellence Workshop Manual. Charleston, W.Va.: AEL. *Available from:* AEL, P.O. Box 1348, Charleston, WV 25325. Phone: 1-800-624-9120.

Stiggins, R.J. (1994). *Student-Centered Classroom Assessment.* Riverside, N.J.: Macmillan. *Available from:* Macmillan Publishing Company, 100 Front Street, Box 500, Riverside, NJ 08075-7500. Phone: 800-257-5755. ISBN # 0-02-417350-9.

Stiggins, R.J., E. Quellmalz, and E. Rubel. (1988). *Measuring Thinking Skills in the Classroom.* Washington, D.C.: National Education Association (NEA). *Available from:* NEA Professional Library, P.O. Box 509, West Haven, CT 06516. Phone: 800-229-4200. ISBN # 0-8106-2011-3.

Testing in American Schools: Asking the Right Questions. (1992). Washington, D.C.: Congress of the United States. Office of Technology Assessment. *Available from:* U.S. Government Printing Office, Superintendent of Documents, Mail Stop SSOP, Washington, DC 20402-9328. Phone: 202-783-3238. ISBN# 0-16-036161-3.

Wiggins, G. (1993). *Assessing Student Performance: Exploring the Purposes and Limits of Testing.* San Francisco: Jossey-Bass. *Available from:* Jossey-Bass Publishers (See information listed previously). ISBN # 1-55542-592-5.

Wisconsin FAST Plants: Information *Available from:* University of Wisconsin-Madison, Department of Plant Pathology, FAST Plants, 1630 Linden Drive, Madison, WI 53706. Phone: 608-263-2634.
Materials *Available from:* Carolina Biological Supply Company, 2700 York Rd., Burlington, NC 27215. Phone: 1-800-334-5551.

Yancy, Kathleen Blake. (Ed.). (1992). *Portfolios in the Writing Classroom.* Urbana, Ill.: National Council of Teachers of English. *Available from:* NCTE (See information previously listed). ISBN # 0-8141-3645-1.

ANNOTATED BIBLIOGRAPHIES

Comprehensive sets of annotated bibliographies on performance assessment have been prepared by Judith Arter and Ann Davis at the Northwest Region Educational Laboratory (NWREL). These bibliographies are organized by subject areas (reading, mathematics, science, social studies, and writing) and topics (portfolios), and are available for a modest fee to cover duplication and mailing costs.

Available from: Northwest Region Educational Laboratory (NWREL), The Test Center, 101 S.W. Main Street, Suite 500, Portland, OR 97204. Phone: 503-275-9562.

PROFESSIONAL DEVELOPERS TOOL KIT

A Consortium of the national Regional Educational Laboratories has produced an excellent resource entitled, *A Tool Kit for Professional Developers: Alternative Assessment in Mathematics and Science.* Packaged in a three-ring binder, the Tool Kit contains a wealth of materials related to performance assessment, including workshop modules, transparency masters, sample performance tasks and scoring rubrics, a database of assessment developers, and an extensive set of annotated bibliographies of print and audiovisual resources. While the focus is on mathematics and science, many of the staff development suggestions are applicable to other content areas.

Available from: NWREL (See address listed above), Document Reproduction Service. Phone: 503-275-9519.

ALTERNATIVE ASSESSMENT DATA BASE

The National Center for Research on Evaluation, Standards and student testing (CRESST) has compiled a database containing lists of over 250 developers of new assessments. While the database includes descriptions of the assessments and contact information for the developers, it does not include the assessments themselves. The database is available on a Macintosh disk in Hypercard.

Available from: CRESST, UCLA Graduate School of Education, 405 Hilgard Avenue, Los Angeles, CA 90024. Phone: 213-825-4711.

VIDEOTAPE RESOURCES ON PERFORMANCE ASSESSMENT

prepared by
Jay McTighe, Director
Maryland Assessment Consortium

Standards NOT Standardization

Volume I—Re-thinking Assessment: Provocations and Issues
Volume II—Re-thinking Assessment: The District
Volume III—Re-thinking Assessment: The Classroom
Volume IV—*Re-thinking Assessment: The School*
This four-volume series serves as the centerpiece for a series of seminars on raising the standards of student performance through attention to "authentic" assessments. Each volume contains two videotapes and a comprehensive manual providing detailed suggestions for seminar leaders.
Available from: Center for Learning, Assessment, and School Structure, 648 The Great Road, Princeton, NJ 08540. Phone: 609-252-1211.

Is This What You Want From Me? Scoring Performance Assessments (21 minutes)

This video introduces teachers, administrators, parents, and others to two types of scoring tools commonly used with performance assessments—rubrics and task-specific keys. These criterion-based scoring tools are described and illustrated through classroom applications. Viewers observe several options for using these tools to promote, as well as measure, learning: (1) teachers presenting rubrics and keys to students before they engage in performance tasks; (2) teachers involving students in helping to identify criteria and develop the scoring tools; and (3) teachers and students using scoring tools to evaluative student work. The video includes a leaders' guide containing suggested pre- and post-viewing discussion questions and a glossary of key terms.
Available from: Maryland Assessment Consortium, 115 East Church Street, Frederick, MD 21701. Phone: 301-694-1337.

Developing Performance Tasks (45 minutes)

This recording of a presentation by Jay McTighe, director of the Maryland Assessment Consortium, documents a practical, step-by-step process for designing performance assessment tasks and related scoring rubrics. The presentation illustrates the use of a set of templates for performance task design. The video is accompanied by a 30-page handout containing the task design templates, an example of a performance task de-

veloped using this process, and a set of task review criteria.
Available from: Maryland Assessment Consortium (See previous listing).

Teaching and Testing in Maryland Today: Education for the 21st Century (14 minutes)

This video was developed for use with school staffs, parents, community members, and Boards of Education. It provides an overview of the new role of performance-based instruction and assessment in the context of Maryland's standards/outcomes-based educational reforms.
Available from: Maryland Assessment Consortium (See previous listing).

Redesigning Assessment

Tape 1—*Redesigning Assessment: Introduction (24 minutes)*
Tape 2—*Redesigning Assessment: Performance Assessment (32 minutes)*
Tape 3—*Redesigning Assessment: Portfolios (40 minutes)*
This three-set videotape series features classroom illustrations of performance assessment in action with comments by students, teachers, administrators, and national experts. Each videotape includes a Facilitator's Guide offering suggestions for using the videos as part of a workshop for professional staff, parents, and Boards of Education.
Available from: Association for Supervision and Curriculum Development, 1250 North Pitt Street, Alexandria, VA 22314. Phone: 703-549-9110.

What's New in School—A Parent's Guide to Performance Assessment (14 minutes)

This videotape is designed to introduce parents, community members, and Boards of Education to the rationale for, and the practices of, performance assessment. The video features examples of performance tasks, projects, and portfolios being used in elementary and secondary schools with comments by students, teachers, and parents. The accompanying Leader's Guide offers suggestions for using the video with various groups.
Available from: Association for Supervision and Curriculum Development (See previous listing).

Performance Assessment in the Classroom

Part 1: *Performance-Based Assessment and Instruction (29 minutes)*
Part 2: *Creating Performance Tasks (31 minutes)*
These two videotapes are designed to introduce teachers, administrators, and parents to the key princi-

ples of performance-based assessment and instruction. The program invites the viewer to consider 10 key questions related to the design and use of classroom performance tasks. Numerous classroom examples and comments by teachers make this a practical and fast-paced resource for staff development.

Available from: The Video Journal of Education, 549 West 3560 South, Salt Lake City, UT 84115-4225. Phone: 800-572-1153.

Program Assessment in the Classroom

Program 1: *Reflections of Learning (29 minutes)*
Program 2: *Utilizing Portfolios (29 minutes)*
These two videotapes feature Bena Kallick, a noted expert on portfolio assessment. The program emphasizes the use of portfolios to document learning and stimulate self-evaluation by students. A variety of classroom examples illustrates the use of portfolio assessment in different subject areas and grade levels.

Available from: The Video Journal of Education (See previous listing).

Performance-Based Assessment in Quality Elementary and Middle Schools (15 minutes)

This videotape describes the 3 Ps of performance-based assessment—performance tasks, projects, and portfolios. These three approaches are illustrated through classroom applications with comments by students, teachers, and administrators. The package includes an information booklet and a set of workshop materials (including transparencies) for use in staff or parent meetings.

Available from: National Association of Elementary School Principals (NAESP), 1615 Duke Street, Alexandria, VA 22314-3483. Phone: 800-386-2377.

Mathematics Assessment: Alternative Approaches (71 minutes)

This video was produced in cooperation with South Carolina Television as a companion to the book, Mathematics Assessment: Myths, Models, Good Questions, and *Practical Suggestions* by Jean Stenmark. Through classroom examples and expert commentary, the program explores teachers' implementations of a variety of assessment methods in their classrooms. A viewer's guide is included.

Available from: National Council of Teachers of Mathematics, 1906 Association Drive, Reston, VA 22091-1593. Phone: 800-235-7566.

Student Growth: Directions for Assessing and Communicating Learning (16 minutes)

This video describes the use of a portfolio system in Edmonton Public Schools for assessing six essential learning outcomes identified by the district. The video shows examples of portfolio review conferences with staff, students, and parents.

Available from: Edmonton Public Schools, Center for Education, 1 Kingsway, Edmonton, Alberta, Canada T5H 4G9. Attn: Terry Terlesky. Phone: 403-429-8228.

Writing Assessment: Issues and Answers

This videotape is part of a training package for a 3-hour workshop on direct assessment of writing based on teacher evaluations of student writing samples. Holistic, analytic, and primary trait scoring are demonstrated. The package includes a user's guide, background reading, and handouts.

Available from: IOX, 5301 Beethoven Street, Suite 109, Los Angeles, CA 90066-7061. Phone: 310-822-3275.

Writing Assessment: Training in Analytic Scoring

This videotape is part of a training package for a 7-hour workshop. Viewers learn to use a six-trait analytical scoring model to assess writing competencies. Participants have opportunities to apply each criterion to actual samples of student writing. The package includes a user's guide, background reading, and handouts.

Available from: IOX (See previous listing).

Developing Assessments Based on Observations and Judgment

This videotape is part of a training package for a 3-hour workshop. Viewers learn how to develop assessments based on observation and judgment. Participants also learn how to evaluate the quality of their own assessments so as to avoid common problems. The package includes a user's guide, background reading, and handouts.

Available from: IOX (See previous listing).

The California Learning Record (23 minutes)

This video was produced by the California Department of Education to introduce the California Learning Record (CLR), a developmentally appropriate portfolio assessment process for young children. Filmed in schools with Chapter I programs in the San Diego Unified School District, the program shows parents, teachers, and students making contributions to the CLR.

Available from: California Department of Education, Bureau of Publications, Sales Unit, P.O. Box 271, Sacramento, CA 95812-0271. Phone: 914-445-1260.

Teacher TV—Episode 11: Alternative Assessment (22 minutes)

Co-produced by the National Education Associate (NEA) and the Learning Channel, this video contains vignettes of teachers using "alternative" methods for assessing student learning. One example describes the use of a computer and scanner for assembling a digital portfolio at the elementary level. A second vignette illustrates how a teacher involved her student in peer evaluation as part of a science fair project.

Available from: NEA Professional Library, P.O. Box 509, New Haven, CT 06516. Phone: 800-229-4200.

Alternatives for Measuring Performance (60 minutes)

On November 21, 1991, the North Central Regional Educational Laboratory broadcast a national teleconference on assessment to sites throughout the United States. This videotape of the teleconference profiles two schools utilizing innovative assessment. A discussion by a distinguished panel of assessment experts follows. The videotape is accompanied by a 36-page guidebook that describes the characteristics of effective assessments, criteria for valid performance assessments, and recommended resources.

Available from: IRI/Skylight Publishing, Inc., 200 East Wood Street, Suite 500, Palatine, IL 60067. Phone: 800-348-4474, ext. 220.

The Arts PROPEL Video Handbook (65 minutes)

Arts PROPEL was initiated to develop nontraditional models of assessment appropriate for students engaged in the visual arts, music, and imaginative writing. This video accompanies the Arts PROPEL Handbook for Visual Arts and provides an overview to the Arts PROPEL project. The program includes sections on PROPEL's guiding principles, students engaged in long-term visual arts projects, and the use of portfolios as vehicles for communication and reflection. Teacher testimonials lend authenticity and practicality to the project.

Available from: Harvard Project Zero, Longfellow Hall, 13 Appian Way, Cambridge, MA 02138. Phone: 800-235-2132.

Indexes

For Teachers and Administrators

Index of Graphics Other Than Assessment Lists